THE LAW COMMISSION

PRIVITY OF CONTRACT: CONTRACTS FOR THE BENEFIT OF THIRD PARTIES

CONTENTS

SECTION B: PRELIMINARY ISSUES

PART III: ARGUMENTS FOR REFORM

PART IV: PRECEDENTS FOR REFORM

PART V: THE FORM OF THE LEGISLATION

PART VI: THE THIRD PARTY RULE AND CONSIDERATION

SECTION C: CENTRAL REFORM ISSUES

PART VII: THE TEST OF ENFORCEABILITY

PART VIII: DESIGNATION, EXISTENCE, AND ASCERTAINABILITY OF THIRD PARTY

PART IX: VARIATION AND CANCELLATION

THE LAW COMMISSION

Item 1 of the Sixth Programme of Law Reform: The Law of Contract

PRIVITY OF CONTRACT: CONTRACTS FOR THE BENEFIT OF THIRD PARTIES

To the Right Honourable the Lord Mackay of Clashfern, Lord High Chancellor of Great Britain

SECTION A
BACKGROUND

PART I
INTRODUCTION

1.1 In 1995 in the Court of Appeal in *Darlington Borough Council v Wiltshier Northern Ltd*[1] Steyn LJ, in criticising the present law, said the following:-

> The case for recognising a contract for the benefit of a third party is simple and straightforward. The autonomy of the will of the parties should be respected. The law of contract should give effect to the reasonable expectations of contracting parties. Principle certainly requires that a burden should not be imposed on a third party without his consent. But there is no doctrinal, logical, or policy reason why the law should deny effectiveness to a contract for the benefit of a third party where that is the expressed intention of the parties. Moreover, often the parties, and particularly third parties, organise their affairs on the faith of the contract. They rely on the contract. It is therefore unjust to deny effectiveness to such a contract. I will not struggle with the point further since nobody seriously asserts the contrary.[2]

1.2 In this Report we make recommendations for the reform of that part of the doctrine of privity of contract which lays down that a contract does not confer rights on someone who is not a party to the contract (hereinafter referred to as the "third party rule"). Our proposals will mean, for example, that subsequent purchasers or tenants of buildings can be given rights to enforce an architect's or building contractor's contractual obligations without the cost, complexity and inconvenience of a large number of separate contracts;[3] that an employer can take out medical expenses insurance for its employees without there being doubts as to whether the employees can enforce the policy against the insurance company;[4] that a life insurance policy taken out for one's stepchild or cohabitee is enforceable (subject to a term to the

---

[1]   [1995] 1 WLR 68.

[2]   *Ibid*, at p 76. For other calls for reform, see paras 2.63-2.69 below.

[3]   See paras 3.12-3.19 below.

[4]   See paras 3.25-3.26 and 7.32 below.

contrary) by that named beneficiary;[5] and that a contractual clause limiting or excluding one's liability to a third party (for example, the promisee's subsidiary company or sub-contractor or employee) will be straightforwardly enforceable by that third party.[6]

1.3 The Law Commission first became interested in this subject after the Commission's creation in 1965.[7] Item 1 of the First Programme of Law Reform was the codification of the law of contract. Item 3 included the topic of third party rights. A substantial amount of work was done on this topic in conjunction with work on consideration. At that time it was felt that reform of privity could not usefully be undertaken without reform of the doctrine of consideration. The relationship between the doctrines of privity and of consideration is discussed in Part VI below, where we explain why we believe that reform of the third party rule can be profitably undertaken without reassessing the entire doctrine of consideration.

1.4 In 1973 work was suspended on the production of a contract code[8] which, in its draft form, would have provided for the creation of rights in third parties.[9] The Law Commission's strategy since then has been to tackle problems in the law of contract as separate projects.[10] In arriving at the view that a project on privity was justified, we were influenced by, for example, the continued judicial and academic criticism of the doctrine,[11] by the work of Commonwealth law reform bodies,[12] by insights gained

---

[5] See paras 3.25-3.26 and 7.34 below. The Married Women's Property Act 1882 extends only to spouses and children.

[6] See paras 2.19-2.35, 3.20, 7.10 and 7.43 below.

[7] This project now comes within Item 1 of the Sixth Programme of Law Reform, Law Com No 234.

[8] 8th Annual Report 1972-1973, Law Com No 58, paras 3-4.

[9] See H McGregor, *Contract Code drawn up on behalf of the English Law Commission* (1993) ss 641ff.

[10] Exemption Clauses: Second Report (1975) Law Com No 69; Scot Law Com No 39 (see the Unfair Contract Terms Act 1977); Report on Contribution (1977) Law Com No 79 (see the Civil Liability (Contribution) Act 1978); Implied Terms in Contracts for the Supply of Goods (1979) Law Com No 95 (see the Supply of Goods and Services Act 1982); Pecuniary Restitution on Breach of Contract (1983) Law Com No 121; Minors' Contracts (1984) Law Com No 134 (see the Minors' Contracts Act 1987); The Parol Evidence Rule (1986) Law Com No 154; Implied Terms in Contracts for the Supply of Services (1986) Law Com No 156; Sale and Supply of Goods (1987) Law Com No 160; Scot Law Com No 104 (see the Sale and Supply of Goods Act 1994); Rights of Suit in Respect of Carriage of Goods by Sea (1991) Law Com No 196; Scot Law Com No 130 (see the Carriage of Goods by Sea Act 1992); Contributory Negligence as a Defence in Contract (1993) Law Com No 219; Firm Offers (1975) Law Com Working Paper No 60; Penalty Clauses and Forfeiture of Monies Paid (1975) Law Com Working Paper No 61.

[11] See paras 2.63-2.69 below.

[12] See paras 4.5-4.14 below.

from our work on the rights of buyers of goods carried by sea,[13] and by a more cautious judicial approach in the late 1980s and early 1990s to tort liability for pure economic loss.[14] In short we had little doubt that the continued existence of the third party rule represented a pressing problem for the English law of contract.

1.5   In Consultation Paper No 121,[15] we set out the current law on the third party rule, the case for its reform, and the main issues that would need to be dealt with in any reform. In an Appendix, we gave an account of the way in which the problem has been dealt with in other jurisdictions. Our provisional conclusion was that the law ought to be reformed and that the reform should be embodied in a detailed legislative scheme. The principal feature of that scheme (that is, the test of enforceability) would be that a third party should be able to enforce a contract where the parties intended that the third party should receive the benefit of the promised performance and also intended to create a legal obligation enforceable by the third party.

1.6   The Consultation Paper attracted 102 replies. A clear majority accepted the validity of our arguments in favour of reform. Our provisional proposals were particularly welcomed by the legal profession and some other professional bodies, academic lawyers, consumer organisations, and the insurance and banking industries. While it was to be expected that the subject of the Consultation Paper would be of great interest to academic lawyers, the wide range of responses from non-academic lawyers and non-lawyers reflects the degree to which the third party rule still causes significant difficulties in practice.

1.7   The minority who opposed the proposals outlined in the Consultation Paper did so in reliance on four main general arguments.[16] First, that reform was unnecessary because the rule caused few problems in practice given that those who were affected by it could use various devices, described below,[17] to get round the third party rule. Secondly, that no legislative reform could hope adequately to deal with all the diverse situations where the third party rule is relevant. Thirdly, that the existing legal regime, while complicated, achieved certainty, and that reform would only result in

---

[13]   Rights of Suit in Respect of Carriage of Goods by Sea (1991), Law Com No 196; Scot Law Com No 130 (see the Carriage of Goods by Sea Act 1992).

[14]   See, eg, *Caparo Industries Plc v Dickman* [1990] 2 AC 605; *Murphy v Brentwood District Council* [1991] 1 AC 398.

[15]   Privity of Contract: Contracts for the Benefit of Third Parties (1991) (hereinafter referred to as Consultation Paper No 121).

[16]   The main opposition to the proposals in the Consultation Paper came from some, although by no means all, of the twenty or so responses from the construction industry. Professor Burrows presented a revised version of our proposals in a lecture to the Society of Construction Law on 4 April 1995; and a copy of that lecture was sent to members of that society inviting comments. The response to that lecture, both at the time and subsequently, suggests that our final recommendations will not be opposed by the construction industry.

[17]   See paras 2.8-2.62 below.

uncertainty and litigation. Fourthly, that the proposals for reform might lead to contracting parties being bound to third parties when this was not their true intention.

1.8   We disagree with the view that the third party rule does not cause significant problems in practice.[18] We cannot ignore those who do not have access to (good) legal advice and, in any event, our proposed reforms will provide a simpler way of affording a third party the right to enforce a contract than the present convoluted techniques. This will not only save the parties costs, it will also save the taxpayer the needless litigation costs caused by the complexity of the present law.   Nevertheless the response of the minority who opposed the proposed reform was invaluable in requiring us to reassess whether our proposals were too uncertain and would result in the imposition of unintended liabilities. In certain respects - and especially as regards the test of enforceability - we have modified our provisional recommendations in an attempt to allay those kinds of fears.   We should emphasise, at the outset, that our recommendations are not concerned to override the allocation of liability within contracts but rather rest on an underlying policy of effectuating the contracting parties' intentions.   At root our recommendations would enable the parties to create enforceable third party rights in contract without the complexities of the devices presently used to circumvent the privity doctrine.

1.9   Our general approach has been to devise moderate reform proposals which can be expected to gain wide support. Some more radical possibilities have been put to one side for fear that the central reform would otherwise be endangered. For example, we do not in this report recommend a special test of enforceability for third parties who are consumers;[19] we do not propose a reform of insurance contracts that goes as far as section 48 of the Australian Insurance Contracts Act 1984;[20] and we do not seek to recast the decision of the House of Lords in *White v Jones*[21] by bringing the claims of disappointed beneficiaries under negligently drafted wills within our proposed Act.[22]

1.10   It has also been important in our thinking that, while we believe that a detailed legislative scheme is the best means of reforming privity, we have no desire to hamper judicial creativity in this area. For example, we have left to the developing common law, what the rights of promisees should be in contracts for the benefit of third parties;[23] and we have left open for the judges to decide what the rights of a joint

---

[18]   See paras 3.5-3.6 and especially 3.9-3.27 below.

[19]   See paras 7.54-7.56 below.

[20]   See paras 12.22-12.25 below.

[21]   [1995] 2 AC 207.

[22]   See paras 7.19-7.27 below.

[23]   See paras 5.12-5.17 below.

promisee, who has not provided consideration, should be.[24] In general terms, we see our draft Bill as achieving at a stroke and with certainty and clarity what a progressive House of Lords might well itself have brought about over the course of time. While the draft Bill departs from a long-established common law rule, we hope that it will not be seen as cutting across the underpinning principles of the common law.

1.11   The arrangement of this Report is as follows. In Part II we examine the present law and calls for reform. In Part III we present the case for reform. Part IV looks at precedents for reform. In Parts V and VI we examine the form of the legislation and the relationship between our reform and the consideration doctrine. In Parts VII to XIV we set out the important issues raised by any reform. In each of Parts VII to XIV, we comment on the responses received to the provisional proposals in our Consultation Paper, and then make detailed proposals for dealing with the issues raised. Part XV contains a summary of our recommendations. A draft Bill to give effect to our recommendations is to be found in Appendix A. Certain statutes from other jurisdictions to which we commonly refer are reproduced in Appendix B. Appendix C contains a list of those who responded to the Consultation Paper. Appendix D lists those who participated at a conference examining Consultation Paper No 121 held at the Institute of Advanced Legal Studies.

1.12   We gratefully acknowledge the assistance of the following people, who helped us with various aspects of this paper:-

Professor Jack Beatson, Rouse Ball Professor of English Law at Cambridge University, who was the Law Commissioner in charge of this project until October 1994 and who has subsequently continued to provide invaluable advice and assistance to us in bringing this Report to fruition; Professor Hugh Beale, University of Warwick, Professor Aubrey Diamond QC, Notre Dame University, and Professor Sally Wheeler, University of Leeds, who together formed our advisory working party; Professor Guenter Treitel QC, Vinerian Professor of English Law at Oxford University, who gave generously of his time and expertise in the final stages of this project; Sir Wilfred Bourne QC who carried out the analysis of consultation; Professor Roy Goode QC, Norton Rose Professor of English Law at Oxford University; Lord Justice Saville; Mr Justice Longmore; Mr Justice Rix; Michael Brindle QC; Stewart Boyd QC; V V Veeder QC; David Foxton; Toby Landau; Frances Paterson; Michael Marks Cohen; Alexander Green; Bruce Harris; Alex Maitland Hudson; Dr Malcolm Clarke, St John's College, Cambridge; Dr Gerhard Dannemann, Centre for the Advanced Study of European and Comparative Law, University of Oxford; Professor Richard Sutton, New Zealand Law Commission.

---

[24] See paras 6.9-6.12 below.

PART II
THE PRESENT LAW AND CALLS FOR REFORM

1. The Present Law

(1) A Brief Statement of the Third Party Rule in Contract

2.1 A contract or its performance can affect a third party.[1] However, the doctrine of privity means that, as a general rule, a contract cannot confer rights or impose obligations arising under it on any person except the parties to it.[2] This Report is concerned with *the conferral of rights* on third parties (including whether a third party should be able to claim the benefit of an exclusion clause contained in a contract to which he is not a party); and, as we have indicated above,[3] references in it to the "third party rule" are to this aspect of the privity doctrine. It was provisionally recommended in the Consultation Paper[4] that the present rule should be retained whereby, subject to a few exceptions,[5] parties to a contract cannot *impose an obligation* on a third party. There was no dissent from this by consultees.[6] It would be an unwarranted infringement of a third party's liberty if contracting parties were able, as a matter of course, to impose burdens on a third party without his or her consent. Our proposed reforms do not, therefore, seek to change the 'burden' aspect of the privity doctrine or the exceptions to it.

(2) Development of the Third Party Rule

2.2 It is generally agreed that the modern third party rule was conclusively established in 1861 in *Tweddle v Atkinson*.[7] In *Drive Yourself Hire Co (London) Ltd v Strutt*,[8] Denning LJ said:

---

[1] As when C guarantees a debt owed by A to B and A pays, thus releasing C who thereby indirectly gains a benefit. See Treitel, *The Law of Contract* (9th ed, 1995) p 551.

[2] Before *Donoghue v Stevenson* [1932] AC 562, the privity doctrine was seen as precluding actions in tort by third parties arising from negligence by a party to a contract in carrying it out: *Winterbottom v Wright* (1842) 10 M & W 109; 152 ER 402.

[3] See para 1.2 above.

[4] Consultation Paper No 121, paras 5.36-5.37, 6.17.

[5] The exceptions include agency, restrictive covenants running with land, restrictive covenants running with goods (see, eg, *Lord Strathcona SS Co v Dominion Coal Co* [1926] AC 108), bailment (eg, *Morris v CW Martin & Sons Ltd* [1966] 1 QB 716; *Singer (UK) Ltd v Tees and Hartlepool Port Authority* [1988] 2 Lloyd's Rep 164, 167-168; *The Captain Gregos (No 2)* [1990] 2 Lloyd's Rep 395, 405; *KH Enterprise (cargo owners) v Pioneer Containers (owners), The Pioneer Container* [1994] 2 AC 324), and the Carriage of Goods by Sea Act 1992, s 3.

[6] Although a few consultees did suggest further exceptions that, at least at this stage, we consider are better left to common law development (eg that the situations in which exclusion clauses bind third parties should be extended).

[7] (1861) 1 B & S 393; 121 ER 762.

[8] [1954] 1 QB 250.

It is often said to be a fundamental principle of our law that only a person who is a party to a contract can sue on it. I wish to assert, as distinctly as I can, that the common law in its original setting knew no such principle. Indeed, it said quite the contrary. For the 200 years before 1861 it was settled law that, if a promise in a simple contract was made expressly for the benefit of a third person in such circumstances that it was intended to be enforceable by him, then the common law would enforce the promise at his instance, although he was not a party to the contract.[9]

2.3 Denning LJ cited several cases to support his view. In *Dutton v Poole*,[10] a son promised his father that, in return for his father not selling a wood, he would pay £1000 to his sister. The father refrained from selling the wood, but the son did not pay. It was held that the sister could sue, on the ground that the consideration and promise to the father may well have extended to her on account of the tie of blood between them.[11] In *Marchington v Vernon*,[12] Buller J said that, independently of the rules prevailing in mercantile transactions,[13] if one person makes a promise to another for the benefit of a third, the third may maintain an action upon it. In *Carnegie v Waugh*,[14] the tutors and curators of an infant, C, executed an agreement for a lease with A, for an annual rent to be paid to C. It was held that C could sue on the instrument, even though he was not a party to it. In addition, there is a respectable line of 16th and 17th century authority allowing an intended beneficiary a right of action.[15] These cases often involved similar facts. The fathers of a potential bride and groom would agree to pay a sum of money to the groom if he married, the bride's father subsequently reneging on the agreement. In several of these cases it was held that, not only could the groom

---

[9] [1954] 1 QB 250, 272.

[10] (1678) 2 Lev 210; 83 ER 523. This decision was supported, obiter, by Lord Mansfield in *Martyn v Hind* (1776) 2 Cowp 437, 443; 98 ER 1174, 1177.

[11] The report discloses disagreement in the King's Bench during the argument, on the grounds that the daughter was privy neither to the promise nor the consideration. Nevertheless, the decision was upheld in the Exchequer Chamber: (1679) T Raym 302; 83 ER 156.

[12] (1797) 1 Bos & P 101, n (c); 126 ER 801, n (c). This case was described as "but a loose note at Nisi Prius" by counsel in the interesting case of *Phillips v Bateman* (1812) 16 East 356, 371; 104 ER 1124, 1129, where A, in the face of a run on a banking house, promised to support the bank with £30,000, whereupon note holders stopped withdrawing their money. When the bank subsequently stopped paying out, A was held not liable to an action by individual holders of bank notes.

[13] The case itself involved a bill of exchange.

[14] (1823) 1 LJ (OS) KB 89.

[15] A Simpson, *A History of the Common Law of Contract* (1975), pp 477-478. See also V Palmer, "The History of Privity - The Formative Period" (1500-1680) (1989) 33 Am J Leg Hist 3; D Ibbetson; "Consideration and the Theory of Contract in Sixteenth Century Common Law" in J Barton (ed), *Towards a General Law of Contract* (1990), 67, 96-99. Cf V Palmer, *The Paths to Privity - The History of Third Party Beneficiary Contracts at English Law* (1992).

sue to recover the amount promised, but that his father, the promisee, could not sue because he had no interest in performance.[16]

2.4   In spite of these cases favouring actions by third party beneficiaries, it is not accurate to say that the third party rule was entirely a 19th century innovation. There were other 16th and 17th century cases where a third party was denied an action on the grounds that the promisee was the only person entitled to bring the action.[17] There were also cases where the reason given why the third party could not sue was because he was a stranger to the consideration, that is, he had given nothing in return for the promise.[18] These cases typically involved the following facts. B owed money to C. A would agree with B to pay C in return for B doing something for A, such as working or conveying a house. A would not pay, and C would sue A. C would lose because he or she had given nothing for A's promise.

2.5   Thus, by the mid-19th century there appeared to be no firm rule either way in English law. The position was to be clarified in *Tweddle v Atkinson*.[19] The facts involved an agreement by the fathers of a bride and groom to pay the groom a sum of money. When the bride's father failed to pay, the groom sued unsuccessfully. Wightman J said that no stranger to the consideration could take advantage of a contract though made for his benefit. Crompton J said that consideration must move from the promisee.[20]

2.6   The authority of *Tweddle v Atkinson* was soon generally acknowledged. In *Gandy v Gandy*,[21] Bowen LJ said that, in spite of earlier cases to the contrary, *Tweddle v*

---

[16]   *Lever v Heys* Moo KB 550; 72 ER 751; also *Levet v Hawes* Cro Eliz 619, 652; 78 ER 860, 891; *Provender v Wood* Het 30; 124 ER 318; *Hadves v Levit* Het 176; 124 ER 433. In an altogether different scenario in *Rippon v Norton* Cro Eliz 849; 78 ER 1074, A promised B that his son would keep the peace against B and B's son (C). A's son thereafter assaulted B's son. B, alleging medical expenses and loss of the services of his son, failed in his action against A, even though he was the promisee. It was said that the son (C) was the person who should have sued, which he later did successfully: Cro Eliz 881; 78 ER 1106.

[17]   *Jordan v Jordan* (1594) Cro Eliz 369; 78 ER 616 (C gave a warrant to B to arrest A for an alleged debt. A promised B that, in return for not arresting him, he would pay the debt. C failed in his action, on the ground, inter alia, that the promise had been made to B); *Taylor v Foster* (1600) Cro Eliz 776; 78 ER 1034 (A, in return for B marrying his daughter, agreed to pay to C an amount which B owed to C. In an action by B against A, it was held that B was the person to sue, being the promisee).

[18]   *Bourne v Mason* (1669) 1 Ventr 6; 86 ER 5; *Crow v Rogers* (1724) 1 St 592; 93 ER 719; *Price v Easton* (1833) 4 B & Ad 433; 110 ER 518. Although in the former two cases, the reason why C failed was because he was a stranger to the consideration, *Price v Easton* contains seeds of more modern doctrine: whereas Denman CJ said that no consideration for the promise moved from C to A, Littledale J said that there was no privity between C and A.

[19]   (1861) 1 B & S 393; 121 ER 762.

[20]   The earlier cases allowing children to be considered a party to their father's consideration were considered obsolete. *Dutton v Poole* (1678) T Raym 302; 83 ER 156, being a decision of the Exchequer Chamber could not be overruled by the Queen's Bench, but was nonetheless not followed.

[21]   (1885) 30 ChD 57, 69.

Atkinson had laid down "the true common law doctrine". In *Dunlop Pneumatic Tyre Co Ltd v Selfridge & Co Ltd*,[22] the House of Lords accepted that it was a fundamental principle of English law that only a party to a contract who had provided consideration could sue on it. Despite several attempts by Denning LJ to allow rights of suit by third party beneficiaries,[23] the House of Lords reaffirmed the general rule in *Midland Silicones Ltd v Scruttons Ltd*.[24] Viscount Simonds said:

> [H]eterodoxy, or, as some might say, heresy, is not the more attractive because it is dignified by the name of reform. ...If the principle of *jus quaesitum tertio* is to be introduced into our law, it must be done by Parliament after a due consideration of its merits and demerits.[25]

2.7　Although the House of Lords has subsequently strongly criticised the rule,[26] it has refrained from any judicial abrogation of it. Thus the general rule remains that a third party cannot enforce a contract made for its benefit.

(3) Existing Exceptions to, or Circumventions of, the Third Party Rule[27]

(a) Trusts of the Promise[28]

2.8　A chose in action may be the subject matter of a trust. Hence a promise by A to B to pay a sum of money to C may be construed as constituting B a trustee of the promise by A for the benefit of C. If so, C (as beneficiary of the trust) can sue to enforce the promise. Thus equity allows a third party to enforce a contract where this can be construed as creating a completely constituted trust in his or her favour. The third party is not then relying merely on a contract made by others. However, the cases

---

[22]　[1915] AC 847.

[23]　*Smith and Snipes Hall Farm Ltd v River Douglas Catchment Board* [1949] 2 KB 500; *Drive Yourself Hire Co (London) Ltd v Strutt* [1954] 1 QB 250.

[24]　[1962] AC 446 (Lord Denning dissenting).

[25]　At pp 467-468.

[26]　See *Beswick v Beswick* [1968] AC 58, 72; *Woodar Investment Developments Ltd v Wimpey Construction UK Ltd* [1980] 1 WLR 277, 291, 297-298, 300. See also dicta of Lord Diplock in *Swain v Law Society* [1983] 1 AC 598, 611; and of Lord Goff in *The Pioneer Container* [1994] 2 AC 324, 335 and *White v Jones* [1995] 2 AC 207, 262-263. See generally paras 2.63-2.69 below.

[27]　Two consultees pointed out to us that deed polls (under which a person can undertake an obligation to another person without that other person having to be a party to the document) are quite frequently used in the commercial world as a means of evading privity, particularly where the beneficiaries belong to a large and fluctuating class. Deed polls cannot be varied once executed. See generally *Sunderland Marine Insurance Co v Kearney* (1851) 16 QB 925; 117 ER 1136; *Norton on Deeds* (2nd ed, 1928) p 27 ff.

[28]　See generally, J Hornby, "Covenants in Favour of Volunteers" (1962) 78 LQR 228; W Lee, "The Public Policy of Re Cook's Settlement Trusts" (1969) 85 LQR 213; J Barton, "Trusts and Covenants" (1975) 91 LQR 236; R Meager and J Lehane, "Trusts of Voluntary Covenants" (1976) 92 LQR 427; C Rickett, "The Constitution of Trusts: Contracts to Create Trusts" (1979) 32 CLP 1; C Rickett, "Two Propositions in the Constitution of Trusts" (1981) 34 CLP 189.

demonstrate that the notion of a trust of the promise is confined within narrow limits. It has only been applied to promises to pay money or to transfer property, and attempts to apply it to other forms of contractual obligation have failed.[29] Most importantly, it must be established that the promisee intended to create a trust. The courts were once prepared to infer this from the simple intention to benefit a third party,[30] an approach which reached its high water mark in *Les Affréteurs Réunis SA v Leopold Walford (London) Ltd.*[31] But in the majority of cases since then they have refused to draw that inference and have instead required a clear indication that a trust was intended.[32] The consequence has been that in recent times this exception has rarely been of assistance to a third party.

2.9   We think it most unlikely that the reasoning of a majority of the Court of Appeal in *Darlington Borough Council v Wiltshier (Northern) Ltd*[33] will herald a swing back to the old approach to trusts of a promise. In that case, A (Wiltshier) entered into a contract with B (Morgan Grenfell) for the benefit of C (Darlington); and B had entered into a contract with C to assign the benefit of its contract with A to C. The majority considered that, by analogy to early trust cases like *Lloyd's v Harper*,[34] B was a "constructive trustee" of the benefit of its rights against A for C. Hence B could have recovered from A substantial damages as representing C's loss; and, on assignment by B to C, C was entitled to the substantial damages that B would itself have been entitled to. It should be emphasised that this was an alternative ground for the decision. As we explain below, the principal reasoning of the Court of Appeal was based on an application of the rule in *Dunlop v Lambert*.[35]

(b) Covenants Concerning Land

2.10   The law allows certain covenants (whether positive or restrictive) to run with land so as to benefit (or burden) people other than the original contracting parties. The

---

[29]   See *Southern Water Authority v Carey* [1985] 2 All ER 1077, 1083; *Norwich City Council v Harvey* [1989] 1 WLR 828; *Chitty on Contracts* (27th ed, 1994), paras 18-045-18-054.

[30]   Eg *Tomlinson v Gill* (1756) Amb 330, 27 ER 221; *Fletcher v Fletcher* (1844) 4 Hare 67, 67 ER 564; *Lloyd's v Harper* (1880) 16 ChD 290; *Re Flavell* (1883) 25 ChD 89.

[31]   [1919] AC 801. See M MacIntyre, "Third Party Rights in Canadian and English Law" (1965) 2 UBCL Rev 103, 104-105.

[32]   See *Re Engelbach* [1924] 2 Ch 348; *Vandepitte v Preferred Accident Insurance Corpn of New York* [1933] AC 70; *Re Clay's Policy* [1937] 2 All ER 548; *Re Foster* [1938] 3 All ER 357; *Re Sinclair's Life Policy* [1938] Ch 799; *Re Schebsman* [1944] Ch 83 (see also Treitel, *The Law of Contract* (9th ed, 1995) p 578 n 99).

[33]   [1995] 1 WLR 68, 75 per Dillon LJ (with whom Waite LJ agreed); Steyn LJ, at p 81, found it unnecessary to consider this point. See paras 2.42-2.45, below.

[34]   (1880) 16 ChD 290. In *Lloyd's v Harper*, however, both James LJ (at p 315) and Lush LJ (at p 321) seemed to regard as important the fact that this approach was necessary in order to permit effective functioning of the common practice in existence in insurance transactions at Lloyd's.

[35]   (1839) 6 Cl & F 600; 7 ER 824. See paras 2.39-2.46 below.

relevant covenant may relate to freehold land or leasehold land. The law relating to the running of covenants is an illustration of where, for commercial and ethical reasons, the privity of contract doctrine has been departed from through the development of a separate body of "non-contractual" principles (here the principles being categorised as belonging to the law of real property).

2.11 The law on covenants relating to leasehold land has recently been reformed by the Landlord and Tenant (Covenants) Act 1995.[36] The effect of the 1995 Act can be briefly explained in the following four points:-

(i) The benefit and burden of covenants in a lease granted prior to 1996 would pass on an assignment of the lease or reversion so as to benefit or bind the assignee of the lease or the reversion, provided that the covenant "touched and concerned" the land.[37] As a result of the Landlord and Tenant (Covenants) Act 1995, in relation to leases granted after 1995, the benefit and burden of *all* covenants in a lease passes on an assignment of the lease or reversion unless the covenant is expressed to be personal.[38] It is now for the parties to decide whether a covenant is to be regarded as personal. It is no longer for the court to try to decide it objectively according to whether it is thought to "touch and concern" the land.

(ii) Where, prior to 1996, L granted a lease to T and T then sublet to S, the burden of the covenants in the headlease did *not* bind S, the sublessee, because there was no privity of estate[39] between L and S. This was subject to an exception. If the covenant was a restrictive covenant, it would bind S as an equitable property right, provided that, where the title was unregistered, he had notice of the covenant (as he would in practice)[40] or, where the title was registered, in any event.[41] In leases granted after 1995, this rule is codified. A restrictive covenant in the headlease binds any sublessee automatically.[42]

(iii) Where, prior to 1996, L granted a lease to T and T then sublet to S, S *could* enforce the benefit of any landlord covenants which touched and concerned the land against L, despite the absence of privity of contract. This is because the

---

[36] Based on the recommendations made in Landlord and Tenant Law: Privity of Contract and Estate (1988) Law Com No 174.

[37] *Spencer's Case* (1583) 5 Co Rep 16a; 77 ER 72 (leases); Law of Property Act 1925, ss 141-142 (reversions).

[38] Landlord and Tenant (Covenants) Act 1995, s 3(6).

[39] Which simply means the relationship of landlord and tenant.

[40] See Law of Property Act 1925, s 44; *White v Bijou Mansions Ltd* [1937] Ch 610.

[41] Land Registration Act 1925, s 23(1)(a).

[42] Landlord and Tenant (Covenants) Act 1995, s 3(5).

benefit of such covenants was annexed under section 78 of the Law of Property Act 1925 and could be enforced by a person with a derivative interest.[43] In a lease granted after 1995, this is no longer possible.[44] S cannot enforce any covenant in the headlease against L.

(iv) For leases granted prior to 1996, the original tenant and landlord remained liable for a breach of covenant in the lease despite assignment. For leases granted after 1995 the original tenant[45] will generally be released from covenants in the lease once the lease has been assigned.[46] This aspect of the reforms is concerned to cut back a normal feature of privity of contract rather than being concerned with the exception to privity of contract constituted by covenants running with land.

2.12 As regards covenants relating to freehold land (which are unaffected by the 1995 Act) any such covenants entered into after 1926 which touch and concern the land will in most cases be automatically annexed to the land of the covenantee under section 78 of the Law of Property Act 1925.[47] According to the wording of that section, where the covenant in question is *positive* it may then be enforced by the covenantee, his successors in title and those who derive title under him or them (such as mortgagees and lessees). Squatters (who are not successors in title) or licensees (who have no title) cannot enforce such an annexed covenant. Where the covenant is restrictive, *any* owner or occupier for the time being can enforce the annexed covenant even though he or she may be a squatter or licensee. There will be few covenants made after 1926 which are not annexed in this way.[48]

(c) Tort of Negligence

2.13 The tort of negligence can be viewed as an exception to the third party rule where the negligence in question constitutes the breach of a contract to which the plaintiff is not

---

[43] *Smith v River Douglas Catchment Board* [1949] 2 KB 500 (lessee able to enforce annexed freehold covenant on the wording of s 78). As it is clear that s 78 applies to leases as well as to freeholds: *Caerns Motor Services Ltd v Texaco Ltd* [1994] 1 WLR 1249, S must be able to enforce the covenant against L.

[44] Law of Property Act 1925, s 78 does not apply to such leases (Landlord and Tenant (Covenants) Act 1995, s 30(4)) and this effect of that section is not replicated: cf Landlord and Tenant (Covenants) Act 1995, s 15.

[45] Somewhat different provisions apply in respect of an assignment of the reversion by the landlord. The landlord must apply to the tenant to be released from the landlord covenants. If the tenant refuses to do so, the court may release the landlord if it considers it reasonable to do so. See Landlord and Tenant (Covenants) Act 1995, ss 6-8.

[46] Landlord and Tenant (Covenants) Act 1995, ss 3 and 5; although under s 16 a tenant may enter into an "authorised guarantee agreement" to guarantee compliance with the covenants by the assignee.

[47] *Federated Homes Ltd v Mill Lodge Properties Ltd* [1980] 1 WLR 594.

[48] It is probably only those which are expressed to be capable of passing solely by express assignment: *Roake v Chadha* [1984] 1 WLR 40.

a party. For example, the classic case of negligence, *Donoghue v Stevenson*,[49] established that where A supplies goods to B under a contract with B, A may owe a duty to C in respect of personal injury or damage to property caused by defects in those goods. But the right not to be injured or to have one's property damaged by another's negligence exists independently of any contractual undertaking by A. It is only in a very wide sense, therefore, that standard examples of the tort of negligence constitute exceptions to the third party rule.

2.14 Of more direct interest are cases of pure economic loss recovery in the tort of negligence where the basis of the third party's claim appears to be the failure by A properly to perform a contract made with B.[50] In other words, cases where the basis of the third party's tort claim appears not to be independent of the rights conferred by the contract. For example, in *Ross v Caunters*,[51] an improperly executed will deprived a prospective beneficiary of an intended benefit, and the prospective beneficiary was able to recover in tort against the negligent solicitor. It can be argued that the remedy in tort effectively served to enforce a contract benefiting a third party at the suit of the third party. The third party was awarded the expectation loss of the benefits that he would have received under the will. This decision was confirmed by the House of Lords in *White v Jones*,[52] where solicitors were held to be negligent and liable to a prospective beneficiary for the loss of the intended legacy (an expectation loss), when they failed to draw up a will before the testator died. The decision was based on an extension of the principle of assumption of responsibility in *Hedley Byrne and Co Ltd v Heller and Partners Ltd*.[53] Lord Goff[54] was of the opinion that in allowing such liability to be imposed, there had been "no unacceptable circumvention of established principles of the law of contract".[55] But, whether acceptable or not,[56] it does seem to us that the decision is best analysed as allowing a third party to enforce a contract by

---

[49] [1932] AC 562.

[50] For discussion of the relationship between contract and tort in this type of situation, see: A Jaffey, "Sub-Contractors - Privity and Negligence" [1983] CLJ 37; J Holyoak, "Tort and Contract after *Junior Books*" (1983) 99 LQR 591; A Jaffey, "Contract in Tort's Clothing" (1985) 5 LS 77; B Markesinis, "An Expanding Tort Law - The Price of a Rigid Contract Law" (1987) 103 LQR 354; W Lorenz and B Markesinis, "Solicitors' Liability Towards Third Parties: Back Into the Troubled Waters of the Contract/Tort Divide" (1993) 56 MLR 558.

[51] [1980] Ch 297.

[52] [1995] 2 AC 207.

[53] [1964] AC 465; see [1995] 2 AC 207, 268.

[54] Who gave the most detailed of the majority speeches.

[55] [1995] 2 AC 207, 268. Lord Goff saw the decision as giving effect to the considerations of "practical justice".

[56] We discuss the decision further in paras 7.19-7.27, 7.36 and 7.48 below.

pursuing an action in tort.[57] A further example is *Junior Books Ltd v Veitchi Ltd*.[58] Here the owners of a factory were allowed to recover expectation loss from a subcontractor, in that they were allowed to recover the cost of either replacing or repairing a negligently constructed factory floor. The owners' claim can again be viewed as being one by a third party beneficiary of a contract (here between the sub-contractor and the head-contractor) to enforce the benefit which was contracted for.

(d) Agency

2.15   Many contracts are made through intermediaries and will be subject to the law of agency. Agency is the relationship which exists between two persons, one of whom (the principal) expressly or impliedly consents that the other should act on his behalf, and the other of whom (the agent) similarly consents so to act or so acts.[59]   One consequence of this relationship is that the principal acquires rights (and liabilities) under contracts made by the agent on his behalf with third parties. Although one can normally say, without undue fiction, that the principal is the real party to the contract concluded by his agent, agency can also be viewed as an exception to the privity doctrine in that the principal, albeit a third party to the contract concluded by his agent, is able to sue (and be sued) on it. The doctrine of the undisclosed principal is particularly controversial.[60] If an agent within his authority contracts in his own name and purportedly on his own behalf, the undisclosed principal may in certain circumstances intervene to sue and be sued on the contract.[61] The other party who has no knowledge of the principal's existence may thus find that he has made a contract with a person of whom he has never heard, and with whom he never intended to contract.[62]

---

[57]   Lord Mustill (dissenting) was clearly of the opinion that the beneficiaries were effectively seeking to enforce a contract to which they were not a party: "...the intended beneficiaries did not engage the solicitor, undertake to pay his fees or tell him what to do. Having promised them nothing he has broken no promise. They nevertheless fasten upon the circumstance that the solicitor broke his promise to someone else..."; [1995] 2 AC 207, 278.

[58]   [1983] 1 AC 520. It should be noted that since it was decided, *Junior Books* has come to be seen as unreliable authority and has consistently been confined to its facts: "The consensus of judicial opinion, with which I concur, seems to be that the decision ... cannot be regarded as laying down any principle of general application in the law of tort or delict", *D & F Estates Ltd v Church Commissioners* [1989] AC 177, 202, per Lord Bridge. Cf *Murphy v Brentwood DC* [1991] 1 AC 398; *White v Jones* [1995] 2 AC 207.

[59]   *Bowstead and Reynolds on Agency* (16th ed, 1996) para 1-001.

[60]   See, for example, Treitel *The Law of Contract* (9th ed, 1995) p 645 ff; Cheshire, Fifoot and Furmston's *Law of Contract* (12th ed, 1991) p 489; *Chitty on Contracts* (27th ed, 1994) para 31-058.

[61]   *Bowstead and Reynolds on Agency* (16th ed, 1996), para 8-069.

[62]   Atiyah, *An Introduction to the Law of Contract* (5th ed, 1995) p 366. Cf R Goode, *Commercial Law* (2nd ed, 1995) p 181.

(e) Assignment

2.16   Except when personal considerations are at its foundation,[63] the benefit of a contract may be assigned (that is transferred) to a third party.[64] The assignment is effected through a contract between the promisee under the main contract (that is, the assignor) and the third party (that is, the assignee). In addition to assignment by an act of the parties, there exists assignment by operation of law.[65] The assent of the promisor is not necessary for an assignment. Assignment may therefore deprive promisors of their chosen contracting party, although safeguards are imposed to protect promisors. While an equitable assignment is usually fully effective even without notice,[66] notice is desirable and there are circumstances in which failure to give notice may leave the equitable assignee unable to exercise rights enjoyed by the assignor.[67] In addition, an assignee takes "subject to equities",[68] that is, subject to any defences which the promisor has and any defects in the assignor's title. The effect of assignment is that the promisor is faced with an action brought on the contract by a person whom he did not regard as a party and whom he may not have intended to benefit. The practical importance of assignment is considerable; the whole industry of debt collection and credit factoring depends upon it.

2.17   In considering reform of the third party rule, assignment constitutes a particularly significant exception. For if, immediately after a contract for a third party's benefit is made, the promisee assigns his rights under it to that third party, the third party can enforce the contract and the promisee loses all right to enforce, vary or cancel the contract. There is a thin divide between (i) making a contract for the benefit of a third party; and (ii) making a contract for the benefit of a third party and, immediately thereafter, assigning that benefit to the third party (especially where the third party does not provide consideration). If an immediate assignment is valid, there can hardly be fundamental objections to allowing the third party to sue without an assignment. It also follows that in considering the details of reform it is instructive to consider the rules of assignment dealing with, for example, the defences and counterclaims

[63]   *Farrow v Wilson* (1869) LR 4 CP 744.

[64]   Cheshire, Fifoot & Furmston's *Law of Contract* (12th ed, 1991) ch 16; Treitel, *The Law of Contract* (9th ed, 1995) ch 16; *Chitty on Contracts* (27th ed, 1994), ch 19.

[65]   For instance, when a party to a contract is declared bankrupt, rights of action forming part of his estate are "deemed to have been assigned" to his trustee in bankruptcy: Insolvency Act 1986, s 311(4).

[66]   *Gorringe v Irwell India Rubber and Gutta Percha Works* (1887) 34 Ch D 128.

[67]   The failure to give notice of the equitable assignment of an option may mean that the option is not exercisable by the assignee: *Warner Bros Records Inc v Rollgreen Ltd* [1976] QB 430: cf *Three Rivers DC v Bank of England* [1995] 3 WLR 650. Notice of a statutory assignment must be in writing: Law of Property Act 1925, s 136(1).

[68]   Cheshire, Fifoot & Furmston's *Law of Contract* (12th ed, 1991) pp 516-7; Treitel, *The Law of Contract* (9th ed, 1995) p 605 ff; *Chitty on Contracts* (27th ed, 1994), paras 19-039-19-045.

available to the promisor (the principle is that an assignee takes "subject to equities"), and joinder of the original promisee (joinder of the assignor is sometimes necessary).[69]

(f) Collateral Contracts

2.18   A contract between two parties may be accompanied by a collateral contract between one of them and a third party.[70] A collateral contract may in effect allow a third party to enforce the main contract (between A and B). For instance, where C buys goods from B, there may be a collateral contract between C and the manufacturer in the form of a guarantee. Collateral contracts have been used as a means of rendering exclusion clauses enforceable by a third party;[71] and are extensively used in the construction industry as a way of extending to subsequent owners or tenants the benefits of a builder's or architect's or engineer's contractual obligations.[72] Strictly speaking, of course, a collateral contract is not an exception to the third party rule in that the 'third party' is a party to the collateral contract albeit not a party to the main contract.

(g) Techniques Used to Enable Third Parties to Take the Benefit of Exclusion Clauses

2.19   A problematic issue, that has been raised in numerous cases, has been the extent to which third parties to contracts may take the benefit of clauses in those contracts excluding or limiting liability for loss or damage. The tangled case law in this area provides an excellent illustration of the tension between, on the one hand, the formal adherence by the judiciary to the privity doctrine, which would prevent third parties taking the benefit of exclusion clauses, and the judiciary's desire to find ways round the doctrine so as to effect the contracting parties' intentions.

2.20   In the first leading case of the twentieth century,[73] *Elder, Dempster & Co Ltd v Paterson, Zochonis & Co Ltd*,[74] the question was whether, as a defence to a shipper's action in tort for negligently stowing cargo, shipowners could rely on an exclusion clause in the bills of lading, despite the fact that the contract of carriage was between the shipper

---

[69]   See *Chitty on Contracts* (27th ed, 1994), paras 19-002, 19-022-19-023.

[70]   Cheshire, Fifoot & Furmston's *Law of Contract* (12th ed, 1991) pp 64-65; Treitel, *The Law of Contract* (9th ed, 1995) pp 534-536; Atiyah, *An Introduction to the Law of Contract* (9th ed, 1995) pp 97-100. *Shanklin Pier Ltd v Detel Products Ltd* [1951] 2 KB 854; *Wells (Merstham) Ltd v Buckland Sand and Silica Ltd* [1965] 2 QB 170; *Charnock v Liverpool Corpn* [1968] 1 WLR 1498.

[71]   See paras 2.24-2.30 below.

[72]   See paras 3.12-3.19 below.

[73]   For 19th century cases, which normally involved carriage by rail, see eg, *Hall v North Eastern Railway Company* (1875) 10 QB 437, a case where the reasoning has been described as artificial but face-saving for privity. See Treitel, *The Law of Contract* (9th ed, 1995) p 568. See also *Bristol and Exeter Ry v Collins* (1859) 7 HLC 194; 11 ER 78; *Martin v Great Indian Peninsular Ry* (1867) LR 3 Ex 9; *Foulkes v Metropolitan District Ry Co* (1880) 5 CPD 157.

[74]   [1924] AC 522.

and the charterer. The House of Lords held that they could do so, although the reasoning on which the result was based has proved very difficult to understand.[75]

2.21 Perhaps the most significant point[76] is that some of their Lordships seemed to accept a principle of vicarious immunity, according to which a servant or agent who performs a contract is entitled to any immunity from liability which his employer or principal would have had. Hence, although the shipowners may not have been privy to the contract of carriage (between shipper and charterer) they took possession of the goods on behalf of, and as agents for, the charterers and so could claim the same protection as their principals.[77]

2.22 Although the principle of vicarious immunity was subsequently generally accepted by the lower courts,[78] it did not survive the decision of the House of Lords (Lord Denning dissenting) in *Midland Silicones Ltd v Scruttons Ltd*.[79] The defendant stevedores, engaged by the carrier, negligently damaged a drum containing chemicals. When the cargo-owners sued in tort, the stevedores unsuccessfully attempted to rely on a limitation clause contained in the bill of lading between the carriers and the

[75] Lord Reid in *Midland Silicones Ltd v Scruttons Ltd* stated that the task of extracting a *ratio* from the case was "unrewarding" [1962] AC 446, 479. See also *Johnson Matthey & Co Ltd v Constantine Terminals Ltd* [1976] 2 Lloyd's Rep 215, 219 (per Donaldson J, "something of a judicial nightmare") and *The Forum Craftsman* [1985] 1 Lloyd's Rep 291, 295 (per Ackner LJ, "heavily comatosed, if not long-interred"). See also Treitel, *The Law of Contract* (9th ed, 1995) pp 568-569; N Palmer, *Bailment* (2nd ed, 1991) pp 1638-1640. *Carver's Carriage by Sea* (13th ed, 1982) p 529, refers to the case as a "mystery". *Scrutton on Charterparties* (19th ed, 1984) p 251 n 36, contends that no general principle is to be extracted from the case.

[76] For the alternative line of reasoning see Lord Sumner, [1924] AC 522, 564, with whom Lord Dunedin and Lord Carson agreed. Lord Sumner talked of there being a "bailment on terms" which appears to mean that by entrusting the goods to the shipowners, the shipper may be taken to have impliedly agreed that the shipowner received the goods on the terms of the bill of lading which included the exemption from liability for bad storage. Lord Goff has recently given some support to this line of thinking in *obiter dicta* in *The Pioneer Container* [1994] 2 AC 324, 339-340 and, most importantly, in *The Mahkutai* [1996] 3 WLR 1 (see para 2.33 below).

[77] This was the basis of Scrutton LJ's judgment in the Court of Appeal: [1923] 1 KB 421, 441, and was supported by Viscount Cave, at p 534, with whom Lord Carson agreed. See also Viscount Finlay, at p 548.

[78] See, for instance, Scrutton LJ in *Mersey Shipping & Transport Co Ltd v Rea Ltd* (1925) 21 Lloyd's Rep 375; *Pyrene Co Ltd v Scindia Steam Navigation Co Ltd* [1954] 2 QB 402. For a discussion of the *Pyrene* case, see Consultation Paper No 121, para 5.37. But cf *Cosgrove v Horsfall* (1945) 62 TLR 140 (where *Elder, Dempster* was not cited) and *Adler v Dickson* [1955] 1 QB 158.

[79] [1962] AC 446. It should be noted that Art IV bis rule 2 of the Hague-Visby Rules, enacted in the UK by the Carriage of Goods by Sea Act 1971, provides that servants or agents of the carrier (but not independent contractors, eg stevedores, employed by it) are to have the benefit of the exceptions and limitations of liability given to the carrier under the Hague-Visby Rules themselves. Similar provisions are contained in the Geneva Convention on the Contract for the International Carriage of Goods By Road (CMR) (implemented in England by the Carriage of Goods by Road Act 1965); in the Warsaw Convention (implemented in England by the Carriage by Air Act 1961); and in the Berne Convention Concerning International Carriage by Rail 1980 (COTIF) (implemented in England by the International Transport Convention Act 1983): see para 12.14, note 21, below.

cargo-owners. The majority of the House of Lords confirmed English law's adherence to the privity of contract doctrine and was not prepared to hold that the principle of vicarious immunity was the *ratio* of *Elder, Dempster*.[80]

2.23 However, the possibility of third party stevedores taking advantage of exemption clauses was not entirely ruled out. Lord Reid said that there could exist a contract between the shipper and the stevedore made through the agency of the carrier, provided certain conditions were met:[81] (i) the bill of lading makes it clear that the stevedore is intended to be protected by the provisions therein;[82] (ii) the bill of lading makes it clear that the carrier, in addition to contracting on its own behalf, is also contracting as agent for the stevedore; (iii) the carrier has authority from the stevedore so to act, or perhaps later ratification by the stevedore would suffice; (iv) there is consideration moving from the stevedore.

2.24 Lord Reid's speech encouraged the use of "Himalaya" clauses,[83] which purport to extend the defences of the carrier to servants, agents and independent contractors engaged in the loading and unloading process. In *New Zealand Shipping Co Ltd v A M Satterthwaite & Co Ltd (The Eurymedon)*,[84] the Privy Council considered the extent to which such an exclusion clause contained in a bill of lading could be relied on by the third party stevedore, an independent contractor employed by the carrier, who was sued by the consignees of goods for negligently damaging the goods while unloading them.

2.25 The majority of the Privy Council gave effect to the clause by regarding the shipper as having made an offer of a unilateral contract to the stevedores to unload the goods on terms incorporating the exclusion clause. This offer was accepted by the stevedores by commencing work. In the words of Lord Wilberforce, the bill of lading:

---

[80] Lord Denning, in his dissenting speech, [1962] AC 446, 487-488, argued that, if the buyer is able to sue a sub-contractor (eg a stevedore) in tort for what was in truth a breach of the main contract, and the stevedore is not allowed the benefit of the terms of that contract, there exists an easy way for the buyer to avoid the terms of the main contract. He held that the stevedores could take advantage of the exclusion clause, since the earlier decision of the House in *Elder, Dempster & Co Ltd v Paterson, Zochonis & Co Ltd* [1924] AC 522 had determined this point in favour of stevedores.

[81] [1962] AC 446, 474.

[82] The exclusion clause was expressed to exclude the liability of the "carrier", and the stevedores suggested that the word "carrier" could be read as including stevedores. This proposition was rejected by a majority of their Lordships: see [1962] AC 446, 471 (*per* Viscount Simonds), 474 (*per* Lord Reid), 495 (*per* Lord Morris).

[83] So called after the vessel in *Adler v Dickson* [1955] 1 QB 158.

[84] [1975] AC 154. Although sometimes overlooked, the negligence claim in the case was being brought by the buyers (consignees) not the shipper. The buyers were held to be bound by the shipper's contract with the stevedore by reason of a so-called *Brandt v Liverpool* [1924] 1 KB 575 contract which arose when the buyers presented the bill of lading and took delivery. See Treitel, *The Law of Contract*, (9th ed 1995) p 570-571.

... brought into existence a bargain initially unilateral but capable of becoming mutual, between the shipper and the [stevedores], made through the carrier as agent. This became a full contract when the [stevedores] performed services by discharging the goods. The performance of these services for the benefit of the shipper was the consideration for the agreement by the shipper that the [stevedores] should have the benefit of the exemptions and limitations contained in the bill of lading.[85]

2.26   The exclusion clause in question was expressed to be entered into by the carrier as agent for its servants, agents and independent contractors, and therefore "the exemption is designed to cover the whole carriage from loading to discharge, by whomsoever it is performed: the performance attracts the exemption or immunity in favour of whoever the performer turns out to be".[86] Further,

In the opinion of their Lordships, to give the appellant the benefit of the exemptions and limitations contained in the bill of lading is to give effect to the clear intentions of a commercial document, and can be given within existing principles. They see no reason to strain the law or the facts in order to defeat these intentions. It should not be overlooked that the effect of denying validity to the clause would be to encourage actions against servants, agents and independent contractors in order to get round exemptions... .[87]

2.27   Nevertheless, the reasoning of Lord Wilberforce in *The Eurymedon* has been criticised as artificial,[88] primarily because it effectively rewrites the Himalaya clause, which was

---

[85]   [1975] AC 154, 167-8.

[86]   [1975] AC 154, 167.

[87]   [1975] AC 154, 169. Lord Wilberforce emphasised the difficulty of analysing many of the common transactions of daily life within the classical "slots" of offer, acceptance and consideration; [1975] AC 154, 167. In dissenting speeches, Viscount Dilhorne and Lord Simon of Glaisdale emphasised that artificial reasoning should not be employed in contractual interpretation with the effect of rewriting contractual provisions. Viscount Dilhorne stated that "...clause 1 of the bill of lading was obviously not drafted by a layman but by a highly qualified lawyer. It is a commercial document but the fact that it is of that description does not mean that to give it efficacy, one is at liberty to disregard its language and read into it that which it does not say and could have said or to construe the English words it contains as having a meaning which is not expressed and which is not implied." [1975] AC 154, 170. At p 172, he referred with approval to the judgment of Fullagar J in *Wilson v Darling Island Stevedoring and Lighterage Co Ltd* (1956) 95 CLR 43, 70, where Fullagar J decried the seeming anxiety of some courts and judges to save grossly negligent people from the normal consequences of their negligence, despite the established tendency of the law to construe exclusion clauses strictly.

[88]   See generally F Reynolds, 'Himalaya Clause Resurgent' (1974) 90 LQR 301; B Coote, 'Vicarious Immunity by an Alternative Route - II' (1974) 37 MLR 453; N Palmer, 'The Stevedore's Dilemma: Exemption Clauses and Third Parties - I' [1974] JBL 101; A Duggan, 'Offloading the Eurymedon' (1974) 9 Melbourne ULR 753; F Rose, 'Return to Elder Dempster?' (1975) 4 Anglo-Am LR 7; G Battersby, 'Exemption Clauses and Third Parties: Recent Decisions' (1978) 28 U of Toronto LJ 75; S Waddams, Comment (1977) 55 Can Bar Rev 327; P Davies and N Palmer, 'The Eurymedon Five Years On' [1979] JBL 337. For discussion of whether the better analysis is a unilateral or a bilateral contract, see N Palmer,

an agreement between the shipper and the carrier and from which it is difficult to detect an offer of a unilateral contract made by the shipper to the stevedore.[89]

2.28 *The Eurymedon* was not received with enthusiasm in other jurisdictions,[90] and in *Port Jackson Stevedoring Pty Ltd v Salmond and Spraggon (Australia) Pty Ltd (The New York Star)*,[91] the High Court of Australia sought to restrict its application.[92] Unloaded goods were stolen from the stevedores' possession, and the consignees sued the stevedores in negligence. The stevedores unsuccessfully attempted to rely on a Himalaya clause in the bill of lading. Stephen and Murphy JJ thought that, as a matter of policy, a decision in favour of the consignees would encourage carriers to insist on reasonable diligence on the part of their employees and contractors. Furthermore, a policy of extending protection to stevedores would merely benefit shipowning nations to the detriment of those countries, such as Australia, which relied on these fleets for their import and export trade. The Privy Council unanimously reversed the High Court of Australia. It warned against confining *The Eurymedon* to its facts, and stated that in the normal course of events involving the employment of stevedores by carriers, accepted principles enabled and required stevedores to enjoy the benefit of contractual provisions in the bill of lading.[93]

2.29 In other contexts the courts have been less attracted by this unilateral contract device though similar results have been achieved by other means. In *Southern Water Authority v Carey*,[94] engineering subcontractors, who were being sued in the tort of negligence,

---

Bailment (2nd ed, 1991) pp 1610-1611. In *The Mahkutai* [1996] 3 WLR 1, Lord Goff referred to, and appeared to support, Barwick CJ's description, in *The New York Star* [1979] 1 Lloyd's Rep 298, of the contract as bilateral.

[89] Since the carrier desires the result that holders of the bill of lading should not sue his servants or independent contractors, he can achieve this by procuring that they promise not to sue, by contracting to indemnify the servants or agents against claims, and by making it clear to the consignor and holder of the bill that he has done so. The carrier would then be able to obtain the staying of any action against the third party in breach of this agreement. See F Reynolds (1974) 90 LQR 301, 304.

[90] It was distinguished by the Supreme Court of British Columbia in *The Suleyman Stalskiy* [1976] 2 Lloyd's Rep 609, and by the Kenyan High Court in *Lummus Co Ltd v East African Harbours Corpn* [1978] 1 Lloyd's Rep 317, 322-323, because it was not shown that the carrier had authority to contract on behalf of the stevedore. See also *Herrick v Leonard and Dingley Ltd* [1975] 2 NZLR 566.

[91] [1981] 1 WLR 138 (PC). See N Palmer, *Bailment* (2nd ed, 1991) pp 1600-1601, for the view that the case might have been decided on the basis of bailment.

[92] Even though they were considering a situation in which all four of Lord Reid's conditions could be said to have been satisfied.

[93] At p 143. Treitel, *The Law of Contract* (9th ed, 1995) pp 571-572, submits that the principle of *The Eurymedon* should not be confined to cases where carriers and stevedores are associated companies or where there is some previous connection between them. He accepts that the protection of Himalaya clauses does not cover acts wholly collateral to contractual performance, see *Raymond Burke Motors Ltd v The Mersey Docks and Harbour Co* [1986] 1 Lloyd's Rep 155 (goods damaged while they were stored and not during any loading or unloading).

[94] [1985] 2 All ER 1077.

sought to rely on an exclusion clause in the main contract between the employer and the head-contractors which excluded liability on the part of all subcontractors, agents and independent contractors. Judge David Smout QC, sitting as an Official Referee, doubted that unilateral contract reasoning could be applied beyond the specialised practice of carriers and stevedores and described it as "uncomfortably artificial".[95] In particular, *The Eurymedon* was held inapplicable because it could not be said that the head-contractors were agents for the subcontractors. Nevertheless, effect was given to the exclusion clause in an alternative way by finding that it negatived the duty of care which would otherwise have existed.[96] A similar result was achieved in *Norwich City Council v Harvey*,[97] where a building was damaged by fire as a result of the negligence of the sub-contractor. The main contract provided that the building owner was to bear the risk of damage by fire, and the sub-contractor contracted on the same terms and conditions as in the main contract. The owner sued the sub-contractor in tort. The Court of Appeal held that, although there was no direct contractual relationship between the owner and the subcontractor, nevertheless they had both contracted with the main contractor on the basis that the owner had assumed the risk of damage by fire. Hence, the subcontractor owed the owner no duty of care in respect of the damage which occurred. May LJ said:

> I do not think that the mere fact that there is no strict privity between the employer and the subcontractor should prevent the latter from relying upon the clear basis upon which all the parties contracted in relation to damage to the employer's building caused by fire, even when due to the negligence of the contractors or subcontractors.[98]

---

[95] At p 1084.

[96] The judge applied the speech of Lord Wilberforce in *Anns v Merton London Borough Council* [1978] AC 728, 751-752 to determine whether a duty of care in tort arose between the client and the subcontractors. He found that sufficient proximity existed to render it reasonably foreseeable by the subcontractors that a failure by them to exercise care would lead to loss or damage to the client. He then asked whether there were any considerations which suggested that the scope of that duty should be reduced, and said that the contractual exemption clause, which defined the area of risk which the client was entitled to regard the contractors as undertaking responsibility for, meant that no duty of care arose. Although this precise approach to the establishment of duties of care in negligence is now out of favour, the courts will presumably employ similar reasoning to determine whether it is "just and reasonable" to impose a duty of care: see *Caparo Industries plc v Dickman* [1990] 2 AC 605; *Murphy v Brentwood DC* [1991] 1 AC 398.

[97] [1989] 1 WLR 828. See also *Pacific Associates Inc v Baxter* [1990] 1 QB 993 in which the Court of Appeal held that if, contrary to its view, there would otherwise have been a duty of care owed by the defendant engineer (C) to the plaintiff main contractor (A) for pure economic loss, it would have been negatived by the exclusion clause in the contract between A and the employer (B) excluding C's liability to A: see on this case *Chitty on Contracts* (27th ed) para 14-044.

[98] At p 837. This reasoning does not, however, explain the non-liability (at pp 833-834) of the sub-contractor's employee who was also sued. This may be the ghost of *Elder, Dempster* rising from its watery grave, the reasoning being reminiscent of the now rejected doctrine of vicarious immunity; N Palmer, *Bailment* (2nd 1991) pp 1609-1610; C Hopkins 'Privity of Contract: The Thin End of the Wedge?' [1990] CLJ 21, 23.

The reasoning in both cases represents a controversial application of the normal principles for ascertaining whether a duty of care in tort exists. This was particularly so in respect of *Norwich CC v Harvey*, where the finding of a duty of care should have been non-problematic because the harm in question was property damage and not pure economic loss.

2.30 Thus there have been several ways in which third parties have taken the benefit of exemption clauses limiting liability for negligence. These include the now rejected doctrine of vicarious immunity, the unilateral contract device and the idea of a contract limiting the scope of a duty of care in tort. By each of these rather artificial techniques, the courts have striven to achieve commercially workable results, despite the privity doctrine.

2.31 The Supreme Court of Canada has recently gone even further than the English courts in enabling third parties to take the benefit of exclusion clauses by in effect accepting the doctrine of vicarious immunity even where the employee has not been expressly referred to in the exclusion clause. In *London Drugs Ltd v Kuehne & Nagel International Ltd*,[99] the plaintiff bailors entered into a contract of bailment with a warehouseman. The contract contained a limitation clause as follows:

> The warehouseman's liability on any one package is limited to $40 unless the holder has declared in writing a valuation in excess of $40 and paid the additional charge specified to cover warehouse liability.

The bailed goods (an electrical transformer) were damaged through the negligent handling of the warehouseman's employees. In the plaintiffs' claim against the employees in the tort of negligence, the question at issue was whether the employees could rely on the limitation clause in the contract. It should be emphasised that there was no express mention of the employees in that limitation clause.

2.32 A majority of the Supreme Court[100] held that employees could take the benefit of a contractual limitation clause where (i) the limitation of liability clause, expressly or impliedly, extends its benefit to the employees seeking to rely on it; and (ii) the employees seeking the benefit of the limitation of liability clause have been acting in the course of their employment and have been performing the very services provided

---

[99] (1992) 97 DLR (4th) 261. Noted by J Adams and R Brownsword, 'Privity of Contract - That Pestilential Nuisance' (1993) 56 MLR 722; S Waddams, 'Privity of Contract in the Supreme Court of Canada' (1993) 109 LQR 349; J Fleming 'Employee's Tort in a Contractual Matrix: New Approaches in Canada' (1993) OLJS 430; C MacMillan, 'Privity and the Third Party Beneficiary: The Monstrous Proposition' [1994] LMCLQ 22; R Wintemute, 'Don't look to me: The Negligent Employee's Liability to the Employer's Customer' (1994-95) 5 KCLJ 117. See also para 2.67, note 178, below.

[100] Iacobucci J with whom L'Heureux-Dube, Sopinka and Cory JJ concurred; McLachlin J concurred on different grounds; La Forest J dissented in part.

for in the contract between their employer and the plaintiff customer when the loss occurred. On the facts of the case, the majority held that:

> [W]hen all the circumstances of this case are taken into account, including the nature of the relationship between employees and their employer, the identity of interest with respect to contractual obligations, the fact that the appellant knew that employees would be involved in performing the contractual obligations, and the absence of a clear indication in the contract to the contrary, the term 'warehouseman' in s 11(b) of the contract must be interpreted as meaning 'warehousemen'. As such, the respondents are not complete strangers to the limitation of liability clause. Rather, they are unexpressed or implicit third party beneficiaries with respect to this clause.[101]

2.33 Finally, in the very recent case of *The Mahkutai*[102] the question before the Privy Council was whether shipowners, who were not parties to the bill of lading contract, (which was between the charterers, who were carriers, and the cargo-owners, the bill of lading being a charterers' bill) could enforce against the cargo-owners an exclusive jurisdiction clause contained in that contract. The Privy Council held that they could not because the Himalaya clause in the bill of lading, which extended the benefit of all "exceptions, limitations, provision, conditions and liberties herein benefiting the carrier" to "servants, agents and subcontractors of the carrier" did not include the exclusive jurisdiction clause because an exclusive jurisdiction clause is a mutual agreement and does not benefit only one party. Rather the rights conferred entail correlative obligations. Hence there was no question of the third party taking the benefit of the exclusive jurisdiction clause whether by application of the *Eurymedon* principle or under what Lord Goff referred to as the principle of "bailment on terms" deriving from Lord Sumner's speech in the *Elder Dempster* case.[103]

2.34 Of particular importance to this Report, however, was the Privy Council's recognition that, while the *Eurymedon* principle, or something like it, was commercially necessary, the principle rested on technicalities that would continue to throw up difficulties unless and until it was recognised that, in this area, there should be a fully-fledged exception to the third party rule. Lord Goff said the following:

> [T]here can be no doubt of the commercial need of some such principle as this, and not only in cases concerned with stevedores; and the bold step taken by the Privy Council in *The Eurymedon*, and later developed in *The New York Star*, has been widely welcomed. But it is legitimate to wonder whether that development is yet complete. Here their Lordships have in mind not only Lord Wilberforce's

---

[101] (1992) 97 DLR (4th) 261, 369.

[102] [1996] 3 WLR 1.

[103] See para 2.21, note 76, above.

discouragement of fine distinctions, but also the fact that the law is now approaching the position where, provided that the bill of lading contract clearly provides that (for example) independent contractors such as stevedores are to have the benefit of exceptions and limitations contained in that contract, they will be able to enjoy the protection of those terms as against the cargo owners. This is because (1) the problem of consideration in these cases is regarded as having been solved on the basis that a bilateral agreement between the stevedores and the cargo owners, entered into through the agency of the shipowners may, though itself unsupported by consideration, be rendered enforceable by consideration subsequently furnished by the stevedores in the form of performance of their duties as stevedores for the shipowners; (2) the problem of authority from the stevedores to the shipowners to contract on their behalf can, in the majority of cases, be solved by recourse to the principle of ratification; and (3) consignees of the cargo may be held to be bound on the principle in *Brandt v Liverpool Brazil and River Plate Steam Navigation Co Ltd*.[104] Though these solutions are now perceived to be generally effective for their purpose, their technical nature is all too apparent; and the time may well come when, in an appropriate case, it will fall to be considered whether the courts should take what may legitimately be perceived to be the final, and perhaps inevitable, step in this development, and recognise in these cases a fully-fledged exception to the doctrine of privity of contract, thus escaping from all the technicalities with which courts are now faced in English law. It is not far from their Lordships' minds that, if the English courts were minded to take that step, they would be following in the footsteps of the Supreme Court of Canada (see *London Drugs Ltd v Kuehne & Nagel International Ltd*)[105] and, in a different context, the High Court of Australia (see *Trident General Insurance Co Ltd v McNiece Bros Pty Ltd*).[106] Their Lordships have given consideration to the question whether they should face up to this question in the present appeal. However, they have come to the conclusion that it would not be appropriate for them to do so, first, because they have not heard argument specifically directed towards this fundamental question, and second because, as will become clear in due course, they are satisfied that the appeal must in any event be dismissed.[107]

2.35   While our proposed reform would reach the same result as in *The Mahkutai* (because, as we shall explain in Part XIV below, exclusive jurisdiction clauses fall outside our proposals), it would bring about at a stroke what Lord Goff regarded as a desirable development in that it would sweep away the technicalities applying to the enforcement by expressly designated third parties of exclusion clauses.

---

[104] [1924] 1 KB 575.

[105] (1992) 97 DLR (4th) 261.

[106] (1988) 165 CLR 107.

[107] [1996] 3 WLR 1, 11-12.

(h) Promisee's Remedies Assisting the Third Party

2.36 Although not strictly an exception to the third party rule - since it is the promisee suing - in certain circumstances the promisee may be able to assist the third party by recovering substantial damages representing its own loss or, more controversially, loss sustained by the third party; or by being granted specific enforcement of the obligation owed to the third party.

(i) Damages

2.37 Subject to a few exceptions (such as *The Albazero*[108] exception discussed below), the promisee is entitled to damages representing its own loss and not that of the third party.[109] For example, in *Forster v Silvermere Golf and Equestrian Centre Ltd*,[110] the plaintiff owned property which she and her two children occupied. She transferred the property to the defendant, who undertook to construct a house for the plaintiff and her children who could live there rent-free for life. When the defendant broke this undertaking, the plaintiff recovered damages for her own loss. However, she could not claim damages for the loss of rights of occupation after her death which her children would have enjoyed. In *Jackson v Horizon Holidays Ltd*[111] Lord Denning MR had reasoned generally that a contracting party could recover the third party's loss but this approach was firmly rejected by the House of Lords in *Woodar Investment Development Ltd v Wimpey Construction UK Ltd*.[112] A, a buyer of land, had promised B, a seller of land, to pay part of the purchase price to C. Although a majority of the House of Lords (Lords Wilberforce, Keith and Scarman; Lords Salmon and Russell dissenting) held that there had been no breach by A justifying termination by B, all their Lordships indicated that, had B had an action for breach, it could have recovered only its own loss and not C's loss.

2.38 As a promisee will commonly suffer no loss, in a contract made for a third party's benefit, it follows that a promisee can often recover nominal damages only. But this will certainly not always be so.[113] In some circumstances, for example where the promisee required the promisor to pay the third party in order to pay off a debt owed by the promisee to the third party, the promisor's failure to benefit the third party will

---

[108] [1977] AC 774. See para 2.40 below.

[109] The traditional view is also that the promisee will normally be unable to bring an action in debt to enforce payment to him or her of sums due to the third party under the contract, since those sums were by definition not due to the promisee: see *Chitty on Contracts* (27th ed, 1994) para 18-030 and *Coulls v Bagot's Executor and Trustee Co Ltd* (1967) 119 CLR 460, 502. *Quaere* whether the promisee can bring an action for sums due to the third party if the purpose of the claim is for the sums to be paid direct to the third party rather than to the promisee; see A Burrows, *Remedies for Torts and Breach of Contract* (2nd ed, 1994) p 317.

[110] (1981) 125 SJ 397.

[111] [1975] 1 WLR 1468.

[112] [1980] 1 WLR 277.

[113] See, generally, A Burrows, *Remedies for Torts and Breach of Contract* (2nd ed, 1994) p 153.

constitute a substantial pecuniary loss to the promisee.[114] And in *Woodar v Wimpey* one justification for the generous measure of damages given to a father for a ruined family holiday in *Jackson v Horizon Holidays Ltd* was that the father was being fully compensated for his own mental distress.[115]

2.39   In two important recent cases, the House of Lords and Court of Appeal respectively have confirmed and extended an exception to the rule that the promisee recovers its own loss only. In *Linden Gardens Trust Ltd v Lenesta Sludge Disposals Ltd*,[116] the question arose as to the damages which could be recovered by a company (the 'employer') which had contracted for work on its property (the removal of asbestos) but had then, before breach of the works contract, sold the property to a third party (to whom the employer had made an invalid assignment of its contractual rights). The House of Lords held that the employer could recover substantial damages - the cost of curing the defects in the work -despite the fact that it no longer had a proprietary interest in the property by the time of the breach and despite the fact that the cost of the repairs had been borne by the assignee and not by the employer.

2.40   The reasoning of the majority of their Lordships (Lords Keith, Bridge and Ackner agreeing with Lord Browne-Wilkinson) was that the employer could recover the third party's (the assignee's) loss on an application of the exceptional principle applicable to a changed ownership of property established by *Dunlop v Lambert*[117] and *The Albazero*.[118] In *The Albazero* Lord Diplock explained the principle as follows:

> [I]n a commercial contract concerning goods where it is in the contemplation of the parties that the proprietary interests in the goods may be transferred from one owner to another after the contract has been entered into and before the breach which causes loss or damage to the goods, an original party to the contract, if such be the intention of them both, is to be treated in law as having entered into the contract for the benefit of all persons who have or may acquire an interest in the

---

[114]   See *Coulls v Bagot's Executor and Trustee Co Ltd* (1967) 119 CLR 460, 501-502 (per Windeyer J).

[115]   Lords Wilberforce, Russell and Keith all relied on this justification. Lord Wilberforce's alternative explanation, [1980] 1 WLR 277, 283, was that a few types of contract - for example, persons contracting for family holidays, ordering meals in restaurants for a party, hiring a taxi for a group - call for special treatment.

[116]   [1994] 1 AC 85. For notes on this case see, eg, I Duncan Wallace, "Assignment of Rights to Sue: Half a Loaf" (1994) 110 LQR 42; A Tettenborn, "Loss, Damage and the Meaning of Assignment" [1994] CLJ 53; A Berg, "Assignment, Prohibitions and the Right to Recover Damages for Another's Loss" (1994) JBL 129.

[117]   (1839) 6 Cl & F 600; 7 ER 824. In this case, goods had been jettisoned from the defendants' ship in a storm, and the appellant consignor sought to recover damages under the contract notwithstanding the fact that title had passed to the consignee before the goods were lost. The consignor was permitted to recover substantial damages for the carrier's failure to deliver, even though the consignor had parted with property in the goods before the breach occurred.

[118]   [1977] AC 774.

goods before they are lost or damaged, and is entitled to recover by way of damages for breach of contract the actual loss sustained by those for whose benefit the contract is entered into.[119]

The only modification required for the application of this principle to *Linden Gardens* was that the property in question was land and buildings not goods. It should be noted, however, that Lord Browne-Wilkinson in *Linden Gardens* confined the exception to cases where the third party had no direct right of action.

2.41 Lord Griffiths decided *Linden Gardens* on a much wider basis. He took the controversial view[120] that the employer had itself suffered a loss (measured by the cost of repairs) by reason of the breach of contract in that it did not receive the bargain for which it had contracted: whether the employer did, or did not, have a proprietary interest in the subject matter of the contract at the date of breach was irrelevant. He said:

> I cannot accept that in a contract of this nature, namely for work, labour and the supply of materials, the recovery of more than nominal damages for breach of contract is dependent upon the plaintiff having a proprietary interest in the subject matter of the contract at the date of breach...the [promisee] has suffered loss because he did not receive the bargain for which he had contracted...and the measure of damages is the cost of securing the performance of that bargain...The court will of course wish to be satisfied that the repairs have been or are likely to be carried out but if they are carried out the cost of doing them must fall upon the defendant who broke his contract.[121]

Nor did it matter to Lord Griffiths that it was the assignee, and not the employer, who had ultimately borne the cost of repairs for, according to Lord Griffiths, "the law regards who actually paid for the work necessary as a result of the defendant's breach of contract as a matter which is *res inter alios acta* so far as the defendant is concerned".[122]

2.42 In *Darlington BC v Wiltshier Northern Ltd*[123] Darlington BC wished to build a recreational centre on its land, but needed to avoid contravening restrictions on local authority borrowing. Thus an arrangement was reached whereby Morgan Grenfell (Local Authority Services) Ltd ("Morgan Grenfell") contracted with Wiltshier

[119] *Ibid* at 847.

[120] Although it should be noted that the other Law Lords expressed some tentative support for his view.

[121] [1994] 1 AC 85, 96-97.

[122] *Ibid* at 98.

[123] [1995] 1 WLR 68.

Northern Ltd ("Wiltshier") for the latter to build the recreational centre on Darlington BC's land. Darlington BC then entered into a covenant agreement with Morgan Grenfell which provided, inter alia, that Morgan Grenfell would pay Wiltshier all sums falling due under the building contract, that the council would reimburse these monies, and that Morgan Grenfell were not liable to the council for building defects. It also provided that, on request, Morgan Grenfell would assign any rights against Wiltshier to Darlington BC. The rights were duly assigned pursuant to the covenant agreement. The council alleged that Wiltshier's construction work was defective. The Court of Appeal had to decide whether Darlington BC, as the assignee of Morgan Grenfell's rights under the construction contract, could recover substantial damages for the cost of repairs that it had incurred. This in turn depended on whether Morgan Grenfell could have claimed substantial damages. The Court of Appeal, by extending the principle in *Linden Gardens*[124] held that Morgan Grenfell, and hence Darlington BC, were entitled to substantial damages.

2.43   The principle of *Linden Gardens* required extension because, in contrast to the facts of *Linden Gardens* and Lord Diplock's formulation of the principle in *The Albazero*, the original contracting party (Morgan Grenfell) had never had a proprietary interest in the property. It was not therefore a case of the owner at the time of contract transferring ownership before breach. Nevertheless Steyn LJ was able to describe the extension required as a "very conservative and limited" one.[125] In effect the principle becomes that wherever there is the breach of a contract for work on property causing loss to a third party who is an owner of that property, and it was known or contemplated by the parties that a third party was, or would become, owner of the property and that owner has no direct right to sue for breach of contract, the original contracting party, who has the right to sue, can recover substantial damages as representing the owner's loss.

2.44   It should also be noted that Steyn LJ (but not Dillon LJ or Waite LJ) expressed support for Lord Griffiths' wider view in *Linden Gardens*, albeit that he did not agree with Lord Griffiths that there was any need to show an intention to carry out the repairs by someone. On this qualification, however, Steyn LJ's view appears to have been subsequently rejected (albeit without direct reference) by the approach of the House of Lords in *Ruxley Electronics and Construction Ltd v Forsyth*[126] in which a plaintiff's intention to effect repairs was considered a crucial ingredient in deciding whether it was reasonable to claim the cost of repairs when higher than the difference in value.

---

[124]   [1994] 1 AC 85.

[125]   [1995] 1 WLR 68, 80.

[126]   [1996] 1 AC 344.

2.45   As an additional ground for allowing the council's appeal, the majority of the Court in *Darlington* (Dillon LJ, with whom Waite LJ agreed) considered that Morgan Grenfell could be treated as a constructive trustee for Darlington BC of the benefit of its rights under the contract against Wiltshier.[127]

2.46   The effect of these cases has been to enhance a promisee's prospects of recovering substantial damages in a contract made for a third party's benefit. The decisions themselves are confined to confirming and developing *The Albazero* exception; but in addition dicta in the cases controversially suggest that substantial damages may be an appropriate measure of the promisee's own loss in a wider range of situations than has traditionally been thought to be the case.

(ii) Specific Performance and a Stay of Action

2.47   In *Beswick v Beswick*[128] an uncle transferred his business to his nephew who, in return, promised that, after his uncle's death, he would pay £5 a week to his widow. The uncle died and his widow brought an action for specific performance of the nephew's promise. The House of Lords, applying the third party rule, held that while the widow could not maintain a successful action in her personal capacity, she could as administratrix succeed in suing for the estate's loss, though not her own personal third party loss. Most importantly, the Lords held that as administratrix she should be granted specific performance of the nephew's promise rather than being confined to damages. This was on the basis that the administratrix's damages would be nominal[129] and that nominal damages would here be inadequate given that the purpose of the bargain was to benefit the widow. This reasoning opens the door to specific performance being an appropriate remedy for promisees in many contracts for a third party's benefit, where the third party rule would otherwise produce an unjust result. It should be noted, however that there are well-known additional restrictions on specific performance (that is, over and beyond damages having to be inadequate) such as that specific performance will not be ordered of a contract for personal service or where the contract to be enforced is not supported by valuable consideration.

2.48   In the case of a promise *not to sue a third party*, the promisee may assist the third party beneficiary by seeking a stay of any action by the promisor against the third party under section 49(3) of the Supreme Court Act 1981. This preserves the power of the court to stay any proceedings before it, where it thinks fit to do so, whether on its own motion or on the application of any person.

---

[127] See para 2.9 above.

[128] [1968] AC 58.

[129] Lord Pearce alone considered that the damages would be substantial. And see generally para 2.38 above.

2.49   In *Gore v Van der Lann*,[130] the question was whether Liverpool Corporation could restrain the holder of a free bus pass from suing a bus conductor for negligence, given that the free pass contained a clause excluding liability for personal injury on the part of the Corporation or its servants. On the facts, the clause was void under section 151 of the Road Traffic Act 1960. However, the Court of Appeal said that the Corporation could have obtained a stay, if: (i) the clause could have been construed as a promise by Mrs Gore not to sue (which on the facts it was not); and (ii) if the Corporation had a sufficient interest so as to entitle it to a stay, for instance if it had been required to indemnify its servants in respect of torts committed by the latter.[131] In *Snelling v John G Snelling Ltd*,[132] Ormrod J said that it did not follow from *Gore* that there had to be an express promise not to sue. It was sufficient that it was a necessary implication of the agreement that P would not sue.[133]

2.50   In *The Elbe Maru*,[134] a bill of lading provided an undertaking that the holder would not make any claim against the carriers' sub-contractors. Whilst the goods were in the custody of sub-contractors of the carriers, they were stolen. The indorsees of the bill of lading claimed damages against the sub-contractors, the action against the original carriers being time barred. The carriers applied for a stay, which was granted. Unlike *Gore*, this was a clear case of a promise not to sue. However, the remedy being discretionary, Ackner J said that it was not enough to show a clear promise not to sue. But where an applicant could show a real possibility of prejudice if the action were not stayed, as here by being exposed to an action by its agents, the discretion to stay would be exercised in their favour.[135]

2.51   Since it is the promisee who obtains the stay rather than the third party, the above cases are best seen as examples of promisees assisting the third party by enforcing the contract in favour of the third party. They constitute the mirror image of *Beswick v*

---

[130]   [1967] 2 QB 31. See P Davies, 'Mrs Gore's legacy to commerce' (1981) 1 LS 287.

[131]   In *European Asian Bank v Punjab and Sind Bank* [1982] 2 Lloyd's Rep 356, 369, Ackner LJ said that for the promisee to obtain a stay it would be necessary to establish an express or implied promise not to sue and some legal or equitable right to protect, such as an obligation to indemnify D. In these circumstances it would be a fraud on the promisee for the proceedings to continue.

[132]   [1973] QB 87.

[133]   It has been argued that *Snelling* is difficult to reconcile with the requirement of sufficient interest as explained in *Gore*, but is nonetheless consistent with the spirit of *Beswick v Beswick*: *Chitty on Contracts* (27th ed, 1994) para 18-038.

[134]   [1978] 1 Lloyd's Rep 206.

[135]   [1978] 1 Lloyd's Rep 206, 210. In *The Chevalier Roze* [1983] 2 Lloyd's Rep 438, 443, Parker J, having referred to *The Elbe Maru*, respectfully doubted whether it was correct that P had done enough if he merely showed a possibility of prejudice. Where P was seeking to prevent D from asserting a possibly good claim, and where D had raised a triable issue which could not be determined without a further investigation of the facts, he found it difficult to see how it could be a fraud on P to allow D's action to proceed.

Beswick, the difference being that the "specific" remedy in that case was concerned to enforce a positive rather than a negative obligation.

(i) Statutory Exceptions

2.52 This section will outline *some* of the major legislative exceptions[136] to the third party rule.

(i) Life Insurance

2.53 By section 11 of the Married Women's Property Act 1882, a life insurance policy taken out by someone on his or her own life, and expressed to be for the benefit of his or her spouse or children, creates a trust in favour of the objects named in the policy.[137]

(ii) Fire Insurance

2.54 Under section 83 of the Fire Prevention (Metropolis) Act 1774, where an insured house or building is destroyed by fire, the insurer may be required "upon the request of any person or persons interested" to lay out the insurance money for the restoration of the building.[138] This means that a tenant can claim under its landlord's insurance, and a landlord under its tenant's insurance.[139]

(iii) Motor Insurance

2.55 Under section 148(7) of the Road Traffic Act 1988, a person issuing a policy under section 145 of the Act shall be liable to indemnify the persons or classes of person specified in the policy in respect of any liability which the policy purports to cover in the cases of such persons.

(iv) Third Parties' Rights Against Insurers

2.56 A contract of insurance may insure the policy-holder against liability to third parties. By section 1 of the Third Parties (Rights Against Insurers) Act 1930, where an insured

---

[136] For an analogous exception, see *Swain v Law Society* [1983] 1 AC 598 in which the House of Lords interpreted s 37 of the Solicitors Act 1974 as empowering the Law Society to create a contract for the benefit of third parties (its members). Lord Diplock said, at p 611, "[T]he policy of insurance which the Society is empowered to take out and maintain by section 37(2)(b) is a contract which creates a jus quaesitum tertio. It does so by virtue of public law, not the ordinary English private law of contract. This makes it unnecessary in the instant case to have recourse to any of those juristic subterfuges to which courts have, from time to time, felt driven to resort in cases in which English private law is applicable, to mitigate the effect of the lacuna resulting from the non-recognition of a jus quaesitum tertio - an anachronistic shortcoming that has for many years been regarded as a reproach to English private law ...."

[137] The Law Revision Committee recommended that section 11 of the 1882 Act should be extended to all life, endowment and education policies in which a particular beneficiary is named: Sixth Interim Report *Statute of Frauds and the Doctrine of Consideration* (1937) Cmd 5449, para 49. See para 12.22 below.

[138] See *Colinvaux's Law of Insurance* (ed Merkin) (6th ed, 1990) pp 194-195.

[139] See *Vural Ltd v Security Archives Ltd* (1989) 60 P & CR 258, 271-272.

becomes, inter alia, bankrupt or wound up, and before or after that time he incurs liability to a third party, the insured's rights under the contract of insurance are transferred to the third party. In other words, the third party has a direct action against the insurer. However, the third party only has transferred to him the rights which the insured would have had. Difficulties have arisen with the Act which we discuss in Part XII below.[140]

(v) Insurance by Those with Limited Interests

2.57 In general, a person with a limited interest in property can insure and recover its full value, holding any amount above his own interest on account for others similarly interested.[141] Section 14(2) of the Marine Insurance Act 1906 states that a "mortgagee, consignee or other person having an interest in the subject-matter insured may insure on behalf and for the benefit of other persons interested as well as for his own benefit". Likewise, section 47 of the Law of Property Act 1925 provides that any insurance money received by the seller between contract and conveyance shall be held on behalf of the buyer and be paid to him.

(vi) Bills of Exchange

2.58 In general, negotiable instruments (such as bills of exchange, cheques and promissory notes), are transferable by delivery and give to the transferee for value, who acts in good faith, ownership of, or a security interest in, the instrument free from equities. Under the Bills of Exchange Act 1882,[142] the holder of a bill of exchange may sue on the bill in his own name. If a bill of exchange is dishonoured, the drawer, acceptor and indorsers are all liable to compensate the holder in due course.[143]

(vii) Bills of Lading

2.59 Where goods are to be carried by sea, the shipper will typically enter into a contract of carriage with a carrier, which is evidenced by a bill of lading. The goods are then usually consigned to the buyer, to whom the bill will be endorsed. At common law the buyer was not able to sue the carrier on the contract of carriage because there was no privity between them.[144] It was to remedy this defect that the Bills of Lading Act 1855 was passed. Under that Act, however, a buyer only had a right of action under the bill of lading contract if the property in the goods passed by reason of, and at the same time as, endorsement of the bill to him or if the endorsement of the bill played an

---

[140] See paras 12.19-12.21 below.

[141] See Treitel, *The Law of Contract* (9th ed, 1995) p 584.

[142] Section 38(1).

[143] Sections 54-56.

[144] *Thompson v Dominy* (1845) 14 M & W 403; 153 ER 532.

essential causal role in the chain of events by which the property passed to him.[145] The Act was replaced by the Carriage of Goods by Sea Act 1992[146] which separates the right to sue the carrier from the passing of property in the goods under the sale contract. This is achieved, under section 2, by a statutory assignment of the right to sue the carrier. The right is assigned to a holder of a bill of lading or to a person to whom delivery of goods is to be made under a sea waybill or ship's delivery order. By section 3, where those with a title to sue under the statute take or demand delivery of the goods or make a claim against the carrier under the contract of carriage they become subject to the liabilities[147] under the contract but without affecting the liabilities of the original shipper. Where a pledgee takes delivery of the goods and pays any carriage charges such as freight or demurrage, there may come into existence an implied contract between the pledgee and the carrier on the terms of the bill of lading. Such a contract, known as a *Brandt v Liverpool* contract,[148] is a further circumvention of the third party rule.

(viii) Law of Property Act 1925, Section 56(1)

2.60 Whereas at common law, no person could sue on a deed inter partes unless a party to that deed, section 56(1) of the Law of Property Act 1925 states:

> A person may take an immediate or other interest in land or other property, or the benefit of any condition, right of entry, covenant or agreement over or respecting land or other property, although he may not be named as a party to the conveyance or other instrument.

Although Denning LJ, in *Drive Yourself Hire Co (London) Ltd v Strutt*,[149] took the view that this abolished the rule in *Tweddle v Atkinson*,[150] it is clear from *Beswick v Beswick*[151] that section 56(1) does not apply to a mere promise by A to B that money will be paid to C. The exact scope of section 56(1) remains unclear. It may be confined (i) to real property; (ii) to covenants running with the land; (iii) to cases in which the instrument is not solely for the benefit of the third party but purports to

---

[145] *Sewell v Burdick* (1884) 10 App Cas 74 (where an action against the bank by the carrier for unpaid freight, the bank being pledgees of the bill of lading, failed as the bank had no property in the bill and the goods); *The San Nicholas* [1976] 1 Lloyd's Rep 8; *The Sevonia Team* [1983] 2 Lloyd's Rep 640; *The Delfini* [1990] 1 Lloyd's Rep 252.

[146] See Rights of Suit in Respect of Carriage of Goods by Sea (1991) Law Com No 196; Scot Law Com No 130, for the recommendations which led to the Carriage of Goods by Sea Act 1992.

[147] Most importantly in practice the obligation to pay the carrier freight in respect of the cargo.

[148] *Brandt v Liverpool, Brazil & River Plate Steam Navigation Co Ltd* [1924] 1 KB 575; *The Aramis* [1989] 1 Lloyd's Rep 213; *The Captain Gregos (No 2)* [1990] 2 Lloyd's Rep 395.

[149] [1954] 1 QB 250, 274.

[150] (1861) 1 B & S 393; 121 ER 762. See para 2.5 above.

[151] [1968] AC 58.

contain a grant to or covenant with it; (iv) to deeds strictly inter partes.[152] It does appear, however, that a person cannot take the benefit of a covenant under section 56(1) unless he or she or his or her predecessor in title was in existence and identifiable when the covenant was made.[153]

(ix) Companies Act 1985, Section 14

2.61   Under section 14 of the Companies Act 1985, the registered memorandum and articles of association of a company bind the company and its members to the same extent as if they respectively had been signed and sealed by each member.[154]

(x) Package Travel, Package Holidays and Package Tours Regulations 1992[155]

2.62   Where a contract for the provision of a package[156] holiday is made between an organiser or retailer and a consumer,[157] the organiser or retailer is liable to the consumer for the proper performance of the obligations under the contract, whether those services are to be performed by the organiser or retailer or not.[158] The Regulations therefore, inter alia, circumvent the third party rule by giving the beneficiaries of package tour contracts direct rights against the organiser and/or retailer with whom the contract was made.[159] The Regulations also require that contracts for the provision of package holidays should comply with certain formalities and provide certain information,[160] provide for withdrawal from the contract where it is

---

[152]   *Chitty on Contracts* (27th ed, 1994) para 18-057.

[153]   *Ibid*; Megarry & Wade, *The Law of Real Property* (5th ed, 1984) p 764.

[154]   The Law Commission is currently considering section 14 in our work on Shareholders' Remedies.

[155]   SI 1992/3288 implementing EEC Council Directive 90/314 on package travel, package holidays and package tours.

[156]   Defined in Regulation 2(1) to mean "the pre-arranged combination of at least two of the following components when sold or offered for sale at an inclusive price and when the service covers a period of more than twenty-four hours or includes overnight accommodation:- (a) transport; (b) accommodation; (c) other tourist services not ancillary to transport or accommodation and accounting for a significant proportion of the package". The definition does not exclude tailor-made packages, and is not avoided by the submission of separate accounts (Reg 2(1)(i) & (ii)).

[157]   Which means the person who takes or agrees to take the package, any person on whose behalf that person agrees to purchase the package or any person to whom that person or any of the beneficiaries transfer the package (Reg 2(2)).

[158]   Regulation 15.

[159]   Regulation 15(1) read in conjunction with the definition of "consumer" in Regulation 2. The Regulations provide that the organiser or retailer is to be liable unless the damage suffered by the consumer was due to his own fault, or to the unforeseeable failures of a third party or circumstances beyond the control of the organiser or retailer: Regulation 15(2). Certain limitations of liability are permitted: Regulation 15(3) & (4).

[160]   Regulations 4 to 12.

significantly altered or cancelled,[161] and make arrangements for bonding and insurance cover.[162]

2. Calls for Reform

2.63 Whilst it is self-evidently desirable that a complete stranger to a contract should not normally have contractual obligations forced upon him or her, without consent, the third party rule (by which a third party cannot take rights under a contract) has been much criticised. This criticism has come from academics,[163] law reform bodies (including the Law Revision Committee in England[164] and bodies in several Commonwealth jurisdictions[165]) and the judiciary. In this section we focus our attention on calls for reform made by the judiciary in past cases.

2.64 In 1967, in *Beswick v Beswick*,[166] Lord Reid cited with approval the Law Revision Committee's proposals that when a contract by its express terms purports to confer a benefit directly on a third party, it should be enforceable by the third party in its own name. While implying that the way forward was by legislation, he stated that the House of Lords might find it necessary to deal with the matter if there was a further long period of Parliamentary procrastination. In *Woodar Investment Development Ltd v Wimpey Construction UK Ltd*,[167] Lord Salmon (dissenting) regarded the law concerning damages for loss suffered by third parties as most unsatisfactory and hoped that, unless it were altered by statute, the House of Lords would reconsider it.[168] Lord Scarman expressed "regret that [the] House has not yet found the opportunity to reconsider the two rules which effectually prevent [the promisee] or [the third party]

---

[161] Regulations 12 and 13.

[162] Regulations 16ff.

[163] See, eg, A Corbin, 'Contracts for the Benefit of Third Persons' (1930) 46 LQR 12; F Dowrick, 'A *Jus Quaesitum Tertio* By Way of Contract in English Law' (1956) 19 MLR 374; M Furmston, 'Return to *Dunlop v Selfridge*?' (1960) 23 MLR 373; J Wylie 'Contracts and Third Parties' (1966) 17 NILQ 351; B Markesinis, 'An Expanding Tort Law - The Price of a Rigid Contract Law' (1987) 103 LQR 354; R Flannigan, 'Privity - The End of an Era (Error)' (1987) 103 LQR 564; F Reynolds, 'Privity of Contract, the Boundaries of Categories and the Limits of the Judicial Function' (1989) 105 LQR 1; P Kincaid, 'Third parties : Rationalising a Right to Sue' [1989] CLJ 243; J Adams & R Brownsword, 'Privity and the concept of a network contract' (1990) 10 Legal Studies 12; D Beyleveld & R Brownsword, 'Privity, Transitivity and Rationality' (1991) 54 MLR 48; J Beatson, 'Reforming the Law of Contracts for the Benefit of Third Parties: A Second Bite at the Cherry' (1992) 45 CLP 1; H Beale, 'Privity of Contract: Judicial and Legislative Reform' (1995) 9 JCL 103; J Wilson, 'A Flexible Contract of Carriage - The Third Dimension?' [1996] LMCLQ 187; S Whittaker, 'Privity of Contract and the Tort of Negligence: Future Directions' (1996) 16 OxJLS 191; E McKendrick, *Contract Law* (2nd ed, 1994) pp 127-131; J Adams and R Brownsword, *Key Issues in Contract* (1995) ch 5.

[164] Sixth Interim Report (1937) Cmd 5449, paras 41-49. See paras 4.2-4.4 below.

[165] See paras 4.5-4.14 below.

[166] [1968] AC 58, 72.

[167] [1980] 1 WLR 277.

[168] At p 291.

recovering that which [the promisor], for value, has agreed to provide."[169] He reminded the House that twelve years had passed since Lord Reid in *Beswick v Beswick* had called for a reconsideration of the rule, and hoped that all the cases which "stand guard over this unjust rule" might be reviewed.[170] Lord Scarman concluded his judgment with an unequivocal call for reform:

> [T]he crude proposition...that the state of English law is such that neither [the third party] for whom the benefit was intended nor [the promisee] who contracted for it can recover it, if the contract is terminated by [the promisor's] refusal to perform, calls for review: and now, not forty years on.[171]

2.65   In *Forster v Silvermere Golf and Equestrian Centre Ltd*,[172] Dillon J referred to the effects of *Woodar* in the case before him as being a blot on the law and thoroughly unjust. In *Swain v Law Society*,[173] Lord Diplock referred to the general non-recognition of third party rights as "an anachronistic shortcoming that has for many years been regarded as a reproach to English private law".

2.66   More recently, Lord Goff and Steyn LJ have added their influential voices to criticisms of the third party rule. In *The Pioneer Container*[174] Lord Goff called into question the future of the rule, and in *White v Jones*[175] his Lordship said, "[O]ur law of contract is widely seen as deficient in the sense that it is perceived to be hampered by the presence of an unnecessary doctrine of consideration and (through a strict doctrine of privity of contract) stunted through a failure to recognise a jus quaesitum tertio".[176] Steyn LJ's dicta in *Darlington Borough Council v Wiltshier Northern Ltd*[177] - with which we opened this Report - are particularly notable for their forthright treatment of the third party rule.

---

[169] At p 300.

[170] At p 300. Lord Keith, at pp 297-298, also associated himself with Lord Scarman's view.

[171] [1980] 1 WLR 277, 301.

[172] (1981) 125 SJ 397.

[173] [1983] 1 AC 598, 611. See para 2.52, note 136, above.

[174] [1994] 2 AC 324, 335. See also para 2.34 above for Lord Goff's comments, in a more specific context, in *The Mahkutai* [1996] 3 WLR 1.

[175] [1995] 2 AC 207.

[176] [1995] 2 AC 207, 262-263.

[177] [1995] 1 WLR 68, 76. See para 1.1 above. Steyn LJ later went on to say, after referring to our Consultation Paper, that there is a respectable argument that reform is best achieved by the courts working out sensible solutions on a case-by-case basis. "But that requires the door to be opened by the House of Lords reviewing the major cases which are thought to have entrenched the rule of privity of contract. Unfortunately, there will be few opportunities for the House of Lords to do so." [1995] 1 WLR 68, 78.

2.67   Of the criticisms of the third party rule made by the judiciary in other jurisdictions,[178] the judgments in the High Court of Australia in *Trident General Insurance Co Ltd v McNiece Bros Pty Ltd*[179] are particularly clear and rigorous. A company which operated a limestone crushing plant took out a liability insurance policy with the appellants (Trident), which was expressed to cover all contractors at the plant. The respondent contractor (McNiece) fell within the terms of the policy, but when it sought indemnification for damages payable to one of its subcontractors, the appellant insurance company refused to indemnify the respondent on the grounds that the latter was not a party to the contract of insurance.

2.68   The respondent succeeded before the High Court of Australia,[180] in a decision which effectively reversed the decision of the legislature not to make the Insurance Contracts Act 1984[181] retrospective. In doing so, three of the Justices mounted an attack on the doctrine of privity. Mason CJ and Wilson J were of the opinion that "[t]here is much substance in the criticisms directed at the traditional common law rules [of privity]...",[182] and they accepted that reform was needed in the area under consideration, as it was an example of "common law rules which operate unsatisfactorily and unjustly".[183] Toohey J was even more vociferous, stating that the rule is "based on shaky foundations and, in its widest form, lacks support both in logic or jurisprudence".[184] He was of the opinion that,

---

[178]   See, eg, the judgment of Iacobucci J (with whom L'Heureux-Dube, Sopinka and Cory JJ concurred) in *London Drugs Ltd v Kuehne & Nagel International Ltd* (1992) 97 DLR (4th) 261, 340-370. He spoke of the need for reform of the privity rule and, while he did not think it appropriate for the courts to embark on major reform or abolition, he recognised an obligation to ameliorate injustice by the incremental relaxation of the rule in limited circumstances. Having said that, the approach that the majority ultimately advocated is, in our view, a radical one and would appear to go beyond our proposed reform by allowing an employee, even if not expressly identified in the exclusion clause, to rely on it. As Professor John Fleming pertinently observes in 'Employee's Tort in a Contractual Matrix: New Approaches in Canada' (1993) 13 OxJLS 430, 437, "[T]he step from express to implied intent to benefit third parties may not look far, but long experience with 'implication' warns against the slide into fiction. Is the failure to mention employees just an oversight, a drafting glitch, or does it signify that the parties never had a mind to include employees? The most that one can say is that in all probability they would have been included, if the need to do so had occurred to the parties. But this is certainly a long way from the 'necessary implication' postulated by Lord Denning in *Adler v Dickson*". See, generally on the *London Drugs* case, paras 2.31-2.32 above.

[179]   (1988) 165 CLR 107. In *Olsson v Dyson* (1969) 120 CLR 365, 392 Windeyer J in the High Court of Australia spoke of "...the rigidity of the obstacles the common law doctrine of privity of contract places in the way of justice to third parties."

[180]   Brennan and Dawson JJ dissenting.

[181]   See para 12.23 and Appendix B below.

[182]   (1988) 165 CLR 107, 118.

[183]   (1988) 165 CLR 107, 123,

[184]   (1988) 165 CLR 107, 168.

...when a rule of the common law harks back no further than the middle of the last century, when it has been the subject of constant criticism and when, in its widest form, it lacks a sound foundation in jurisprudence and logic and further, when that rule has been so affected by exceptions or qualifications, I see nothing inimical to principled development in this Court now declaring the law to be otherwise...[185]

2.69 In the event, Mason CJ and Toohey and Wilson JJ decided the case on the basis of a specific abrogation of the third party rule in relation to insurance contracts. Two reasons were advanced. First, it would be unjust not to give effect to the contracting parties' intentions. Secondly, it was likely that third party beneficiaries would rely on an insurance policy covering them and not insure separately. Deane and Gaudron JJ favoured the use of a trust and the principle of unjust enrichment[186] respectively, in order to avoid the injustice of the operation of the third party rule, and even the two dissenting judges, Brennan and Dawson JJ, based their dissent on maintaining coherent and gradual development of the common law rather than justifying their decision on the appropriateness of the rule itself.

---

[185] (1988) 165 CLR 107, 170-1.

[186] This is a novel and controversial approach in that the principle against unjust enrichment is being used to protect expectations rather than to reverse benefits acquired at the expense of the plaintiff: see K Soh, "Privity of Contract and Restitution" (1989) 105 LQR 4; I Jackson (1989) 63 ALJ 368.

SECTION B
PRELIMINARY ISSUES

PART III
ARGUMENTS FOR REFORM[1]

1. The Intentions of the Original Contracting Parties are Thwarted

3.1   A first argument in favour of reform, as stated in the Consultation Paper, is that the third party rule prevents effect being given to the intentions of the contracting parties. If the theoretical justification for the enforcement of contracts is seen as the realisation of the promises or the will or the bargain of the contracting parties, the failure of the law to afford a remedy to the third party where the contracting parties intended that it should have one frustrates their intentions, and undermines the general justifying theory of contract.[2]

2. The Injustice to the Third Party

3.2   A second argument focuses on the injustice to the third party where a valid contract, albeit between two other parties, has engendered in the third party reasonable expectations of having the legal right to enforce the contract particularly where the third party has relied on that contract to regulate his or her affairs. In most circumstances this argument complements the above argument based on the intentions of the contracting parties. For in most circumstances the intentions of the contracting parties and the reasonable expectations of the third party are consistent with each other. However, one of the most difficult issues that we face is the extent to which the contracting parties can vary or discharge the contract. That issue can be presented as raising the conflict between these two fundamental arguments for reform. In other words, should the injustice to the third party trump the intentions of the parties *where those intentions change*? As will become clear, we believe that where the injustice to the third party is sufficiently "strong" (that is, where the third party has not merely had expectations engendered by knowledge of the contract but has relied on the contract or has accepted it by communicating its assent to the promisor) it should trump the changed intentions of the contracting parties. That is, the original

---

[1]   Most of the arguments were canvassed in Consultation Paper No 121, paras 4.1-4.35. We do not set out again here the discussion in paras 4.3-4.4 of the Consultation Paper in which possible arguments *for* the third party rule were set out and then refuted one by one. See also paras 1.7-1.8 above.

[2]   See, eg, F Dowrick "A *Jus Quaesitum Tertio* By Way of Contract in English Law" (1956) 19 MLR 374, 390-392; R Flannigan, "Privity - The End of an Era (Error)" (1987) 103 LQR 564, 582-587; C Fried, *Contract as Promise* (1981) pp 44-45 (although Fried argues that acceptance by the third party is essential). *Contra* is P Kincaid, "The UK Law Commission's Privity Proposals and Contract Theory" (1994) 8 JCL 51 who argues that the promise theory underpinning contract dictates that only the promisee can enforce the promise: in our view, this is to take an unnecessarily narrow view of the morality of promise-keeping where a promise is intended to benefit a third party.

parties' right to change their minds and vary the contract should be overridden once the third party has relied on, or accepted, the contractual promise.

3. The Person Who Has Suffered the Loss Cannot Sue, While the Person Who Has Suffered No Loss Can Sue

3.3　In a standard situation, the third party rule produces the perverse, and unjust, result that the person who has suffered the loss (of the intended benefit) cannot sue, while the person who has suffered no loss can sue. This can be illustrated by reference to *Beswick v Beswick*.[3] In that case, as we have seen,[4] the House of Lords held that the widow could not enforce the promise in her personal capacity, since the contract was one to which she was not privy. However, as administratrix of her husband's estate, she was able to sue as promisee, albeit that she could only recover nominal damages because the uncle, and hence his estate, had suffered no loss from the nephew's breach. Hence we see that the widow in her personal capacity, who had suffered the loss of the intended benefit, had no right to sue, while the estate, represented by the widow in her capacity as administratrix, who had suffered no loss, had that right. As it was, a just result was achieved by their Lordships' decision that nominal damages were, in this three party situation, inadequate so that specific performance of the nephew's obligation to pay the annuity to the widow should be ordered in respect of the claim by the administratrix. But where specific performance is not available (for example, where the contract is not one supported by valuable consideration or where the contract is one for personal service) the standard result is both perverse and unjust.

4. Even if the Promisee Can Obtain a Satisfactory Remedy for the Third Party, the Promisee May Not be Able to, or Wish to, Sue

3.4　In *Beswick v Beswick*, the promisee, as represented by the widow as administratrix, clearly wanted to sue to enforce the contract made for her personal benefit. However, in many other situations in which contracts are made for the benefit of third parties, the promisee may not be able to, or wish to, sue, even if specific performance or substantial damages could be obtained. Clearly the stress and strain of litigation and its cost will deter many promisees who might fervently want their contract enforced for the benefit of third parties. Or the contracting party may be ill or outside the jurisdiction. And if the promisee has died, his or her personal representatives may reasonably take the view that it is not in the interests of the estate to seek to enforce a contract for the benefit of the third party.

---

[3]　[1968] AC 58.

[4]　See para 2.47 above.

5. The Development of Non-Comprehensive Exceptions

3.5 A number of statutory and common law[5] exceptions to the third party rule exist. These have been discussed at paragraphs 2.8 to 2.62 above. Where an exception to the third party rule has been either recognised by case-law or created by statute, the rule may now not cause difficulty. Self-evidently, this is not the case where the situation is a novel one in which devices to overcome the third party rule have not yet been tested. We believe that the existence of exceptions to the third party rule is a strong justification for reform. This is for two reasons. First, the existence of so many legislative and common law exceptions to the rule demonstrates its basic injustice. Secondly, the fact that these exceptions continue to evolve and to be the subject of extensive litigation demonstrates that the existing exceptions have not resolved all the problems.

6. Complexity, Artificiality and Uncertainty

3.6 The existence of the rule, together with the exceptions to it, has given rise to a complex body of law and to the use of elaborate and often artificial stratagems and structures in order to give third parties enforceable rights.[6] Reform would enable the artificiality and some of the complexity to be avoided. The technical hurdles which must be overcome if one is to circumvent the rule in individual cases also lead to uncertainty, since it will often be possible for a defendant to raise arguments that a technical requirement has not been fulfilled. Such uncertainty is commercially inconvenient.

7. Widespread Criticism Throughout the Common Law World

3.7 In Part II, we saw that there had been criticism of the third party rule and calls for its reform from academics, law reform bodies and the judiciary. We shall see in Part IV that the rule has been abrogated throughout much of the common law world, including the United States, New Zealand, and parts of Australia. The extent of the criticism and reform elsewhere is itself a strong indication that the privity doctrine is flawed.

8. The Legal Systems of Most Member States of the European Union Allow Third Parties to Enforce Contracts

3.8 A further factor in support of reforming the third party rule in English law is the fact that the legal systems of most of the member states of the European Union recognise and enforce the rights of third party beneficiaries under contracts. In France, for example, the general principle that contracts have effect only between the parties to them[7] is qualified by Art 1121 of the *Code Civil*, which permits a stipulation for the

---

[5] We use this phrase to mean 'non-statutory' or 'judge-made'. Some of the exceptions are equitable.

[6] See, eg, paras 2.27 and 2.34 above.

[7] Art 1165, *Code Civil*. See B Nicholas, *The French Law of Contract*, (2nd ed, 1992), p 169ff.

benefit of a third party as a condition of a stipulation made for oneself or of a gift made to another. The French courts interpreted this as permitting the creation of an enforceable stipulation for a person in whose welfare the stipulator had a moral interest. In so doing, they widened the scope of the Article so as to permit virtually any stipulation for a third person to be enforced by him or her, where the agreement between the stipulator and the promisor was intended to confer a benefit on the third person.[8] In Germany, contractual rights for third parties are created by Art 328 of the *Burgerliches Gesetzbuch* permitting stipulations in contracts for performances to third parties with the effect that the latter acquires the direct right to demand performance, although the precise scope of these rights depends on the terms and circumstances of the contract itself.[9] Surveying the member states of the European Union, we are aware that the laws of France, Germany, Italy,[10] Austria,[11] Spain,[12] Portugal,[13] Netherlands,[14] Belgium,[15] Luxembourg,[16] and Greece,[17] recognise such rights (as does Scotland);[18] whereas only the laws of England and Wales (and Northern Ireland) and the Republic of Ireland[19] do not.[20] With the growing recognition of the need for harmonisation of the commercial law of the states of the European Union - illustrated most importantly by the work being carried out by the Commission on European Contract Law under

---

[8] For further detailed discussion of the *stipulation pour autrui* in French law, see B Nicholas, *The French Law of Contract* (2nd ed, 1992) p 181ff; Consultation Paper No 121, Appendix, paras 24-27. See also, generally, S Whittaker, "Privity of Contract and the Law of Tort: the French Experience" (1995) 15 OxJLS 327.

[9] See Consultation Paper No 121, Appendix paras 28-29.

[10] Art 1411, Italian Civil Code 1942.

[11] Art 881, Austrian Civil Code 1811.

[12] Art 1257 par 2, Spanish Civil Code 1889.

[13] Art 443, Portuguese Civil Code 1966.

[14] Book 6 art 253, Dutch Civil Code 1992.

[15] Who apparently followed the French Civil Code model: see *International Encyclopedia of Comparative Law* (ed Kötz), Vol VII, ch 13, para 13-12.

[16] Again modelled on the French Civil Code: see n 15 above.

[17] Art 411, Greek Civil Code 1941.

[18] See W McBryde, *The Law of Contract in Scotland* (1987), ch 18. See also Consultation Paper No 121, Appendix paras 22-23.

[19] See Consultation Paper No 121, Appendix para 21. Although in the Republic of Ireland, as in England and Wales, exceptions to the doctrine permitting the creation of enforceable third party benefits exist: see Married Women's Status Act 1957, s 8(1).

[20] We have obtained no conclusive information regarding the law in the Scandinavian member states of the EU, Denmark, Finland and Sweden, although we understand that in Denmark third party rights are enforced: see *Principles of European Contract Law, Part I : Performance, Non-performance and Remedies* (ed O Lando and H Beale) (1995), Art 2.115 Notes.

the chairmanship of Professor Ole Lando[21] - it seems likely that there will be ever increasing pressure on the UK to bring its law on privity of contract into line with that predominantly adopted in Europe.

9. The Third Party Rule Causes Difficulties in Commercial Life

3.9   Lest it be erroneously thought that the third party rule nowadays causes no real difficulties in commercial life, or that the case for reform is purely theoretical rather than practical, we have chosen two types of contracts - construction contracts and insurance contracts - to illustrate some of the difficulties caused by the rule.[22]

(1) Construction Contracts

3.10   Both simple construction contracts involving only an employer and a builder, and complex construction contracts involving several main contractors, many subcontractors and design professionals are affected by the third party rule.

3.11   Simple construction contracts illustrate the difficulties which can arise when one contracting party agrees to pay for work to be done by another contracting party which will benefit a third party to the contract. Say, for example, a client contracts with a builder for work to be done on the home of an elderly relative. If the work is done defectively, it is only the client who has a contractual right to sue the builder for its failure to deliver the promised performance. On traditional principles, and subject to the decisions in *Linden Gardens Trust v Lenesta Sludge Disposals Ltd*[23] and *Darlington BC v Wiltshier Northern Ltd,*[24] the client can often only recover nominal damages, since he or she will have suffered no direct financial loss as a result of the builder's failure to perform.[25] The elderly relative could not himself or herself sue for breach of contract, and the tort of negligence does not normally allow the recovery of pure economic loss.[26] Therefore the elderly relative could not recover the cost of repairs in

---

[21]   The first part of the Commission's work, *Principles of European Contract Law, Part I: Performance, Non-performance and Remedies* (ed O Lando and H Beale) was published in 1995. Art 2.115 headed "Stipulation in favour of a Third Party" allows third parties to be given legally enforceable rights. It should be noted that in 1989 the European Parliament passed a Resolution requesting that a start be made on the preparatory work for drawing up a European Code of Private Law. The preamble to the Resolution states that "...unification can be carried out in branches of private law which are highly important for the development of the single market, such as contract law..." (Resolution of 26 May 1989, OJEC No C 158/401, 26 June 1989).

[22]   For practical difficulties in relation to shipping contracts (but see now the Carriage of Goods by Sea Act 1992), sale of goods contracts, contracts to pay money to a third party and contractual licences, see Consultation Paper No 121, paras 4.8-4.11, 4.19-4.21, 4.23-4.24, 4.26.

[23]   [1994] AC 85.

[24]   [1995] 1 WLR 68. See paras 2.39-2.46 above.

[25]   See para 2.38 above.

[26]   Eg, *Murphy v Brentwood DC* [1991] 1 AC 398.

the tort of negligence and, if forced to move to alternative accommodation while the repairs were being carried out, could not recover consequent loss and expense either.

3.12 In complex construction projects, there will be a web of agreements between the participants in the project, allocating responsibilities and liabilities between the client (and sometimes its financiers), the main contractor, specialist sub-contractors and consultants (architects, engineers and surveyors). Most significant construction projects in the UK are carried out under one of three major contractual procurement routes,[27] and so the documentation used is very often highly standardised.

3.13 The third party rule means that only the parties within each contractual relationship can sue each other. The unfortunate result is that one cannot in the 'main' contracts simply extend the benefit of the architect's and engineer's duties of care and skill, and the contractor's duties to build according to the specifications, to subsequent purchasers or tenants of the development, or to funding institutions who might suffer loss as a result of the defective execution of the works. This cannot be achieved under the present third party rule without either joining the third party in question into the contract which contains these obligations, which in the case of a subsequent purchaser or tenant is impractical, since their identity may be unknown at the commencement of the works, or even for a long time afterwards, or executing a separate document - a "collateral warranty" - extending the benefit of the duties in question. Were it not for these collateral warranties, the third party rule would prevent contractual actions by subsequent owners of completed buildings against the architect, engineer, main contractor or subcontractor whose defective performance may have caused loss or damage to them.[28]

3.14 In an effort to overcome the privity deficiency of the law of contract, attempts were earlier made by subsequent owners of defective premises to sue in tort, and the expansion of the categories of negligence following *Hedley Byrne & Co v Heller & Partners Ltd*,[29] and particularly *Anns v Merton London Borough Council*,[30] initially

---

[27] In 1987, 52% of work was undertaken on lump sum contracts with firm bills of quantities, whether for private or public clients, such as the Joint Contracts Tribunal Standard Form of Building Contract, 1980 edition ("JCT 80") or the JCT Intermediate Form of Contract, 1984 edition ("IFC 84"). 12% of work was carried out on design and build contracts, such as the JCT Standard Form of Building Contract with Contractor's Design, 1981 edition ("CD 81"). 9% was carried out under management works contracts, such as the JCT Management Works Contract, 1987 edition ("MC 87"). The method of procurement will depend on factors such as the design route chosen for the project, the client's objectives and requirements, the funding arrangements chosen, and external factors such as economic risk and demographic trends: Ashworth, *Contractual Procedures in the Construction Industry* (2nd ed, 1991) pp 37-39, 47-48.

[28] Similar problems apply when the third parties seeking rights of suit are tenants with full repairing leases, and who are therefore under a contractual obligation to the landlord of the building to maintain its fabric.

[29] [1964] AC 465.

[30] [1978] AC 728.

resulted in such claims being successful.[31] However, the law is now set against the recovery in negligence of economic loss caused by defective construction. In *D & F Estates Ltd v Church Commissioners for England*,[32] it was held that a builder was not liable in tort to a subsequent purchaser in respect of the cost of repair of defects to a building. The House of Lords then overruled *Anns v Merton LBC* in *Murphy v Brentwood District Council*[33] in holding that a local authority, which negligently failed to ensure that the builder complied with relevant by-laws and building regulations, owed no duty of care in tort as regards defects in the building causing pure economic loss; and, in a decision handed down on the same day, confirmed the approach taken in the *D & F Estates Ltd* case in relation to builders.[34] As a result of these cases, a subsequent owner or purchaser now has little protection in tort.

3.15   A typical collateral warranty given by an architect, engineer or main contractor excludes consequential economic loss and limits the defendant's liability, having regard to other claims of the warrantee, to a just and equitable proportion of the third party's loss. A typical warranty in favour of a finance house will also contain provisions permitting the finance house to take over the benefit of the contractor's or architect's or engineer's appointment contracts on condition of payment of liabilities, if the main finance contract is determined for any breach on the part of the employer, so that the finance house could ensure the continuance of work on the development notwithstanding some breach of the loan agreement by which the original employer was financed. There will also be provisions permitting the finance house, purchaser or tenant a licence to copy and use for specified purposes any designs or documents that are the property of the contractor or architect or engineer, and a clause undertaking that the contractor, architect or engineer will maintain professional indemnity insurance in a specified sum for a specified period. Finally, the warranty will normally permit assignment by the finance house, purchaser or tenant without any consent of the warrantor being required. These collateral warranties are generally supported by separate nominal consideration or are made under deed and thus are not tied to consideration in the main contract.

3.16   It is important to add that, where the benefit of the obligations undertaken by the warranty are assigned to sub-financiers or further purchasers or tenants down the line, this can give rise to further difficulties arising from the law of assignment. In particular, there is the difficulty as to whether an assignee can recover full damages, which was in issue in *Linden Gardens Trust Ltd v Lenesta Sludge Disposals Ltd*[35] and

---

[31]   See *Salmond & Heuston on the Law of Torts* (eds Heuston and Buckley) (20th ed, 1992) p 288ff, esp 295-296.

[32]   [1989] AC 177.

[33]   [1991] 1 AC 398.

[34]   *Department of the Environment v Thomas Bates and Son Ltd* [1991] AC 499.

[35]   [1994] 1 AC 85.

Darlington Borough Council v Wiltshier Northern Ltd[36] and which led to the application, and extension, of an exception to the normal rule on quantification of damages.[37]

3.17   Our proposed reforms would enable contracting parties to avoid the need for collateral warranties by simply laying down third party rights in the main contract. Moreover, our proposed reforms would enable the contracting parties to mirror the terms in existing collateral warranties. Although this involves 'jumping ahead' to some details of our proposed reforms, it is worth explaining this latter point in some detail. Applying our conditional benefit approach discussed in Part X below, there is no reason why the architects' engineers' and contractors' liability to the third party could not be limited, as it presently is under collateral warranty agreements, so as to exclude consequential loss and so as to be limited to a specified share or a just and equitable share of the third party's loss.[38] As regards defences, a claim by a third party under our proposed legislation, as we examine in Part X below, will be subject to defences and set-offs arising from, or in connection with, the contract and relevant to the particular contractual provision being enforced by the third party and which would have been available against the promisee. But this is a default rule only and the contracting parties can provide for a wider or a narrower sphere of operation for defences and set-offs, if they so wish. So the present position under collateral warranties, whereby the claim is subject to defences arising under the main contract, is, or can be, replicated. What about variation of the contract by the original contracting parties? A collateral warranty, once executed, may not be varied without the consent of the benefited third party purchaser, tenant or finance house. Our proposals are, on the face of it, more flexible in that the contracting parties can vary the contract without the third party's consent until the third party has relied on the contract or has accepted it. In practice, however, this ability to vary is not likely to be of any great advantage to the contracting parties because, assuming that the promisor could reasonably be expected to have foreseen that the third party would rely on the contract, they would only be certain that it was safe to vary or cancel the original contract if they first communicated with the third party to ensure that there has been no reliance. It should be stressed that when we refer to variation, we are referring to variation of the contract. The work in building contracts is commonly subject to variation and, if so, would obviously continue to be variable irrespective of the third party's reliance or acceptance.[39]

---

[36]   [1995] 1 WLR 68.

[37]   See paras 2.39-2.46 above.

[38]   In contrast to limitations in collateral warranties, limitation clauses will not be subject to ss 2(2) or 3 of the Unfair Contract Terms Act 1977 where an action is brought by a third party under our proposed Act: see paras 13.9-13-13 below.

[39]   See para 9.37, note 30, below. Note also that, as explained at paras 9.37-9.42 below, our proposals would allow the parties, expressly, to reserve the right to vary irrespective of reliance or acceptance by the third party.

3.18   So, in our view, our proposals would enable the contracting parties to replicate the advantages of collateral warranties without the inconvenience of actually drafting and entering into separate contracts. Moreover, our proposals may carry a limited degree of extra flexibility as regards variation.

3.19   A further advantage of our legislative reform, as against collateral warranty agreements, is that it would not be necessary to assign the benefit of a provision extending the contractor's or architect's duty of care to sub-financiers and other purchasers and tenants down the line, since these persons could simply be named as potential beneficiaries of the clause by class. Thus, the difficulties caused by quantification of damages in claims under assigned collateral warranty agreements would be entirely removed.

3.20   The main contract between the client and main contractor may also contain exclusion clauses limiting the liability of the main contractor for certain types of defective performance. The main contractor may have entered into these clauses on its own behalf and on behalf of subcontractors, in an effort to enable subcontractors to take advantage, in actions against them in the tort for negligence, of the limitations and exemptions contained in such clauses. As we have seen, the exception to the third party rule, developed in *New Zealand Shipping Ltd v A M Satterthwaite & Co Ltd*,[40] may not necessarily work in this context albeit that the courts have sometimes allowed third parties to take advantage of the exclusion clause by regarding it as negativing the duty of care that would otherwise have arisen.[41] A reform of the privity rule would permit contractors and clients straightforwardly and uncontroversially to extend the benefit of exclusion clauses in their contract to employees, sub-contractors and others.

3.21   Further problems may arise as regards payment obligations. At present, when a main contractor fails to pay a subcontractor for work performed, the subcontractor will have no right to sue the client directly for payment, although the client will be entitled to take the benefit of the subcontractor's work. It may be that the participants in a construction project might wish to provide for payment direct by the client to the subcontractor for work performed under a subcontract,[42] and to give the subcontractor a corresponding right to sue the client for the agreed sum once the work is performed. Even if such a right were expressly provided for, the present third party rule would prevent such an express term from being enforceable by the subcontractor against the client, unless the subcontractor and client are in a contractual relationship.

---

[40]   [1975] AC 154. See paras 2.24-2.26 above.

[41]   *Southern Water Authority v Carey* [1985] 2 All ER 1077; *Norwich City Council v Harvey* [1989] 1 WLR 828; *Pacific Associates Inc v Baxter* [1990] 1 QB 993. See para 2.29 above.

[42]   JCT 80 (clauses 35.13.3-35.13.5) and Form NSC (Employer/Nominated Subcontractor's Agreement) 2a, clause 6(1), create a duty on the part of the client to pay nominated subcontractors direct.

3.22   Employers may make arrangements with contractors which are designed by both parties to benefit neighbours with regard to issues such as noise, access and working hours. The intended recipients of these benefits may be protected via the tort of nuisance but reform of the third party rule would enable the parties to give the neighbours the right to enforce the contract which would give them additional, and often significantly better, protection than in tort.

3.23   Our attention has also recently been drawn to the difficulties caused by the third party rule in the offshore oil and gas industry, which provide an excellent example of the anomalies and inconsistencies generated by the rule in practice. We understand that for many years, major oil companies and their advisers have attempted to minimise litigation arising from drilling contracts in the North Sea. This has largely been achieved by the use of cross indemnities between oil companies and contractors, which to be effective, must not only benefit the parties to the contracts in question but also all other companies in their respective groups, their employees, agents, sub-contractors and co-licensees. This is because, for example, it will often be unclear at the outset of a project which member of a client company's group will operate a platform and will thus be caused loss by any failings on the part of the contractor. An indemnity should therefore ideally benefit all companies likely to be affected. It is generally impractical for more than a handful of the beneficiaries of the indemnities given to be made parties to the contract. Moreover, careful drafting of the indemnity is necessary to ensure that those made parties to the indemnity can recover losses actually sustained by other group companies and beneficiaries. At present therefore, the third party rule is circumvented by making the parties to the contract agents or trustees for the other beneficiaries. Some devices used have become even more complex than those commonly employed in the construction industry, with webs of mutual cross-indemnities, back to back indemnity agreements, and incorporation of all main contract provisions into sub-contracts. We understand that there is concern among legal advisers as to the validity of these circumventions of privity. Our proposed reform will permit contractors and employers straightforwardly to extend the benefit of indemnity and exemption clauses contained in a contract to other companies in a group, employees, sub-contractors and others.

(2) Insurance Contracts

3.24   There are several common situations where one party takes out an insurance policy for the benefit of another. The third party rule would prevent the third party enforcing the contract of insurance against the insurer. The inconvenience of this has led to a number of statutory inroads. For example, by section 11 of the Married Women's Property Act 1882, a life insurance policy taken out by someone on his or her own life, and expressed to be for the benefit of his or her spouse or children, creates a trust in favour of the objects named in the policy. By section 148(7) of the Road Traffic Act 1988 a person covered by a liability insurance policy for motor accidents, even though taken out by someone else (for example, by a spouse or employer) is able to enforce that policy against the insurer. And under other legislation dealing, for example, with fire insurance and situations where the insured party becomes insolvent, third parties are given rights to enforce insurance contracts even though they are not expressly designated in them.[43]

3.25   There are, however, still a number of insurance contracts where legislation has not intervened to give third party beneficiaries a right to enforce the contract against the insurer. For example, a life insurance policy taken out for the benefit of dependants other than spouses and children, for example a co-habitee or a parent or a stepchild, falls outside the Married Women's Property Act 1882 and appears, therefore, not to be enforceable by those dependants. If a company takes out liability insurance covering the liability of its subsidiary company, and its contractors and sub-contractors, only the company itself would have the right to enforce the insurance contract.[44] Again, if an employer takes out private health insurance, to cover medical expenses, on behalf of its employees, the employees would have no right to enforce the insurance contract so as to ensure reimbursement of expenses incurred.[45] If in these circumstances the employer is insolvent or, because of a transfer of undertakings, has no interest in the contract, the employee has no legal standing to force the insurance company to pay in the event of a claim under the policy and the liquidator in the employer's insolvency may not wish to pursue such a claim. Even if the employer is solvent and wishes to sue, the employer may have difficulty in securing an adequate remedy as, in an action for damages, it can normally only recover its own loss which will usually be nil.[46]

3.26   In Australia, section 48 of the Insurance Contracts Act 1984 allows third parties to enforce insurance contracts where they are named as beneficiaries or as "covered by the policy". We explain in Part XII why our recommendations for reform in this project do not go quite so far as the Australian legislation.[47] Nevertheless our reform proposals will enable an insurer and assured, by an express term, to confer enforceable rights on third parties (for example, employees): and contracts of insurance which purport to confer a benefit on an expressly designated third party will be enforceable

---

[43]   See paras 2.54 and 2.56 above.

[44]   Cf *Trident General Insurance Co Ltd v McNiece Bros Pty Ltd* (1988) 165 CLR 107. See paras 2.67-2.69 above.

[45]   Cf *Green v Russell* [1959] 2 QB 226; see para 7.51 below. A *Which?* report, April 1992, "Income When You're Ill" 224, 227 draws attention to the problem for employees of enforcing an insurance policy taken out by an employer.

[46]   These types of situation are not within the strict ratio of *Linden Gardens Trust Ltd v Lenesta Sludge Disposals Ltd* [1994] 1 AC 85 or *Darlington Borough Council v Wiltshier Northern Ltd* [1995] 1 WLR 68 (discussed above in paras 2.39-2.46). However they might appear to fall within the scope of these decisions, in that it was envisaged that the fruits of the contract would be enjoyed by a third party, and "it could be foreseen that damage caused by a breach would cause loss to a [non-contracting party] and not merely to the original contracting party", [1994] 1 AC 85, 114, per Lord Browne-Wilkinson.

[47]   See paras 12.23-12.25 below.

by a third party subject to this being contrary to the parties' intentions on a proper construction of the contract.

3.27   We should add, finally, that, if renegotiated on the same terms after our proposals come into force,[48] the well-known agreement between the Motor Insurers' Bureau and the Secretary of State for the Environment, whereby the Bureau agrees to pay to a victim of a road accident any unsatisfied judgment against an uninsured (or untraceable) driver, would prima facie be enforceable by a victim (although of course, in any renegotation, the MIB might decide to insert a term to the effect that the agreement is not to be enforceable by the third party). The third party rule means that, at present, the agreement is unenforceable by the victims[49] although the Bureau's practice is not to rely on the doctrine of privity as a defence.[50]

10. Conclusion

3.28   For the reasons articulated above, we believe that a reform of the third party rule is necessary. Contracting parties may not, under the present law, create provisions in their contracts which are enforceable directly by a third party unless they can take advantage of one of the exceptions to the third party rule. Our basic philosophy for reform is that it should be straightforwardly possible for contracting parties to confer on third parties the right to enforce the contract.

3.29   We therefore recommend that:

(1)   the rule of English law whereby a third party to a contract may not enforce it should be reformed so as to enable contracting parties to confer a right to enforce the contract on a third party.

3.30   Following on from this, we need to clarify at the outset what we mean by the "right to enforce the contract". In the Consultation Paper we provisionally recommended that rights which may be created in favour of a third party should extend (a) both to the right to receive the promised performance from the promisor where this is an appropriate remedy and to the right to pursue any remedies for delayed or defective performance, and (b) to the right to rely on any provisions in the contract restricting or excluding the third party's liability to a contracting party as if the third party were a party to the contract.[51] We explained that the first part of this recommendation states the central point that the third party beneficiary is to be entitled to performance

---

[48]   Our proposed Act will not apply to contracts made before the coming into operation of the Act: see paras 14.20-14.21 below.

[49]   Although the agreement may be specifically enforced by the Minister: *Gurtner v Circuit* [1968] 2 QB 587.

[50]   See, eg, *Hardy v Motor Insurers' Bureau* [1964] 2 QB 745; *Albert v Motor Insurers' Bureau* [1972] AC 301; *Persson v London Country Buses* [1974] 1 WLR 569. See, generally, Treitel, *The Law of Contract* (9th ed, 1995) p 585.

[51]   See Consultation Paper No 121, paras 5.17-5.18, 6.6.

of the promise, or damages for its non-performance. The second part of the recommendation allows third parties to be able to take advantage of exemption clauses agreed for their benefit, thus achieving the result reached in *The Eurymedon*[52] and *The New York Star*[53] more directly.

3.31 Consultees generally agreed with this provisional recommendation, although a few academic lawyers raised doubts as to whether this was the appropriate way to deal with exclusion clauses. While we continue to agree with our provisional recommendation, we would now formulate the recommendation in slightly different language.[54]

3.32 We therefore recommend that:

(2) **a right to enforce the contract means (1) a right to all remedies given by the courts for breach of contract (and with the standard rules applicable to those remedies applying by analogy) that would have been available to the third party had he been a party to the contract, including damages, awards of an agreed sum, specific performance and injunctions; and (2) a right to take advantage of a promised exclusion or restriction of the promisor's rights as if the third party were a party to the contract.** (Draft Bill, clause 1(4) and 1(5))

3.33 There are three points of clarification concerning this recommendation:

(i) By emphasising the remedies *given by the courts* for breach of contract we mean to exclude termination (or discharge) of a contract for substantial breach by the promisor. Termination is a self-help, not a judicial, remedy.[55] We believe that the third party should not be entitled to terminate the contract for breach as this may be contrary to the promisee's wishes or interests.

(ii) By emphasising the remedies for breach of contract, we mean to exclude restitutionary remedies, such as the recovery of money had and received for total failure of consideration, which an innocent party can claim once he has validly

---

[52] [1975] AC 154.

[53] [1981] 1 WLR 138. See paras 2.24-2.30 above.

[54] The main equivalent provision in the New Zealand legislation is s 8 of the Contracts (Privity) Act 1982 which reads as follows: "The obligation imposed on a promisor by section 4 of this Act may be enforced at the suit of the beneficiary as if he were a party to the deed or contract, and relief in respect of the promise, including relief by way of damages, specific performance, or injunction, shall not be refused on the ground that the beneficiary is not a party to the deed or contract in which the promise is contained or that, as against the promisor, the beneficiary is a volunteer". "Beneficiary" and "benefit" are defined in s 2. See Appendix B below

[55] A Burrows, *Remedies for Torts and Breach of Contract* (2nd ed, 1994) p 1.

terminated a contract for breach.[56] We do not consider that the third party can establish that the promisor has been unjustly enriched at *his* expense (where this latter phrase means "by subtraction from the third party").[57]

(iii) By treating the third party for the purposes of this recommendation as if he had been a party to the contract, and by stressing that the rules as to the remedies are to apply by analogy, we mean to make clear that, for example, the third party is entitled to (substantial) damages for his own loss, that he cannot recover loss that is too remote, that he is under a duty to mitigate his loss, and that he may be awarded specific performance (unless, for example, the contract is not supported by valuable consideration or is a contract for personal service or the third party has fallen foul of the doctrine of laches). It should also be noted, although this is in any event the position in standard two-party contracts,[58] that it will of course be the defendant's (the promisor's) contemplation that will be crucial for the purposes of the contractual remoteness of damage test.

---

[56] Goff and Jones, *The Law of Restitution* (4th ed, 1993) pp 407-409, 412-424; P Birks, *An Introduction of the Law of Restitution* (revised ed, 1989) chapter 7; A Burrows, *Remedies for Torts and Breach of Contract* (2nd ed, 1994) pp 307-308; A Burrows, *The Law of Restitution* (1993) pp 397-398.

[57] P Birks, *An Introduction to the Law of Restitution* (revised ed, 1989) pp 23-24, 40-44, 313-315; A Burrows, *The Law of Restitution* (1993) pp 16-17, 376.

[58] This is made clear in cases subsequent to *Hadley v Baxendale* (1854) 9 Exch 341, 156 ER 145, such as *Victoria Laundry (Windsor) Ltd v Newman Industries Ltd* [1949] 2 KB 528 and *Koufos v Czarnikow Ltd, The Heron II* [1969] 1 AC 350.

PART IV
PRECEDENTS FOR REFORM

4.1 In deciding on the form, and details of our proposals, we have derived great help from the recommendations for abrogation of the third party rule made by the Law Revision Committee in England, the legislative reforms enacted in New Zealand and in some jurisdictions in Australia, and the departure from the traditional common law approach brought about by the judiciary in the United States. In this Part, we examine some of the illuminating central features of these 'precedents' for reform.[1]

1. The Law Revision Committee Report

4.2 In 1937, the Law Revision Committee, chaired by Lord Wright MR, presented its Sixth Interim Report.[2] Among the topics addressed by the Committee in this Report was the common law's rejection of a *ius quaesitum tertio*. The Committee's Report stated that England was almost alone among modern systems of law in its rigid adherence to the application of the third party rule, and that experience had demonstrated that the rule was apt to lead to hardship thus necessitating exceptions from it.[3] The Committee regarded the trust exception, illustrated by the line of cases following *Tomlinson v Gill*,[4] as the most important, and said that, if this doctrine had been applied in all cases, it would be possible to say that English law did have a *ius quaesitum tertio*. However the application of the exception had been limited by other cases,[5] and therefore "the law on this point is uncertain and confused. For the ordinary lawyer it is difficult to determine when a contract right 'may be conferred by way of

---

[1] The relevant legislation in Western Australia, Queensland and New Zealand is set out in Appendix B. The law on contracts for the benefit of third parties in several other jurisdictions was set out in the Appendix to Consultation Paper No 121. We have also found of help and interest the Ontario Law Reform Commission, *Report on Amendment of the Law of Contract* (1987) ch 4 and, especially, the clear and elegant Report of the Manitoba Law Reform Commission Report No 80, *Privity of Contract* (1993). The former concluded that a detailed legislative scheme was not the appropriate method of reform; rather there should be a simple abrogation of the third party rule by statute, with the details left to the courts. The latter proposed a draft Bill based on the New Zealand Contracts (Privity) Act 1982, with some amendments. Neither report has yet been implemented.

[2] Law Revision Committee, Sixth Interim Report, *Statute of Frauds and the Doctrine of Consideration*, (1937) Cmd 5449.

[3] Law Revision Committee, Sixth Interim Report, para 41.

[4] (1756) Ambler 330, 27 ER 221. See also *Gregory and Parker v Williams* (1817) 3 Mer 582; 36 ER 224; *Lamb v Vice* (1840) 6 M & W 467; 151 ER 495; *Robertson v Wait* (1853) 8 Exch 299, 155 ER 1360; *Lloyd's v Harper* (1880) 16 Ch D 290; *Les Affréteurs Réunis Société Anonyme v Leopold Walford (London) Ltd* [1919] AC 801. See Law Revision Committee, Sixth Interim Report, para 42.

[5] *In Re Empress Engineering Company* (1880) 16 Ch D 125, 127 per Jessel MR "I know of no case where, when A simply contracts with B to pay money to C, C has been held entitled to sue A in equity"; *Dunlop Pneumatic Tyre Co Ltd v Selfridge and Co Ltd* [1915] AC 847, 853 per Viscount Haldane LC; *Vandepitte v Preferred Accident Insurance Corporation of New York* [1933] AC 70 (PC). See Law Revision Committee, Sixth Interim Report, para 43.

property', in Viscount Haldane's phrase, and when it may not".[6] The Report concluded that "there is a strong argument for attempting to frame a rule which will be more easily understandable".[7] A further practical reason for reform was that the enforcement of a *ius quaesitum tertio* by way of trust involved the addition of the trustee as a party to all legal proceedings to enforce the trust, which was wasteful and unnecessary, as the third party's position was more analogous to an assignee of a contractual right than to a beneficiary of a trust.[8]

4.3 The Committee then went on to consider the circumstances in which third party rights should arise, and considered that there should be three important limitations. First, no third party right should be acquired unless given by the express terms of the contract.[9] Secondly, the promisor should be able to raise any defences against the third party which he or she would have been able to raise against the promisee. Thirdly, the right of the promisor and promisee to vary or cancel the contract at any time should be preserved unless the third party had received notice of the agreement and had adopted it either expressly or by conduct. The Committee therefore recommended that:

> where a contract by its express terms purports to confer a benefit directly on a third party, the third party shall be entitled to enforce the provision in his own name, provided that the promisor shall be entitled to raise as against the third party any defence that would have been valid against the promisee. The rights of the third party shall be subject to cancellation of the contract by the mutual consent of the contracting parties at any time before the third party has adopted it either expressly or by conduct.[10]

---

[6] Law Revision Committee, Sixth Interim Report, para 44.

[7] *Ibid.*

[8] Law Revision Committee, Sixth Interim Report, para 46. The Committee also thought that an important practical reason for reform was the increasing role played by documentary letters of credit in world trade. The Committee concluded that "it is very undesirable that the validity in law of a commercial contract of such importance should remain in doubt": Law Revision Committee, Sixth Interim Report, para 45. Of course, the legal validity of documentary letters of credit is now well-settled. Our Consultation Paper concluded that documentary letters of credit were valid through an exception to the doctrine of consideration, and did not constitute infringements of the third party rule: see Consultation Paper No 121, para 3.32; *Hamzeh Malas & Sons v British Imex Industries Ltd* [1958] 2 QB 127.

[9] The Law Revision Committee was adamant that no third party right should be acquired by implication (eg, because the performance of the contract would benefit the third party). See Law Revision Committee, Sixth Interim Report, para 47.

[10] Law Revision Committee, Sixth Interim Report, para 48.

The Committee also recommended that the provisions of section 11 of the Married Women's Property Act, 1882, should be extended to all life, endowment and education policies, in which a particular beneficiary is named.[11]

4.4   As we shall see,[12] the Report of the Law Revision Committee was directly influential in promoting reform to the third party rule in Western Australia which, like Queensland, did not have a separate Law Reform Commission Report on the third party rule before introducing reform. However, its recommendations on the third party rule (and on the doctrine of consideration) have, of course, not been implemented in England.[13]

2. Abrogation of Third Party Rule in Other Common Law Jurisdictions

(1) Western Australia

4.5   Section 11 of the Western Australian Property Law Act 1969, in line with the proposal of the English Law Revision Committee, amended the third party rule by providing that:

> ...where a contract expressly in its terms purports to confer a benefit directly on a person who is not named as a party to the contract, the contract is...enforceable by that person in his own name... .[14]

All defences which would have been available to the promisor had the third party been a party to the contract are available in an action by the third party,[15] and in any action on the contract by the third party, all parties to the contract must be joined.[16] Further, the legislation permits the enforcement of all terms of the contract against the third party which are "in the terms of the contract...imposed on the [third party] for the benefit of the [promisor]".[17] The legislation also permits variation or cancellation of the contract by the contracting parties at any time until the third party adopts it either expressly or by conduct.[18]

---

[11]   Law Revision Committee, Sixth Interim Report, para 49. In its section on consideration, the Law Revision Committee included a recommendation that the rule that consideration must move from the promisee should be abolished: see para 37.

[12]   See paras 4.5-4.7 below.

[13]   For possible reasons for inaction, see J Beatson, 'Reforming the Law of Contracts for the Benefit of Third Parties - A Second Bite at the Cherry' (1992) 45(2) CLP 1, 14-15.

[14]   Western Australia Property Law Act 1969, s 11(2) (W Austl Acts 1969, No 32).

[15]   Western Australia Property Law Act 1969, s 11(2)(a).

[16]   Western Australia Property Law Act 1969, s 11(2)(b). This requirement was criticised by the New Zealand Contracts and Commercial Law Reform Committee, see para 4.6, below.

[17]   Western Australia Property Law Act 1969, s 11(2)(c).

[18]   Western Australia Property Law Act 1969, s 11(3).

4.6 . The New Zealand Contracts and Commercial Law Reform Committee[19] made a number of criticisms of the Western Australian legislation:

(i)   it does not appear to permit enforcement by third parties who are not in existence or ascertained at the time of formation of the contract;[20]

(ii)   it seems to require express naming of the third party;

(iii)   it seems to exclude implied terms in favour of third parties;

(iv)   it requires the joinder of each person named as a party to the contract in any proceedings commenced by the third party;

(v)   it does not clearly express the necessity for the promisor and promisee to have intended to confer a legal right on the third party.

4.7   It should be noted that the Western Australian legislation does not provide for the situation where, instead of paying the third party, the promisor pays the promisee. If the third party is to be regarded as having an independent right under the contract, the fact that the promisor has performed in favour of the promisee should not *necessarily* eliminate the third party's right to performance. In *Westralian Farmers Co-Operative Ltd v Southern Meat Packers Ltd*,[21] the Supreme Court of Western Australia found that, where the plaintiff third party had established the existence of a contractual payment term in its favour, and the defendant claimed that it had already made payment to the original promisee, the plaintiff third party could nevertheless maintain its claim to payment. We address the issue of overlapping claims by the third party and by the promisee in Part XI below.

(2) Queensland

4.8   The third party rule was abrogated by statute in Queensland in 1974. Section 55 of the Queensland Property Law Act 1974[22] provides that:

> A promisor who, for a valuable consideration moving from the promisee, promises to do or to refrain from doing an act or acts for the benefit of a

---

[19]   New Zealand Contracts and Commercial Law Reform Committee, *Privity of Contract* (1981) pp 49-50.

[20]   We are not entirely convinced that this and the following point are accurate criticisms of the Western Australian legislation. The fact that the third party is "a person not named as a party" does not necessarily mean that it is only where the third party is named that he can enforce the contract.

[21]   [1981] WAR 241. See Consultation Paper No 121, Appendix, para 3. See also J Longo, 'Privity and the Property Law Act: *Westralian Farmers Co-Operative Ltd v Southern Meat Packers Ltd*' (1983) 15 University of Western Aust LRev 411.

[22]   Queensland Stat No 76 of 1974, s 55.

beneficiary shall, upon acceptance by the beneficiary, be subject to a duty enforceable by the beneficiary to perform that promise.[23]

Prior to acceptance, the promisor and promisee may vary or discharge the terms of the promise without the beneficiary's consent.[24] After acceptance, the promisor's duty to perform in favour of and at the suit of the beneficiary becomes enforceable, and the promise may only be varied with the consent of the promisor, promisee and beneficiary.[25] On acceptance, the beneficiary is bound to perform any acts that may be required of him by the terms of the promise.[26] Defences that can normally be raised against an action to enforce a promissory duty can be raised by the promisor against the beneficiary.[27] The section defines what constitutes an "acceptance" so as to render a promise enforceable by the beneficiary,[28] and which "promises" will be capable of giving rise to rights in third party beneficiaries.[29] Unlike the Western Australian legislation, discussed above, the Queensland legislation does not require that the contract expressly purports to confer a benefit on the third party.[30] And it imposes no obligation to join all parties in any action by the third party.[31]

(3) New Zealand

4.9   In 1981, the New Zealand Contracts and Commercial Law Reform Committee presented a Report on the third party rule, which appended draft legislation to implement the recommended reforms.[32] The Report gave a brief account of the

[23]   Queensland Property Law Act 1974, s 55(1). The New Zealand Contracts and Commercial Law Reform Committee, *Privity of Contract* (1981) p 52 regarded the Queensland legislation as "deficient in not providing that the duty may be created by deed as well as by simple contract."

[24]   Queensland Property Law Act 1974, ss 55(2).

[25]   Queensland Property Law Act 1974, s 55(3)(a) and (d).

[26]   Queensland Property Law Act 1974, s 55(3)(b).

[27]   Queensland Property Law Act 1974, s 55(4).

[28]   Queensland Property Law Act 1974, s 55(6)(a):"'acceptance' means an assent by words or conduct communicated by or on behalf of the beneficiary to the promisor, or to some person authorized on his behalf, in the manner (if any), and within the time, specified in the promise or, if no time is specified, within a reasonable time of the promise coming to the notice of the beneficiary".

[29]   Queensland Property Law Act 1974, s 55(6)(c): "'promise' means a promise - (i) which is or appears to be intended to be legally binding; and (ii) which creates or appears to be intended to create a duty enforceable by a beneficiary...".

[30]   Although the promise must appear to be intended to confer a legal right enforceable by the third party: see note 29 above.

[31]   If criticisms (i) and (ii) in paragraph 4.6 above are accurate, the Queensland legislation also differs in that the beneficiary need not be named or in existence or identified at the time of the contract: see s 55(6)(b). See Ontario Law Reform Commission, *Report on Amendment of the Law of Contract* (1987) pp 62-64; Manitoba Law Reform Commission, *Privity of Contract* (1993) Report No 80 pp 32-34.

[32]   New Zealand Contracts and Commercial Law Reform Committee, *Privity of Contract* (1981).

existing common law of New Zealand,[33] which was virtually identical to that of England and Wales. The Report then considered developments in other jurisdictions, including the absence of a third party rule in most civilian systems[34] and its abrogation, either by the courts or by statute, in the United States, Israel, Western Australia and Queensland. The Committee considered arguments that the practical difficulties caused by the rule, and the devices adopted for avoiding its operation in particular circumstances, were insufficient to justify a fundamental change in the law, but refuted the contention that the intentions of the contracting parties could usually be achieved by the courts. The Report said:[35]

> We are not convinced by such arguments. We have looked in vain for a solid basis of policy justifying the frustration of contractual intentions...[W]e are left with a sense of irritation like that which, we suspect, motivated the majority of the Privy Council in *New Zealand Shipping Co Ltd v Satterthwaite & Co Ltd*,[36] to say, '...to give the appellant the benefit of the exemptions and limitations contained in the bill of lading is to give effect to the clear intentions of a commercial document...' ...The case for reform is completed, in our opinion, by the observations of Lord Scarman (sometime Chairman of the English Law Commission) in *Woodar Investment Development Ltd v Wimpey Construction (UK) Limited.*[37]

4.10   The New Zealand Committee therefore recommended that a third party should be given a right to enforce a contract where a promise contained in a deed or contract confers, or purports to confer, a benefit on that third party.[38] The New Zealand Committee's recommendations were substantially implemented in the New Zealand Contracts (Privity) Act 1982, although one of the changes is that the 1982 Act, in contrast to the draft Contracts (Privity) Bill annexed to the Committee's Report, includes a requirement that the third party should be designated in the contract in order to obtain an enforceable right.

4.11   The Act, in section 4, provides that:

> Where a promise contained in a deed or contract confers, or purports to confer, a benefit on a person, designated by name, description or reference to a class,

---

[33]   *Ibid*, paras 2.1-2.3.

[34]   The Report, at para 3.1, considered the law of France, Germany, South Africa, Denmark, Norway and Scotland.

[35]   New Zealand Contracts and Commercial Law Reform Committee, *Privity of Contract* (1981), paras 6.2-6.3.

[36]   [1975] AC 154, 169.

[37]   [1980] 1 WLR 277, 300-301. Lord Scarman's observations are set out above at para 2.64.

[38]   *Privity of Contract* (1981) Appendix C, Draft Contracts (Privity) Act, clause 4.

who is not a party to the deed or contract...the promisor shall be under an obligation, enforceable at the suit of that person, to perform that promise.

Thus the section starts from the premise that all promises benefiting sufficiently designated third parties are to be enforceable at the suit of that third party. The section is not limited to express promises, and extends equally to implied promises. However the section goes on to provide that it does not apply:

to a promise which, on the proper construction of the deed or contract, is not intended to create, in respect of the benefit, an obligation enforceable at the suit of that person.

4.12   Section 4 thus creates a reverse onus of proof in respect of the contracting parties' intention to create a legally enforceable obligation in favour of the third party. It is up to them to establish that their promise was not intended to have this effect. The New Zealand Act therefore controls liability by the requirement that the third party be sufficiently designated in the contract and by resting liability on the intentions of the contracting parties to confer a right of enforceability (albeit under a reversed burden of proof).

4.13   The Act goes on to provide that promises benefiting third parties may not be varied or cancelled without the third party's consent once the third party has either (i) materially altered his position in reliance on the promise;[39] (ii) obtained judgment on the promise; or (iii) obtained an arbitration award on the promise.[40] However, where there is an express provision permitting variation in other circumstances, which is known to the third party, such variation is permitted.[41]

4.14   In 1993, the New Zealand Law Commission considered the operation of the Act,[42] and concluded that most of the problems which had arisen in its operation concerned the scope of what became section 4, and particularly the requirement of designation. These caused difficulties particularly in connection with pre-incorporation contracts and contracts involving nominees. The New Zealand Law Commission examined the decisions under the Act, but recommended no changes to it. The precise difficulties identified by the Commission will be discussed in Part VIII of this Report when we consider designation, and existence, of the third party.

---

[39]   Or his position has been materially altered by the reliance of any other person on the promise.

[40]   New Zealand Contracts (Privity) Act 1982, s 5.

[41]   New Zealand Contracts (Privity) Act 1982, s 6. For the New Zealand approach to defences, see para 10.7 below.

[42]   New Zealand Law Commission, *Contract Statutes Review*, NZLC R 25, (1993), pp 217-218.

(4)   United States

4.15   There is a vast literature on third party rights in the United States,[43] which no short account can adequately summarise. The following paragraphs merely highlight some of the main difficulties revealed by the case law.

4.16   Since the decision of the New York Court of Appeals in *Lawrence v Fox*,[44] it has become generally accepted that a third party is able to enforce a contractual obligation made for his benefit. However, the problem of defining what is meant by a third party beneficiary has never adequately been solved. Section 133 of the first Restatement of Contracts published in 1932 distinguished donee beneficiaries, creditor beneficiaries, and incidental beneficiaries: only donee and creditor beneficiaries could enforce contracts made for their benefit. A person was a "donee beneficiary" if the purpose of the promisee was to make a gift to him, or to confer upon him a right not due from the promisee. A person was a "creditor beneficiary" if performance of the promise would satisfy an actual or asserted duty of the promisee to him. A person was an "incidental beneficiary" if the benefits to him were merely incidental to the performance of the promise.

4.17   It became apparent that a number of third party beneficiaries did not fall within the "donee" and "creditor" categories,[45] such that some courts simply disregarded the categorisation approach and allowed beneficiaries to recover who were neither creditors nor donees.[46] The inflexibility of the categorisation approach led to changes in the second Restatement of Contracts published in 1981, under which intended beneficiaries, who can enforce contracts, are contrasted with incidental beneficiaries, who cannot. Section 302 of the Restatement (Second) provides:

> "(1)   Unless otherwise agreed between promisor and promisee, a beneficiary of a promise is an intended beneficiary if recognition of a right to performance in the beneficiary is appropriate to effectuate the intention of the parties and either

---

[43]   See the standard accounts in *Corbin on Contracts*, Vol 4, and *Williston, A Treatise on the Law of Contracts*, Vol 2, which well illustrate the complexity of American law. See also, eg, D Summers, 'Third Party Beneficiaries and the Restatement (Second) of Contracts' (1982) 67 Cornell L Rev 880; S De Cruz, 'Privity in America: A Study in Judicial and Statutory Innovation' (1985) 14 Anglo-Am L Rev 265; H Prince, 'Perfecting the Third Party Beneficiary Standing Rule under Section 302 of the Restatement (Second) of Contracts' (1984) 25 Boston College L Rev 919; A Waters, 'The Property in the Promise: A Study of the Third Party Beneficiary Rule' (1985) 98 Harvard L Rev 1109. See also the Ontario Law Reform Commission's Report on Amendment of the Law of Contract (1987), pp 55-58.

[44]   20 NY 268 (1859).

[45]   In a private construction context, subcontractors were neither donee nor creditor beneficiaries: D Summers, 'Third Party Beneficiaries and the Restatement (Second) of Contracts' (1982) 67 Cornell L Rev 880, 884.

[46]   *Ibid.* For an example of a third party taking the benefit of an exclusion clause as a third party beneficiary, see *Carle & Montanari Inc v American Export Isbrandtsen Lines Inc* 275 F Supp 76 (1967).

(a)   the performance of the promise will satisfy an obligation of the promisee to pay money to the beneficiary;[47] or

(b)   the circumstances indicate that the promisee intends to give the beneficiary the benefit of the promised performance.[48]

(2)   An incidental beneficiary is a beneficiary who is not an intended beneficiary."[49]

4.18   However, the Restatement (Second) fails properly to explain the distinction between intended and incidental beneficiaries, given that "the parties, or more simply the promisee, may intend a third party to receive a benefit but not intend that party to have standing to enforce the promise".[50] The "intent to benefit" test has, in practice, failed to achieve consistent results,[51] in particular in the field of public service contracts.[52]

4.19   Other difficult questions under the Restatement (Second) include the following. Should reference be made to the contract alone, or to all the prevailing circumstances when determining whether the appropriate intention exists?[53] Some states have adopted a requirement that the intent to benefit the third party be expressed within the contract. However, even in the states that have adopted this strict test of intent, the requirement has not been consistently applied.[54]

4.20   A further problem is the question of whose intent is relevant to establish a third party right. Section 302(1) refers to the intention of the parties, although section 302(1)(b)

---

[47]   Eg where B promises A to discharge a debt owed by A to C.

[48]   Eg where B promises A to make a gift to C.

[49]   Eg where B promises A to build a structure which has the effect of enhancing the value of C's land.

[50]   H Prince, 'Perfecting the Third Party Beneficiary Standing Rule under Section 302 of the Restatement (Second) of Contracts' (1984) 25 Boston College L Rev 919, 979.

[51]   There have been several varieties of the "intent to benefit" test: the contract must have been for the "sole and exclusive" benefit of the third party; the "primary intention" of the promisee must have been to benefit the third party; the contract must have been "necessarily" for the benefit of the third party; the direct benefit must have been "express or unmistakeable" or "sufficiently immediate": Prince, *ibid*, pp 934-937.

[52]   A Waters, "The Property in the Promise: A Study of the Third Party Beneficiary Rule" (1985) 98 Harvard L Rev 1109, 1186-1188.

[53]   In *Beckman Cotton Company v First National Bank of Atlanta* 666 F 2d 181 (1982), by considering the surrounding circumstances the court was able to confer a right of enforcement on a third party beneficiary, although not named in the contract.

[54]   See H Prince, 'Perfecting the Third Party Beneficiary Standing Rule under Section 302 of the Restatement (Second) of Contracts' (1982) Boston College L Rev 919, 926-931.

refers to the promisee's intention. Different jurisdictions apply different tests:[55] some require proof only of the promisee's intention; others focus upon the intent of both parties, and some have adopted a midway position, requiring that the promisor should have reason to know of the promisee's intent to contract for a benefit to a third party.[56]

4.21 On the question whether the contracting parties may vary or revoke their promise, section 311 of the Restatement (Second) provides that the contracting parties may create rights that cannot be modified, but that otherwise they are free to modify unless the beneficiary "materially changes his position in justifiable reliance on the promise or brings suit on it or manifests assent to it at the request of the promisor or promisee".

---

[55] *Ibid*, p 931.

[56] On one view, only the promisee's intention should be relevant, since the promisor's motivation for entering into the contract will frequently be the considerations he receives from the promisee. However, this is not invariably so: the promisor may have an interest in seeing that the third party is benefited, as where he is a relative: *Re Stapleton-Bretherton* [1941] Ch 482.

PART V
THE FORM OF THE LEGISLATION

1. A Detailed Legislative Scheme?

5.1 The Consultation Paper[1] included a consideration of four possible techniques [2] by which reform of the third party rule could be effected:

(i) further exceptions to the third party rule could be made in specific instances;

(ii) the rule preventing the promisee from recovering the third party's loss could be reformed;

(iii) there could be a provision that no third party should be denied enforcement of a contract made for its benefit on the grounds of lack of privity (an enabling provision);

(iv) the law could be reformed by means of a detailed legislative scheme.

5.2 Our provisional recommendation was that reform should be by way of a detailed legislative scheme (that is, option (iv) above). Almost all consultees were in favour of this provisional conclusion.[3] They believed that anything less than a detailed legislative scheme would lead to unacceptable uncertainty. Before confirming our views on this issue, we shall briefly consider the advantages and disadvantages of the various options.

(1) Further Exceptions in Specific Instances

5.3 The first suggestion, that reform might be effected by specific further exceptions to the third party rule, has the advantage that particular needs in particular situations can be directly addressed in detail. Another possible advantage is that exceptions in specific circumstances should leave little room for debate about whether there is an intent to give an enforceable right in particular cases. But to create further situation-specific exceptions misses the point that the third party rule is generally flawed. Creating further specific exceptions will merely serve to make the law more complex while still leaving unacceptable gaps in a third party's rights.

(2) Abolishing the Rule Preventing Recovery by the Promisee of Third Party's Loss

5.4 In the Consultation Paper we accepted that the major advantage of this technique of reform is that it avoids the need to address several difficult questions which arise if

---

[1] Consultation Paper No 121, paras 5.1-5.7.

[2] It was also envisaged that it would be possible to combine some of these possibilities, for instance (i) and (iii).

[3] Including some who did not favour reform.

third parties are given directly enforceable rights, such as: what is the test for enforceability by a third party?; can the original parties vary or rescind the contract?; can the promisee sue in addition to the third party?; is the promisor entitled to rely on defences available against the promisee? However, in our view, this would not be an adequate method of reform, most centrally because the promisee may be either unwilling or unable to enforce a contract made for a third party.

(3) Removal of the Bar to Third Party Enforcement

5.5   The preferred method of reform advocated by the Ontario Law Reform Commission was that "[t]here should be enacted a legislative provision to the effect that contracts for the benefit of third parties should not be unenforceable for lack of consideration or want of privity".[4] The Ontario Commission preferred this approach to a detailed legislative scheme for several reasons:

(i)   it was thought better that the courts should be permitted some flexibility in dealing with the variety of issues which would undoubtedly arise under any reform;

(ii)   since third party beneficiary cases arise in widely different contexts (from contracts to pay money to relatives to contracts involving the extension of defences in bills of lading to stevedores), it was thought that legislation could not satisfactorily deal with all such problems and that anomalies were likely to arise if the same set of rules were to apply to such widely different circumstances;

(iii)   the problem of defining the class of beneficiaries entitled to sue and the question of variation and rescission were regarded as particularly intractable.

5.6   We acknowledged in the Consultation Paper that this method of reform has the attraction of making the change of principle a legislative matter while leaving subsequent development to the courts. However, we also expressed the view that the problems involved are too complex and numerous to lend themselves to an incremental approach. We concluded that this approach would beg many important questions about the detailed application of reform of the third party rule, and that to leave these issues to the courts with no legislative guidance could be said to be an abdication of responsibility when we are aware that they involve questions of principle which will at some stage have to be faced. While this approach undoubtedly achieves flexibility it does so at the expense of clarity and certainty. We felt that the development of the law in the United States, even with the assistance of the Restatements, illustrates some of the disadvantages of such an approach.[5]   We

---

[4]   *Report on Amendment of the Law of Contract* (1987) p 71.

[5]   For the law in the United States, see paras 4.15-4.21 above.

continue to find these arguments to be convincing, and thus reject a simple abolition of the privity rule as a method of reform.

(4) Reform by Means of a Detailed Legislative Scheme

5.7 This was the approach adopted in Western Australia,[6] Queensland,[7] New Zealand,[8] and recommended in Manitoba.[9] On this approach, policy would be determined and provision made for such matters as the contractual provisions that are enforceable by third parties, the rights of contracting parties to vary or discharge the contract, and promisors' defences. The crucial advantage of this approach is its certainty.

5.8 Although the House of Lords could, if a suitable opportunity arose, reconsider the third party rule in English law,[10] the House has on a number of occasions declined to do so. Moreover, one may have to wait a very long time for a suitable case to reach the House of Lords. In any event a legislative reform has the advantage that many of the difficulties of detail identified in the Consultation Paper and in this Report can be addressed and dealt with in a manner not open to the judiciary. In line with the overwhelming view of consultees, we therefore believe that a detailed legislative scheme is the best way to proceed.

5.9 We therefore recommend that:

(3) **the third party rule should be reformed by means of a detailed legislative scheme.**

2. Judicial Development of Third Party Rights

5.10 We should emphasise that we do not wish our proposed legislation - which we believe to be a relatively conservative and moderate measure - to hamper the judicial development of third party rights. Should the House of Lords decide that in a particular sphere our reform does not go far enough and that, for example, a measure of imposed consumer protection is required or that employees (even though not mentioned in the contract) should be able to rely on exclusion clauses that protect their employers under a doctrine of vicarious immunity[11], we would not wish our proposed legislation to be construed as hampering that development.

---

[6] Property Law Act 1969, s 11. See paras 4.5-4.7 above.

[7] Property Law Act 1974, s 55. See para 4.8 above.

[8] Contracts (Privity) Act 1982. See paras 4.9-4.14 above.

[9] Manitoba Law Reform Commission, Report No 80, *Privity of Contract* (1993) p 57. See para 4.1, note 1, above.

[10] As shown by the inroads into the rule made by the courts in other jurisdictions. Eg, Australia (*Trident General Insurance Co Ltd v McNiece Bros Pty Ltd* (1988) 165 CLR 107); Canada (*London Drugs Ltd v Kuehne & Nagel International Ltd* (1992) 97 DLR (4th) 261); USA (*Lawrence v Fox* 20 NY 268 (1859)).

[11] See *London Drugs Ltd v Kuehne & Nagel International Ltd* (1992) 97 DLR (4th) 261. See paras 2.31-2.32 above.

5.11 We therefore recommend that:

(4) the legislation should not be construed as preventing judicial development of third party rights. (Draft Bill, clause 6(1))

3. Reform of The Promisee's Remedies?

5.12 While it is our view that a reform of the rule preventing recovery by the promisee of the third party's loss is not the correct way to reform privity, this seems the most appropriate point in this Report to consider whether, in any event, there should be legislative reform of the promisee's remedies in a contract for a third party's benefit.

5.13 As we have seen in Part II,[12] a promisee's remedies can in some circumstances be of benefit to the third party. The promisee may be able to obtain an order of specific performance[13] or, if the promisor's breach causes loss to the promisee, may obtain substantial damages. If, however, the breach does not cause the promisee any loss and the case is not an appropriate one for specific performance, there will be a difficulty. Normally, the promisee can recover only for his or her own loss and this may mean that he or she will get only nominal damages even if there has been a substantial loss to the third party. The traditional view is also that the promisee will normally be unable to bring an action in debt to enforce payment to him or her of sums due to the third party under the contract, since those sums were by definition not due to the promisee.[14]

5.14 In our Consultation Paper, we did not raise as a specific issue the possibility of reforming the promisee's remedies, albeit that we did provisionally recommend that reform of the rule preventing the promisee from recovering the third party's loss in damages would not be an adequate method of reforming the third party rule.[15] The question we now wish to address, however, is whether, in addition to our central recommendations for reform of the third party rule, we should also recommend reforms to the law on the promisee's remedies.

5.15 We believe that to make specific recommendations in relation to the promisee's remedies in a contract for the benefit of a third party raises matters properly looked at in a more specific review. As the issue was addressed in a rather peripheral manner in our Consultation Paper, we do not believe that it would be appropriate in this Report to make detailed recommendations for its reform. Moreover, in recent years the courts have gone a considerable way towards developing rules which in many appropriate cases do allow the promisee to recover damages on behalf of the third

---

[12] See paras 2.36-2.51 above.

[13] Or, if the promise was not to sue the third party, a stay of action.

[14] See para 2.37, note 109, above.

[15] Consultation Paper No 121, para 5.3.

party. *The Albazero*[16] and *Linden Gardens Trust Ltd v Lenesta Sludge Disposals Ltd*[17] are particularly important in this respect. Our recommendation is that this is a matter at present better left to the evolving common law. Certainly we would not wish to forestall further judicial development of this area of the law of damages.

5.16   Indeed it is important to emphasise that, while our proposed reform will give some third parties the right to enforce contracts, there will remain many contracts where a third party stands to benefit and yet will not have a right of enforceability. Our proposed statute carves out a general and wide-ranging exception to the third party rule but it leaves that rule intact for cases not covered by the statute. On the facts of *Linden Gardens* itself, there would be no question of the third party having a right of enforcement under our proposed reform. The property in question had been sold to the third party after the contract for work on the property had been entered into and there was a clause in the works contract barring assignment of the rights under it. The recognition in that case that the promisee could have recovered damages based on the third party's loss will be as important after the implementation of our proposed reform as it is under the present law; and we would not wish our proposed reform to be construed as casting any doubt on the decisions in *The Albazero, Linden Gardens* and *Darlington BC v Wiltshier Northern Ltd.*[18]

5.17   We therefore recommend that:

(5)   **the remedies available to the promisee in a contract enforceable by a third party should be left to the common law.** (Draft Bill, clause 4)

5.18   The co-existence of an action by a third party to enforce a promised benefit, and the potential ability of the promisee to recover substantial damages for a third party's loss, raise the question of how any overlap between these claims is to be dealt with. We address this in Part XI below.[19]

---

[16]   [1977] AC 774. See para 2.40 above.

[17]   [1994] 1 AC 85. See paras 2.39-2.46 above.

[18]   [1995] 1 WLR 68. See paras 2.42-2.46 above.

[19]   See paras 11.1-11.4, 11.16-11.22 below.

PART VI
THE THIRD PARTY RULE AND CONSIDERATION

1. Introduction and Consultation

6.1 The relationship between the doctrine of consideration and the third party rule has long been debated. We argued in the Consultation Paper[1] that a reform of the third party rule did not require an associated review of the doctrine of consideration. Our view was that the rule that only a party to a contract can enforce it and the rule that consideration must move from the promisee could be distinguished in policy terms: the third party rule determines who can enforce a contract; while the rule that consideration must move from the promisee determines the types of promises that can be enforced. We pointed out that the view that the rules are distinct is supported by authority[2] and by the Report of the Law Revision Committee[3] although it has been questioned by some academics.[4]

6.2 We now wish to address this difficult question again and, in the light of the response of consultees,[5] to discuss it in a little more detail than in the Consultation Paper. In particular, it is now apparent to us that some of this debate has been bedeviled by the ambiguity of the phrase "consideration must move from the promisee". We are also concerned to acknowledge that the belief of some that it is unacceptable to reform privity without reforming consideration is not concerned to deny that it might, at a formal level, be *possible* to do one without the other. Rather the belief is that, at a deeper policy level, the reform of privity involves relaxing the importance attached to consideration.

2. Consideration Must Move From the Promisee

6.3 This maxim is ambiguous. On the one hand, it can be taken to mean that to be binding a promise must be supported by consideration. If A promises B £100, B cannot enforce the promise (unless made under deed) because there is no

---

[1] See Consultation Paper No 121, paras 2.5-2.10.

[2] See, eg, *Tweddle v Atkinson* (1861) 1 B & S 393; 121 ER 262; *Dunlop Pneumatic Tyre Co Ltd v Selfridge and Co Ltd* [1915] AC 847, 853. See also *Kepong Prospecting Ltd v Schmidt* [1968] AC 810, 826.

[3] The Law Revision Committee, Sixth Interim Report, (1937) para 37. See further above, paras 4.2-4.4.

[4] M Furmston, "Return to *Dunlop v Selfridge*" (1960) 23 MLR 373, 382-384; B Coote, "Consideration and the Joint Promisee" [1978] CLJ 301; R Flannigan "Privity - the End of an Era (Error)" (1987) 103 LQR 564, 568-569. Cf H Collins, *The Law of Contract* (2nd ed, 1993) pp 283-292 who supports the view that the third party rule is not inseparably linked with the doctrine of consideration; *Chitty on Contracts* (27th ed, 1994) para 3-032 which accepts the view that the rule that consideration must move from the promisee and the third party rule are not inextricably linked; *Anson's Law of Contract* (ed Guest) (26th ed, 1984) pp 86-87; Treitel, *The Law of Contract* (9th ed, 1995) p 539 is less categorical but also on balance supports this view.

[5] See also E McKendrick, *Contract Law* (2nd ed, 1994) pp 129-130.

consideration for A's promise. The promise is a gratuitous one. This fundamental requirement of consideration could be expressed by saying that B cannot succeed because, although B is a promisee, it has not provided consideration and consideration must move from the promisee.

6.4   In the Consultation Paper, the maxim "consideration must move from the promisee" was essentially used in this first sense of consideration being a necessary requirement for a valid contract. Hence the Paper included the following two passages: "[t]wo of the central questions of policy in the law of contract are: (i) which promises are legally enforceable; and (ii) who can enforce them? The first question is associated with the doctrine of consideration; the second with the doctrine of privity....";[6] "we believe that the third party rule, ie, that third parties cannot enforce contracts made for their benefit, can be reformed without prejudicing the rule that consideration must move from the promisee."[7] Certainly once one has interpreted the maxim that consideration must move from the promisee as meaning merely that consideration is necessary, one can see that, at a formal level, there is no difficulty in reforming privity without altering the need for consideration. That is, one can insist that, provided there is a contract supported by consideration (or made by deed), it may then be enforceable by a third party beneficiary who has not provided consideration.

6.5   But the maxim "consideration must move from the promisee" can also be used to mean, and is probably generally understood to mean, that, even though the promise is supported by consideration, the consideration must move from the plaintiff. That is, the party seeking to enforce the contract must have provided the consideration. Used in this sense one cannot, even at a formal level, reform the privity doctrine while leaving untouched the rule that consideration must move from the promisee. A reform allowing a third party to sue would achieve nothing, or almost nothing, unless there was also a departure from the rule that a plaintiff could not sue on a contract if it has not provided consideration. Used in this sense, the rule that consideration must move from the promisee and the rule of privity that only a party to a contract can enforce it are so closely linked that the essential dispute is whether they are distinguishable at all; whether, in other words, there are two rules or one.

6.6   That dispute ultimately turns on what one means by "a party" to a contract where the contract is supported by consideration rather than being made under deed. It can best be illustrated by reference to the situation of joint promisees. Say, for example, that A promises B and C to pay C £100 if B will do certain work desired by A. If B does the work, and A declines to pay the £100 to C, can C sue? On the face of it, C, not having provided consideration, cannot sue. This can be expressed in one of two ways: either (i) that C cannot sue because, although a party to the contract and privy to it,

---

[6]   Consultation Paper No 121 para 2.1.

[7]   Consultation Paper No 121 para 2.10.

C falls foul of the rule that consideration must move from the promisee; or (ii) that C cannot sue because, not having provided consideration for A's promise, C is not a party to the contract and therefore falls foul of *both* the privity rule and the rule that consideration must move from the promisee (which are merely two ways of expressing exactly the same point).

6.7 Whichever of these two views is taken (and the practical significance of choosing between them seems to relate only to how one deals with joint promisees, which we discuss below) the central point is that the legislation must recognise that if, by "consideration must move from the promisee" one means "consideration must move from the plaintiff" one cannot sensibly reform privity without also departing from that rule.

6.8 We therefore recommend that:

(6) the legislation should ensure that the rule that consideration must move from the promisee is reformed to the extent necessary to avoid nullifying our proposed reform of the doctrine of privity.[8]

3. The Joint Promisee Exception

6.9 A difficult linked issue is how we should deal with the question as to whether a joint promisee can sue even though it has not provided consideration in a contract not made by deed. In other words, how should we deal with the so-called 'joint promisee exception'?[9] The present English law on joint promisees is not entirely clear. However, it seems likely that an English court would apply the approach of the High Court of Australia in *Coulls v Bagot's Executor & Trustee Co Ltd*.[10] In that case, four members of the High Court suggested that a joint promisee could sue despite not having provided consideration[11] (although Windeyer J suggested that one could regard B as having provided consideration *on behalf of C*).[12] Barwick CJ explained that the

---

[8] After discussions with the draftsman, we are satisfied that this recommendation will automatically be met by the central clause of the legislation which gives a third party a right to enforce the contract; such a clause can only be interpreted as also reforming the rule that consideration must move from the promisee (where that rule means that consideration must move from the plaintiff).

[9] This point is left unclear in the legislation enacted in, eg, New Zealand and Western Australia.

[10] (1967) 119 CLR 461. For support in England see, for example, *New Zealand Shipping Co Ltd v A M Satterthwaite & Co Ltd* [1975] AC 154, 180 (per Lord Simon of Glaisdale). See also *McEvoy v Belfast Banking Co Ltd* [1935] AC 24, 43 (per Lord Atkin). See, generally, *Chitty on Contracts* (27th ed, 1994) paras 3-035-3-036 and Treitel, *The Law of Contract* (9th ed) pp 532-533 which draw a distinction between joint, joint and several, and several promises.

[11] On the facts the majority (McTiernan, Taylor and Owen JJ) considered that Mrs Coulls was not a promisee so that this joint promisee exception did not come into play. Barwick CJ and Windeyer J dissented taking the view that Mrs Coulls was a joint promisee.

[12] In his powerful article, "Consideration and the Joint Promise" [1978] CLJ 301, Coote argues that, in a bilateral contract, C can only be regarded as having provided consideration if it has undertaken an obligation to A.

justification for this exception to the need for consideration to move from the promisee was that the promise had been made to C and consideration for the promise had been provided, albeit by B not C. This approach is reminiscent of the view of the Law Revision Committee in 1937. Having cited the joint promisee example given above, the Committee continued, "[W]e can see no reason either of logic or of public policy why A, who has got what he wanted from B in exchange for his promise, should not be compelled by C to carry out that promise merely because C, a party to the contract, did not furnish the consideration".[13]

6.10   We agree that C should have the entitlement to sue A. Indeed, given our reform of the privity doctrine, it would be absurd if this were not so: that is, it would be absurd if a joint promisee had no right to enforce the contract whereas a third party (to whom the promise has not been given or made) would have that right. The much more difficult question, however, is what should be the precise rights of enforcement of the joint promisee (who has not provided consideration)? And, in particular, should such a joint promisee be regarded as a third party within our proposed reforms? The advantage of treating such a joint promisee as a third party is that the absurdity referred to above would be avoided. But there are at least two possible disadvantages of this approach. The first is that it is arguable that a joint promisee should have a more secure entitlement to sue than (other) third parties on the basis that the promise was directly addressed, or given, to him. On this basis, the joint promisee should not have to satisfy the test of enforceability laid down in our proposals (discussed in Part VII below) and ought not to be caught by the provisions allowing variation or cancellation without his consent (discussed in Part IX below). The second disadvantage, and in a sense cutting the other way from the first disadvantage, is that precisely because the promisee is a joint promisee - and is therefore closely connected with the other joint promisee vis-a-vis the promise - it is arguable that traditional rules on joint creditors[14] should apply and some of these rules (for example, requiring joinder of the other joint creditor to any action[15] and allowing one joint creditor to release the promisor provided not in fraud of the other)[16] differ from our proposals for third parties.[17]

6.11   We have found these questions as to the precise rights of a joint promisee who has not provided consideration difficult to resolve. As they were not put out to consultation, and as the position of joint promisees is somewhat peripheral to the central focus of our reform, we think it preferable to leave them to the courts to resolve if and when

---

[13]   Sixth Interim Report (1937) para 37. See para 4.3, note 11 above.

[14]   Treitel, *The Law of Contract* (9th ed, 1995) pp 529-533.

[15]   *Ibid*, p 530.

[16]   *Ibid*, p 532. See also para 11.9, note 8, below.

[17]   For our proposals regarding joinder see paras 14.1-14.5 below. For our proposals regarding releases, see paras 11.7-11.8 and 11.11-11.12 below.

they arise. In line with the implicit assumption of the Consultation Paper,[18] we therefore consider that a joint promisee who has not provided consideration should not count as a third party within our proposed reforms. We adopt this approach in the confident expectation that, particularly in the light of our reforms, the English courts will avoid the absurdity referred to above by accepting the 'joint promisee exception' so that a joint promisee who has not provided consideration will not be left without a basic right to enforce the contract.

6.12 We therefore recommend that:

(7) **without prejudice to his rights and remedies at common law, a joint promisee who has not provided consideration should not be regarded as a third party for the purposes of our reform.** (Draft Bill, clause 8)

4. Reforming Privity Without Reforming Consideration: The Deeper Policy Question

6.13 We have said above that, while at a formal level, it is possible to reform privity without reforming the need for consideration, the question must be addressed at a deeper policy level as to whether this involves relaxing the importance attached to consideration. The argument that a reform of privity does relax the importance of consideration rests on the proposition that a third party who has not provided consideration, and hence not "earned" the promise, should be afforded no better rights than a gratuitous promisee. The fact that someone else has provided consideration for the promise is an irrelevance vis-à-vis the claim by the third party. Yet our proposed reform not only affords a third party better rights than a gratuitous promisee, it also allows the claim of the third party, who has provided no consideration, to trump the rights of the contracting parties, who have provided consideration and hence have earned each other's promise, to vary or cancel the contract.[19]

6.14 This argument can be illustrated by the following hypothetical example. A wants to give a car to C that he is buying from B and also wants to assure C, in advance, that the car will be his. In a first situation, in addition to its contract with B, A makes a gratuitous promise to C. In a second situation A insists on a term of the contract with B being that the car should be delivered, and title should pass, to C. A informs C of that contract for his benefit. It is argued that the position of C, and the justice underpinning whether C can sue A in the first situation or B in the second situation for failure to deliver the car, is indistinguishable. But according to our proposed reform C would be able to sue in the second situation, subject to satisfying the test of enforceability, but not in the first situation.

---

[18] It was implicit in the Consultation paper No 121, paras 2.7, 3.33, that a joint promisee should not count as a third party for the purposes of our proposed reform.

[19] See Part IX below.

6.15   At first blush one can resist this argument by emphasising that to allow a third party to sue is to ensure that the intentions of the parties, who have provided consideration, are upheld. That, in other words, there is a crucial difference between the situation where a promise is supported by consideration, albeit enforced by a third party, and the situation where the relevant promise is gratuitous. The overall coherent policy may be presented as the enforcement of bargains, the upholding of the intentions of those who have provided consideration, not the enforcement of gratuitous promises. But the difficulty then lies in explaining why the third party's right trumps the contracting parties' rights to vary or cancel the contract. True adherence to consideration would appear to dictate that the contracting parties should be free to change their intentions at any time. Yet, as we have argued in Part III and will argue in more detail in Part IX below, our reform recognises that consideration should give way to the need to avoid the injustice of disappointing the reasonable expectations of the third party, where that third party has relied on the contract or has accepted it by communicating its assent to the promisor.

6.16   One possible answer to that difficulty is to draw a distinction between the formation of a contract and its variation or cancellation and to argue that consideration is less important in relation to the latter than to the former. In other words, that in relation to variation but not formation, the intentions of those providing consideration may be overridden by the need not to disappoint the expectations of a gratuitous promisee or a third party beneficiary.

6.17   Alternatively we see no objection to accepting that, while formally, our reform does not affect the requirement of consideration, at a deeper policy level, and within the area of third party rights, it may represent a relaxation of the importance attached to consideration.[20] After all, promises under deed are enforceable without the need for consideration. And there are other established examples in the law of exceptions to the need for consideration: for example, documentary letters of credit, compositions with creditors, and the doctrine of promissory estoppel. The recognition of such exceptions, allied to academic criticisms of the requirement of consideration (in its classic sense of there needing to be a requested counter-performance or counter-promise), suggests that the doctrine of consideration may be a suitable topic for a future separate review by the Law Commission. But for the present we see no practical difficulty in taking the limited step in this paper of recommending what may be regarded as a relaxation of the requirement of consideration to the limited extent necessary to give third parties rights to enforce valid contracts in accordance with the contracting parties' intentions.

---

[20] This is also openly recognised by the New Zealand Contracts and Commercial Law Reform Committee in *Privity of Contract* (1981) para 8.2.4: "The benefit to the third party is, we think, analogous to a gift to him. If the donee of that 'gift' is to be able to enforce it, this right must to that extent relax the doctrine of consideration. We think the doctrine should be relaxed to that extent. In other words, our view is that the consideration necessary to support the contract ought not to have to be provided by the third party; it should be sufficient, we think, that the consideration for the promise be supplied by a party to the contract."

SECTION C
CENTRAL REFORM ISSUES

PART VII
THE TEST OF ENFORCEABILITY

1. Consultation and Our Recommendation

7.1 In the Consultation Paper the test of enforceability was identified as the central issue involved in reform of the third party rule.[1] The test of enforceability provides the answer to the question, "When (ie in what circumstances) does a third party have the right to enforce a contract or contractual provision to which he/she is not a party?" The Consultation Paper set out six possible tests. These were as follows:

(i)   a third party may enforce a contract which expressly in its terms purports to confer a benefit directly on him;[2]

(ii)   a third party may enforce a contract in which the parties intend that he should receive the benefit of the promised performance, regardless of whether they intend him to have an enforceable right of action or not;

(iii)   a third party may enforce a contract in which the parties intend that he should receive the benefit of the promised performance and also intend to create a legal obligation enforceable by him (the "dual intention" test);

(iv)   a third party may enforce a contract where to do so would effectuate the intentions of the parties and either the performance of the promise satisfies a monetary obligation of the promisee to him or it is the intention of the promisee to confer a gift on him;

(v)   a third party may enforce a contract on which he justifiably and reasonably relies, regardless of the intentions of the parties;

(vi)   a third party may enforce a contract which actually confers a benefit on him, regardless of the purpose of the contract or the intention of the parties.

---

[1]   See Consultation Paper No 121, para 5.8.

[2]   This was the test advocated by the Law Revision Committee's Sixth Interim Report (1937), para 48. The Committee did not analyse its proposed test in detail so that it did not clarify whether the contracting parties must have intended to confer a legal right of enforceability: on the face of it there is no such requirement (so that the test is a wide one) but some of our consultees construed the test as laying down that the parties must expressly confer a legal right of enforceability (so that the test is a narrow one).

7.2 It was provisionally concluded in the Consultation Paper that the third party should only be able to enforce a contract where the contracting parties intend that he should receive the benefit of performance and intend to create a legal obligation enforceable by him (the "dual intention" test set out in option (iii) above).[3] It was also provisionally recommended that reform should enable consideration of the circumstances surrounding the making of the contract when deducing the parties' intentions.[4]

7.3 The recommendation of a "dual intention" test drew the most comment from consultees. There were roughly six strands of consultees' opinions. First, the majority of consultees accepted the proposed dual intention test without criticism. Secondly, a substantial minority feared that the proposed dual intention test would lead to unacceptable uncertainty in the law and might lead to unintended liabilities being forced onto contracting parties. Such critics tended, therefore, to reject reform altogether or, if there were to be reform, they tended to prefer the Law Revision Committee's proposal (that is, option (i) above) or something like it. Thirdly, some consultees thought that the second, or "intention to create an enforceable right" limb of the test, was artificial and preferred option (ii) or (vi) above. Fourthly, and somewhat similarly, some consumer interests feared that the second limb would prove difficult to apply to consumer transactions and argued that it should not apply in that field.[5] Fifthly, a few consultees saw the first limb of the test, requiring an intention to benefit a third party, as unnecessary and redundant. Finally, a few consultees, while approving the dual intention test, suggested that to avoid uncertainty in its application, the implementing legislation should contain a series of presumptions for or against the creation of legally enforceable rights in particular circumstances.

7.4 While we continue to believe (along with the majority of consultees) that, of the options set out in the consultation paper, the "dual intention" test is the best approach, we also consider, in the light of the views of some consultees, that it requires modification and clarification in order to provide an acceptable statutory test. This is for two main reasons.

7.5 First, where the parties have expressly conferred legal rights on the third party, we agree with those consultees who suggested that it ought not to be necessary to show additionally that the third party was an intended beneficiary of the contract. Secondly, we agree with the strong view of many consultees that a test of effecting the parties' intentions in the light of the contract and the surrounding circumstances produces unacceptable uncertainty. In other words, while we continue to believe that one must

---

[3]   Consultation Paper No 121, para 5.10.

[4]   Consultation Paper No 121, para 5.12.

[5]   For example, one consultee feared that a strict application of the dual intention test would mean that most consumer sale of goods transactions would not fall within the reform, and thus argued that a looser test was required for such transactions.

seek to effect the parties' intentions to confer legal rights on the third party, we also consider that, to avoid unacceptable uncertainty, one needs a clearer and sharper test for implementing that policy. We have therefore ultimately opted for a test of enforceability which, like the recommendations of the Law Revision Committee in 1937, emphasises the express terms of the contract but also closely follows the New Zealand Contracts (Privity) Act 1982 in relying on a rebuttable presumption of an intention to confer legal rights on a third party.

7.6 We therefore recommend that:

(8) **the test of enforceability should be as follows:**

(a) **a third party shall have the right to enforce a contractual provision where that right is given to him - and he may be identified by name, class or description - by an express term of the contract (the "first limb");**

(b) **a third party shall also have the right to enforce a contractual provision[6] where that provision purports to confer a benefit on the third party, who is expressly identified as a beneficiary of that provision, by name, class or description (the "second limb"); but there shall be no right of enforceability under the second limb where on the proper construction of the contract it appears that the contracting parties did not intend the third party to have that right (the "proviso").** (Draft Bill, clause 1(1) and 1(3) (the first and second limbs), clause 1(2) (the proviso) and clause 7(1) and 7(2)(a))

7.7 Before examining each of the two limbs of our recommended test of enforceability, it is worth emphasising that our recommended test of enforceability rests on the belief that the novel context of third party rights requires a novel approach to contractual intention. In English contract law the intentions of the contracting parties are important in two main areas; (i) intention to create legal relations; and (ii) establishing and construing the terms, express and implied, of the contract. However, the existing law on each of those aspects of contractual intention does not easily lend itself to determining the contracting parties' intentions as regards the legal rights of third parties. The law on intention to create legal relations draws a distinction between commercial and domestic agreements, with a presumption being made in favour of an intention to create legal relations in respect of the former but not in respect of the latter. Such an approach is inappropriate when one is considering the parties' intentions as regards the legal rights of third parties; indeed, as the fear of unintended liabilities has been most keenly impressed upon us in respect of commercial, as opposed to domestic, contracts, a presumption of an intention to create legal rights in third party beneficiaries in commercial but not domestic contracts, would directly undermine our policy objectives.

---

[6] The contractual provision could be implied, albeit that the third party must be expressly identified: see examples 11 and 14 in paras 7.38 and 7.41 below.

7.8 At first sight the concept of an implied term might be thought more fruitful. Indeed we were for some time attracted by the view that the appropriate method of reform was to rely on existing tests for the implication of terms into contracts, namely the "officious bystander" or "business efficacy" tests.[7] The difficulty with the former, however, is that if the test is strictly construed it leads to there being no right of enforceability in even the plainest cases (see examples 1-3 below)[8] where we consider reform to be essential. In particular, on a strict construction of the "officious bystander" test, a term can only be implied where it is clear that *both parties* would have agreed to the term; and, again, the standard requirement that the parties must know the facts upon which the implication is based would appear, analogously, to require the parties to know of the legal difficulties in leaving it to the promisee to enforce the contract. Similarly, it is far from clear that the "business efficacy" test for implying terms can be sensibly applied to the question of whether a third party has the legal right to enforce the contract because a contract will rarely be unworkable simply because a third party has no right to enforce it: the promisee will always have that right. Of course, one might leave the courts to loosen the traditional tests so as to render them more workable in this new context. But this would defeat the whole point of relying on existing tests and would seem to be a recipe for uncertainty and confusion. In any event, to rely on implied terms is to rely on a body of law and tests that are notoriously unclear in their application even in respect of standard two-party contracts. And even analysed as a matter of theory, the implication of terms into contracts ranges from an exercise in construing the true actual intention of the parties through to imposing liabilities on parties subject to their contracting out with no very clear divide between the extremes. Put another way, the line between implied terms in fact (based on the parties' actual intentions) and implied terms in law (based on considerations other than the parties' intentions) is a thin and slippery one.

7.9 Ultimately therefore we have come to the view that a novel approach to contractual intention is required in respect of creating legal rights for third parties that rests neither on the existing law relating to intention to create legal relations nor on implied terms.

2. The First Limb of the Test of Enforceability

7.10 This limb is largely self-explanatory. It is satisfied where the contract contains words such as "and C shall have the right to enforce the contract" or "C shall have the right to sue". In our view, it would also cover an exclusion (or limitation) clause designating third parties (eg "C shall be excluded from all liability to A for damage caused in unloading the goods") because an exclusion clause, as a legal concept, has no meaning unless it is intended to affect legal rights and, where the third party is expressly designated as a person whose liability is excluded, the plain meaning of the exclusion

---

[7] For these tests see, eg, Treitel, *The Law of Contract* (9th ed, 1995) pp 185-188; E McKendrick, *Contract Law* (2nd ed, 1994) pp 152-155.

[8] Paras 7.28-7.30 below.

clause is that the third party is to have the benefit of it without having to rely on enforcement by the promisee.[9] We also tend to think that a clause such as "and the obligation to build to a safe standard shall enure for the benefit of subsequent owners and tenants for a period of ten years" falls within this first limb so as to be enforceable by subsequent owners and tenants. Of course, even express words sometimes give rise to questions of interpretation (as the last example shows) but the great merit of this limb of the test is that it should give rise to very few disputes.

7.11   Although the Law Revision Committee's test of a contract "expressly purporting to confer a benefit directly on a third party" is ambiguous, one interpretation of it, and the one favoured by several consultees, is that it accords with this first limb. Indeed some consultees considered that this first limb should be the *only* test on the basis that anything else is likely to give rise to uncertainty and to some risk of unintended liability. However, in our view, to have a reform based just on this first limb would be excessively narrow. For example, it would not cover the facts of problematic past cases, such as *Beswick v Beswick*.[10] Nor would it cover many other situations (see the examples discussed in paras 7.28-7.34 and 7.39-7.41 below) in which we believe that a third party should have the right of enforceability, consistently with the parties' intentions to confer that right, and yet the parties have not expressly conferred that right. It would also operate to the disadvantage of those who do not have the benefit of (good) legal advice.

7.12   One issue that we have found difficult is whether this first limb should permit the creation of rights of enforcement by third parties *who are not intended to be beneficiaries.* While this question does not arise in respect of our recommended second limb - because the third party must there be an intended beneficiary - it is conceivable that the parties may expressly confer a right of enforceability on a third party who is not to be a beneficiary.

7.13   A few consultees questioned the need for the third party to be a beneficiary. They pointed out that it is not normally a condition for the validity of a contractual provision that it benefits the person seeking to enforce it. And they thought that the meaning of 'benefit' might give rise to (unnecessary) difficulty. Two main examples were given of where the parties might seek to contract to create obligations which would benefit a range of persons not party to the contract but in the interests of simplicity and certainty might wish to confine the ability to enforce the rights arising to a third party who was not a beneficiary. First, A contracts with B to transfer £10,000 to C, which C is to hold on trust for the benefit of D: and C is expressly given the right to enforce A's obligation to B. It was argued that, in that situation, C should

---

[9]   This means that our reform provides a solution to the enforcement of 'Himalaya' clauses by third parties that does not involve any of the complexity or artificiality that the courts have been forced into in order to render such clauses enforceable: see paras 2.24-2.35 above.

[10]   [1968] AC 58. See para 7.46 below.

have the right to enforce the contract even though the performance of A's obligation would be for the benefit of D and (although we do not agree with taking such a narrow interpretation of 'benefit') C could perhaps be said not to "benefit" from the performance by being made a trustee of the benefit. Secondly, A (a developer) and B (the client) might wish to designate C (a management company) as having the right to sue to enforce warranties in the construction contract for D-Z (the tenants). In the light of these sorts of example it was therefore argued that a requirement of "benefit" provided a useful means of identifying the most common category of contracts where third parties should be permitted to enforce contracts, but should not be essential.

7.14 The contrary view was taken by the Scottish Law Commission, in a Memorandum published in 1977 dealing with the ius quaesitum tertio in Scottish law.[11] It said, "Where there is merely title to sue without personal benefit, it may well be that an altogether different legal relationship is established between the three parties involved from that which arises when a contract is concluded with the intention of *benefiting* a *Tertius*...[I]f a person has merely bare title to sue it is difficult (unless he acts in the capacity of agent) to see what patrimonial loss he could establish if he sued for non-performance...[T]he expression *jus quaesitum tertio* seems to have been stretched inaptly to include the type of cases just mentioned...[U]nless the third party designated in a contract as entitled to accept payment or performance is a beneficiary or an agent, mandatory, or trustee, we do not think that he should have a right to sue at all".

7.15 An argument in favour of the Scottish view is that to permit the creation of bare rights to sue would recreate one of the difficulties of the present law, whereby a contracting party in a contract for a third party's benefit, while able to sue, will generally recover no substantial damages because it has suffered no loss. Even if damages are substantial there is some difficulty in deciding whether they can be retained by the contracting party or must be paid over to the third party beneficiary. Our reform seeks to minimise this problem of the contracting party having a bare right to sue by giving the third party beneficiary a right to sue. But if the third party need not be a beneficiary, and yet has the right to sue, those problems would be recreated as between third and fourth parties rather than as between promisee and third party.

7.16 Ultimately, however, we do not consider this to be a strong enough reason for denying giving effect to the expressed intention of the parties. A third party suing for the benefit of a fourth party under our reform will be in no worse position than a contracting party suing for a third party beneficiary under the present law. And while the remedies available to that third party may be inadequate in many situations, in others they will not (for example, specific performance or the award of an agreed sum may be available even if substantial damages are not). In any event, the mere

---

[11] Scottish Law Commission, Memorandum No 38, *Constitution and Proof of Voluntary Obligations: Stipulations in favour of Third Parties* (1977) pp 18-24.

insistence that the third party be a beneficiary does not erase the problem that the primary benefit (and hence primary loss) may be that of a fourth party not the third party. It is our view, therefore, that under the first limb of the test the third party need not be an intended beneficiary of the contractual provision in question.

3. The Second Limb of The Test of Enforceability

(1) General Aspects of the Second Limb

7.17   This limb is concerned to cover those situations where the parties do not expressly contract to confer a legal right on the third party. *In general terms it establishes a rebuttable presumption in favour of there being a third party right where a contractual provision purports to confer a benefit on an expressly designated third party. But that presumption is rebutted where on the proper construction of the contract the parties did not intend to confer a right of enforceability on the third party.* In our view, this second limb achieves a satisfactory compromise between the aims of effecting the intentions of the contracting parties while not producing an unacceptable degree of uncertainty in the law. It is very similar to (and would seem to reach the same results as) the sole test of enforceability in the New Zealand Contracts (Privity) Act 1982. It may also be said to come close to the Law Revision Committee's proposals that the contract must expressly purport to confer a benefit directly on a third party.

7.18   Three features of this second limb are noteworthy:

(i)   Express designation by name, class or description is a necessary *but not a sufficient condition* for raising the rebuttable presumption. Although rare, a third party could be designated in the contractual provision that is sought to be enforced even though no benefit is to be conferred on that third party. For example, an employer may take out an insurance policy to cover loss that *it suffers* where a key employee is injured or ill. Although the employee may be mentioned in the relevant contractual obligation of the insurer to pay the employer ("we promise to indemnify [the employer] against loss suffered through the illness of [the employee]") that contractual obligation does not purport to benefit the third party. Again, if A contracts with B to pay him £1000 on C's death or when C attains the age of 21, it is clear that no benefit is to be conferred on C even though C is expressly designated by name.

(ii)   The contracting parties must intend the third party to be benefited by the particular contractual provision (that is, the contractual provision sought to be enforced) and not some other contractual provision. Say, for example, a building contractor enters into a design and build contract. The fact that the "build obligations" expressly purport to benefit subsequent owners does not mean to suggest that the subsequent owners are intended to be beneficiaries of the "design obligations".

(iii) The presumption of enforceability is rebutted where the proper objective construction of the contract is that the parties did not intend the third party to have the right of enforceability. The onus of proof will be on the contracting parties (usually in practice the promisor), so that doubts as to the parties' intentions will be resolved in the third party's favour. A promisor who wishes to put the position beyond doubt can exclude any liability to the third party that he might otherwise have had. But to allay the fears of the construction industry we should clarify that, even if there is no express contracting out of our proposed reform, we do not see our second limb as cutting across the chain of sub-contracts that have traditionally been a feature of that industry. For example, we do not think that in normal circumstances an owner would be able to sue a sub-contractor for breach of the latter's contract with the head-contractor. This is because, even if the sub-contractor has promised to confer a benefit on the expressly designated owner, the parties have deliberately set up a chain of contracts which are well understood in the construction industry as ensuring that a party's remedies lie against the other contracting party only. In other words, for breach of the promisor's obligation, the owners' remedies lie against the head-contractor who in turn has the right to sue the sub-contractor. On the assumption that that deliberately created chain of liability continues to thrive subsequent to our reform, our reform would not cut across it because on a proper construction of the contract - construed in the light of the surrounding circumstances (that is, the existence of the connected head-contract and the background practice and understanding of the construction industry) - the contracting parties (for example, the sub-contractor and the head-contractor) did not intend the third party to have the right of enforceability.[12] Rather the third party's rights of enforcement in relation to the promised benefit were intended to lie against the head-contractor only and not against the promisor. For similar reasons we consider that the second limb of our test would not normally give a purchaser of goods from a retailer a right to sue the manufacturer (rather than the retailer) for breach of contract as regards the quality of the goods.

(2) Negligent Will-Drafting

7.19   In fixing the boundaries of our proposed reform, we have encountered most difficulty with the situation where a solicitor negligently fails properly to draw up a will thereby causing loss to the intended beneficiaries of the will. Should those beneficiaries have

---

[12]   In a classic statement of the law on the proper construction of a contract in *Reardon Smith Line Ltd v Yngvar Hansen-Tangen* [1976] 1 WLR 989, 995-996 Lord Wilberforce said, "No contracts are made in a vacuum; there is always a setting in which they have to be placed. The nature of what it is legitimate to have regard to is usually described as 'the surrounding circumstances' but this phrase is imprecise: it can be illustrated but hardly defined. In a commercial contract it is certainly right that the court should know the commercial purpose of the contract and this in turn presupposes knowledge of the genesis of the transaction, the background, the context, the market in which the parties are operating".

the right to sue the solicitor under a reform of privity? While we can certainly see the force in allowing those beneficiaries a cause of action, we do not think that this is best rationalised as effecting the parties' intentions to confer that right. Moreover, as the House of Lords in *White v Jones*[13] has now held that the prospective beneficiaries have an action in the tort of negligence against the solicitor, we see no pressing practical need to stretch our facilitative reform in order to achieve what is widely perceived to be the just solution.

7.20   The wording of our proposed reform is therefore not intended to include negligent will-drafting (and analogous) situations. The crucial words are that the promise must be one to *confer a benefit on* the third party. The solicitor's express or implied promise to use reasonable care is not one by which the solicitor is to confer a benefit on the third party. Rather it is one by which the solicitor is to enable the client to confer a benefit on the third party.[14]

7.21   In support of the line here being taken, it is significant that in *White v Jones* neither Lord Goff, giving the leading speech of the majority, nor Lord Mustill, in his dissenting speech, thought that the facts of *White v Jones* would naturally fall within a *jus quaesitum tertio*. Lord Goff said, "It is true that our law of contract is widely seen as deficient in the sense that it is perceived to be hampered by the presence of an unnecessary doctrine of consideration and (through a strict doctrine of privity of contract) stunted through a failure to recognise a jus quaesitum tertio. But even if we lacked the former and possessed the latter, the ordinary law could not provide a simple answer to the problems which arise in the present case, which appear at first sight to require the imposition of something like a contractual liability which is beyond the scope of the ordinary jus quaesitum tertio".[15] And Lord Mustill, dissenting, said: "But even under a much expanded law of contract it is hard to see an answer to the objection that what the testator intended to confer on the new beneficiaries was the benefit of his assets after his death; not the benefit of the solicitor's promise to draft the will".[16]

7.22   Similarly, in New Zealand it was accepted in *Gartside v Sheffield, Young & Ellis*[17] that section 4 of the Contracts (Privity) Act 1982 does not give the disappointed

---

[13]   [1995] 2 AC 207.

[14]   If one were to view the contracting parties as having given the third party the legal right to enforce the contract, one would need to qualify that right by recognising the testator's undoubted power to change his will. That is, the right of enforceability could only come into play once the testator had died without having changed his mind. Yet to regard such a qualification as having been thought through by the contracting parties at the time of contracting seems fictional.

[15]   [1995] 2 AC 207, 262-263.

[16]   Ibid, at p 723.

[17]   [1983] NZLR 37.

beneficiary under a will a right to sue the solicitor. In Cooke J's words, "[O]n an ordinary and natural reading of the key s 4 of that Act, a prospective beneficiary under a proposed will could not invoke the Act. For the contract between the testator and the solicitor would not itself contain a promise conferring or purporting to confer a benefit on the prospective beneficiary. Putting the point in another way, the solicitor has not promised to confer a benefit on him."[18]

7.23 In the Consultation Paper, we invited comments on how best, if at all, to deal with the question of improperly executed wills prejudicing prospective third party beneficiaries.[19] There was an overwhelming view (and this prior to *White v Jones*) that this area should not be treated as an aspect of the law on contracts for the benefit of third parties.[20]

7.24 The distinction that our second limb seeks to draw between a promise to confer a benefit on a third party and a promise of potential benefit to a third party is also strongly supported by Kit Barker in his illuminating article entitled, "Are We up to Expectations? Solicitors, Beneficiaries and the Tort/Contract Divide".[21] He writes:

> [T]he New Zealand model would provide no relief to the disappointed beneficiary in [*White v Jones*].... This is because the action assumes that, for a third party to be able to sue upon a contract, the contract must contain some promise to confer a benefit upon (provide some performance to) her. No such promise, it has rightly been said, is present here. The testator promises to pay the solicitor for his services. The solicitor in the ordinary case promises that he will, in rendering those services, take reasonable care to ensure that the testator is successful in effectuating his beneficial intentions. Both are able to foresee, of course, that if the latter's promise is broken, the testamentary gift may not take effect and the third party may be prejudiced, but neither actually promises to provide the third party with any primary performance at all.
>
> The case is therefore tangibly different from the classic contract for the benefit of third parties, found in *Beswick v Beswick*, where A promises B that he will provide primary performance to C. Here, A promises performance (professional advice) to B, so that B can achieve his desired aim of conferring a benefit on C. The difference between the two situations is not in the direction of the promise which

---

[18] Ibid, at p 42. See also Richardson J at p 49.

[19] Consultation Paper No 121 paras 5.40-5.44, 6.21.

[20] It is noteworthy that a number of consultees thought that the appropriate solution lay in amendments to the law of succession (see on this T Weir, 'A Damnosa Hereditas' (1995) 111 LQR 357 and, for a contrary view, S Cretney, "Negligent Solicitors and Wills: A Footnote" (1996) 112 LQR 54) or in recognising a restitutionary action by the beneficiary against the residuary legatee, rather than in contract or tort.

[21] (1994) 14 OxJLS 137, 142 (emphasis in the original).

is made - in both cases it is made to B - but in its content. In the first instance, A undertakes to transfer performance from himself to C. In the second, he only promises performance to B. Whilst C is clearly an 'intended beneficiary' of A's promise in *Beswick* (because she is to secure from A some performance by virtue of it) in [*White v Jones*]... she is an intended object of A's promise only in the very different sense that A *knows that the standard of his performance to B will have consequences* for her.

7.25   It is our view, therefore, that the negligent will-drafting situation ought to lie, and does lie, just outside our proposed reform. It is an example of the rare case where the third party, albeit expressly designated "as a beneficiary" in the contract, has no presumed right of enforcement. Indeed it is arguable that, by merely adjusting the wording of the second limb to include promises that are "of benefit to" expressly designated third parties, rather than those that "confer benefits on" third parties, we would have brought the negligent will-drafting situation within our reform. But we believe that those words draw the crucial distinction between the situation where it is natural to presume that the contracting parties intended to confer legal rights on the third party and the situation where that presumption is forced and artificial.[22]

7.26   It has also been important in our thinking that, if the negligent will-drafting situation were brought within our reform, it would be impossible to exclude the inter vivos gift situation. Say a solicitor negligently fails to draw up properly the documentation for an inter vivos gift. The donor, believing it to be valid, executes the documents. The mistake comes to light some time later during the lifetime of the donor but after the gift to the intended donee should have taken effect. The donor, by then, having changed his mind, declines to perfect the imperfect gift in favour of the intended donee. If the negligent will-drafting case were within our reform, it is hard to see how this could not be. Yet in this situation, even supporters of *White v Jones* may baulk at giving the third party a right against the solicitor given that the donor can rectify the position should he or she so wish. A duty of care to the third party was denied at first instance in an analogous situation in *Hemmens v Wilson Browne*[23] and certainly in *White v Jones* Lord Goff did not think that the third party should have a claim in this type of inter vivos situation. He said:

---

[22]   In deference to the important arguments of Professor Markesinis, 'An Expanding Tort Law - The Price of a Rigid Contract Law' (1987) 103 LQR 354, we should explain that our reform is based on a model of a contract for the benefit of third parties and does not seek to embrace the wider German concept of a contract with protective effects for third parties. We would be afraid of the uncertainty that the generalised legislative introduction of that German concept would create: see K Barker (1994) 14 OxJLS 137, 143-146. However we would not wish our reform to be construed as preventing the House of Lords embracing that more radical approach in specific situations: see para 5.10 above.

[23]   [1995] Ch 223.

I for my part do not think that the intended donee could in these circumstances have any claim against the solicitor. It is enough, as I see it, that the donor is able to do what he wishes to put matters right. From this it would appear to follow that the real reason for concern in cases such as [*White v Jones*] lies in the extraordinary fact that, if a duty owed by the testator's solicitor to the disappointed beneficiary is not recognised, the only person who may have a valid claim has suffered no loss, and the only person who has suffered a loss has no claim.[24]

7.27   However we must add that, while we consider that negligent will-drafting should fall outside our proposed reform, at a theoretical level we prefer the view that the right of the prospective beneficiaries more properly belongs within the realm of contract than tort. It is very difficult to explain the basis of the claim, which deals with an omission and pure economic loss, as being other than one to enforce the promise of the solicitor (albeit by a party who was not intended to have that right). Had *White v Jones* been decided against the potential beneficiaries, we would have seriously contemplated a separate provision - outside our general reform - giving prospective beneficiaries a right to sue the negligent solicitor for breach of contract. The primary basis of such a provision would have been that a right of action for the beneficiaries is the only way to ensure that the promisee's expectations engendered by the solicitor's binding promise are fulfilled. But given the decision in *White v Jones* the practical need for such a provision has been obviated.

(3)   The Application of the Second Limb of the Test to Various Hypothetical Situations

7.28   1.   A promises B, his father, that in return for the transfer of the family home, A will pay C an annuity of £5,000 per annum for her life. B dies, and A refuses to continue payments. The promise is one by which A is to confer a benefit (£5,000 per annum) on C, who is expressly identified by name. C will therefore have the right to enforce A's promise (subject to A rebutting the presumption by pointing to a term, or other feature of the contractual matrix, showing that A and B did not intend C to have that right).

7.29   2.   B Ltd contracts with A Ltd for the sale of a plot of land. The consideration is to be £100,000 paid to B Ltd and £50,000 paid to C Ltd, which is an associated company of B Ltd. The land is transferred. B Ltd receives its payment but A Ltd, experiencing financial difficulties, refuses to make the payment to C Ltd. The promise is one by which A Ltd is to confer a benefit (£50,000) on C Ltd, which is expressly identified by name. C Ltd could therefore sue A Ltd for breach of the payment obligation (subject to rebuttal by A under the proviso to the second limb).[25]

---

[24]   [1995] 2 AC 207, 262.

[25]   For a discussion of some other issues affecting contracts for the sale of land that are raised by our reform, see paras 14.8-14.11 below.

7.30 3. B owes £5,000 to C. To discharge this debt, B enters into a contract with A that A will carve a sculpture for C. A fails to carve the sculpture. The promise is one by which A is to confer a benefit (the sculpture) on C, who is expressly identified by name. C will therefore have the right to sue A (subject to rebuttal by A under the proviso to the second limb).

7.31 4. B takes out a liability insurance policy with A whereby A agrees to indemnify B and all B's subsidiary companies, contractors and sub-contractors in respect of liabilities incurred in carrying out B's construction contracts. C, a sub-contractor, is held liable in negligence for injuries suffered by a workman and wishes to be indemnified by A under the insurance policy with B. Subject to rebuttal by A under the proviso to the second limb, C would be able to enforce A's promise: A has promised to confer a benefit (indemnity payment) on C, who is expressly identified by class.

7.32 5. B takes out a policy of insurance with A Ltd to cover her employees against medical expenses. The policy provides that payments under it will be made direct to ill employees or, at the discretion of A Ltd, to the provider of the medical services in discharge of an employee's liability to that provider. C, an employee, suffers a disorder and requires hospitalisation. Meanwhile B disappears. C seeks to sue as a beneficiary of B's contract of insurance with A Ltd. Subject to rebuttal by A Ltd under the proviso to the second limb, C would be able to do so: A has promised to confer a benefit (direct payment or the discharge of C's liability to the provider of medical services) on C, who is expressly identified by class.

7.33 6. B takes out a personal accident insurance policy with A Ltd to cover his employees against accidents. By the terms of the policy, payments are to be made to B, receipt by B alone is to be an effectual discharge of A Ltd's liability, and A Ltd is to be entitled to treat B as the absolute owner of the policy. C, an employee, is injured and B is insolvent. C seeks to recover from A Ltd as a beneficiary of B's contract with A Ltd. This is a difficult example.[26] On one view, B retains an absolute discretion whether to hand on to C the payments received from A Ltd and it is therefore difficult to say that under the contract of insurance A purports to confer a benefit on C. Again, one might say that there is a rebuttal by A under the proviso to the second limb. The alternative and, in our opinion, preferable view is that, once received, the money is held by B on trust for C. On that view, the contract does purport to confer a benefit on C (who is expressly identified by class) and one can argue that there is no rebuttal by A under the proviso to the second limb: the channelling of the payment through B is a matter of administrative convenience and does not negate C's right to enforce payment by A to B.

[26] See para 7.51 below.

7.34   7.   B takes out a life insurance policy with A Ltd naming C as the beneficiary of the policy. C has co-habited with B for fifteen years although they are not married. B is killed in a car accident. Subject to rebuttal by A Ltd under the proviso to the second limb, C would be able to enforce the policy on B's death. A Ltd has promised to confer a benefit (payment) on C in the event of B's death, and C is expressly identified by name.

7.35   8.   A Ltd insure B & Co, a firm of solicitors, against professional negligence. C Fund, an intended beneficiary of X's will, has obtained judgment against the firm for its failure to ensure that X's will was drawn up properly and with expedition. B & Co has no assets save its professional indemnity policy. C Fund argues that it can sue A as beneficiary of the firm's insurance cover. It cannot do so. A has not promised to confer a benefit on C, and C has not been expressly identified.

7.36   9.   B is an elderly man with a substantial estate which he plans to leave to his favourite charity, the C Fund. He approaches A & Co solicitors to prepare a will which will achieve these intentions. D, a partner of the firm, negligently fails to take any steps to prepare the will for several weeks, during which time B dies. C Fund, on hearing of this, seeks to sue the solicitors. C cannot enforce A's promise to use reasonable care and expedition in drawing up the will because that promise does not purport to confer a benefit on C. Rather it is a promise to enable B to confer a benefit on C. C will therefore not be able to sue A for breach of contract and will instead have to rely on its cause of action in the tort of negligence as established in *White v Jones*.[27]

7.37   10.   B & Co enters into a contract with A & Co, who are building contractors, to construct a chemical plant. B & Co sell the plant to C & Co, who operate it for a short period before defects in the building allow an escape of poisonous gases. These cause substantial financial losses to farmers, whose livestock must be destroyed. The farmers sue C & Co, who, close to bankruptcy, seek to sue on the contract between A & Co and B & Co. C & Co cannot sue A & Co as A & Co have not promised to confer a benefit on C & Co, who have not been expressly identified. The position would be different if the building contract expressly states that the rights as to the quality of the building work are to enure for the benefit of subsequent owners and/or tenants of the plant. This would probably satisfy the first limb of our test of enforceability but, even if it does not, C & Co would have the right of enforceability under the second limb (subject to rebuttal by A & Co under the proviso) as A & Co have promised to confer a benefit on C & Co (that, as and when occupied by C & Co, the building will be of a particular standard) who are expressly identified by class.

---

[27] [1995] 2 AC 207.

7.38   11.   C Ltd engages B Ltd, a construction company, to construct a new plant for its rapidly expanding publication operations. B Ltd engages A Ltd, a well known subcontracting firm, to lay flooring in the plant. A Ltd fails to provide flooring of an appropriate standard and, through consequent delay to the start of manufacturing operations at its new plant, C Ltd loses a valuable export order. C Ltd could not sue A Ltd for failure to perform its obligations to provide flooring of a suitable standard. Even if there were a promise by A Ltd to confer a benefit (a floor of a particular standard) on C Ltd, who were expressly identified, the right of enforceability is rebutted under the proviso to the second limb. On a true construction of the sub-contract, construed in the light of the head-contract and the understanding and practice of the construction industry, C Ltd is not intended to have a right against A Ltd. Rather C Ltd's right of redress lies against B Ltd for A Ltd's breach (and B Ltd's right of redress lies against A Ltd).[28]

7.39   12.   B engages A to build a conservatory onto his daughter C's house as a birthday present. Through A's failure to use proper care in constructing the conservatory, C's house suffers structural damage and her valuable collection of orchids is ruined. If A has promised to confer the benefit (the building of a conservatory using reasonable care) on C, who has been expressly identified, C will have the right to sue A for breach of that contractual provision (subject to rebuttal by A under the proviso to the second limb).

7.40   13.   Mr B books two rooms in a luxury hotel owned by A Ltd in the Lake District for a two week holiday for himself and his wife and children. On arrival, the hotel has double booked and cannot offer alternative accommodation. Mr B's party are forced to stay in a hotel a long distance away, which, though more expensive, has less celebrated cuisine and few facilities. Mr B's wife and children, who will have been expressly identified, will have a right to sue A Ltd (subject to rebuttal by A Ltd under the proviso to the second limb) for any additional expenses incurred as a result of the hotel's breach of contract, and for the loss of enjoyment resulting from the double booking.[29]

7.41   14.   On Mr and Mrs C's marriage, their wealthy relative B buys an expensive 3 piece suite as a wedding gift from A Ltd, a well known Central London department store with a reputation for quality. She makes it clear when purchasing the 3 piece suite that it is a gift for friends and indeed the delivery slip and instructions show that it is to be sent to Mr and Mrs C's home and should be left with the housekeeper as it is a gift. After 2 weeks of wear the fabric on the suite wears thin and frays, and after 3 weeks, two castors collapse. Subject to rebuttal by A

---

[28]   See para 7.18 point (iii) above.

[29]   This is not a package holiday within the Package Travel, Package Holidays and Package Tours Regulations 1992 (SI 1992/3288): see para 2.62 above.

Ltd under the proviso to the second limb, Mr and Mrs C can sue A Ltd for breach of an implied term in the contract that the goods be of a satisfactory quality.[30] A Ltd have promised to confer a benefit (the suite of satisfactory quality) on Mr and Mrs C,[31] who have been expressly identified by name.

7.42   15.   Again, the above example, save that A Ltd are entirely unaware that the suite is a gift for anyone, and it is delivered to B's home. Mr and Mrs C could not sue A Ltd, since the contract between B and A Ltd does not purport to confer a benefit on Mr and Mrs C, who have not been expressly identified.

7.43   16.   B & Co's standard form of building contract contains an exclusion clause which seeks to exclude the liability to its clients of "all agents, servants, employees and subcontractors" engaged by B & Co in the performance of the contract works for any loss and damage occasioned other than through wilful misconduct. A & Co, a developer using B & Co's services in constructing nuclear power plants, discovers that one of these is built on dangerously unstable ground, and will have to be decommissioned. The surveyor engaged by B & Co to carry out the site survey, Mr C, has clearly been negligent. Mr C has extensive professional indemnity cover. Mr C seeks to claim the benefit of the exclusion clause in A & Co's contract with B & Co to prevent A & Co from recovering against him in tort for negligence. Mr C would succeed under the first limb of our test or, on the basis that the exclusion clause is a promise to confer a benefit (the exclusion of liability) on Mr C, who is expressly identified by class, under the second limb.

7.44   17.   A contracts with B to carry A's packages by road. It is a term of the contract that the value of the packages is "deemed to be not over £100 unless otherwise declared". B sub-contracts with C to carry a package. C loses the package which was worth £1000 and is sued by A in the tort of negligence. C has no rights to enforce the 'deemed value' clause under our proposals because C has not been expressly identified as a beneficiary of that clause. Nor has C been expressly given the right to enforce that clause under the first limb of the test of enforceability.

[30]   Our understanding is that, although delivery is to be made to a third party, the contract will qualify as a contract for the sale of goods to the promisee for the purposes of the Sale of Goods Act 1979 so that the relevant term will be implied by reason of ss 13-14 of the 1979 Act. But it should be noted that to qualify as a contract for the sale of goods within the definition in s 2(1) of the Sale of Goods Act 1979 ("A contract of sale of goods is a contract by which the seller transfers or agrees to transfer the property in goods to the buyer for a money consideration, called the price") one must assume that, although delivery is to be made to the third party, there is a moment in time at which property first passes to the promisee. Although not directly on the point, we have found the following cases of assistance: *E & S Ruben Ltd v Faire Brothers & Co Ltd* [1949] 1 KB 254; *Jarvis v Williams* [1955] 1 WLR 71. Even if we are wrong on this, one can readily assume that, irrespective of the statute, the courts would normally imply a term that the goods be of satisfactory quality.

[31]   If there is to be no delivery to a third party it will normally be difficult to argue that a contract of sale purports to confer a benefit on a third party.

(4)   The Application of the Second Limb of the Test to Some Past Cases.

7.45   How would the second limb of the test of enforceability apply to the facts of some of the most celebrated cases where the third party rule has caused difficulty?

7.46   In *Beswick v Beswick*,[32] the provision of old Mr Beswick's contract with his nephew providing for payment of an annuity to Mrs Beswick would give Mrs Beswick a presumed right of enforceability under our second limb. The nephew promised to confer the benefit (the annuity payments) on Mrs Beswick, who was expressly named. This presumption could only be rebutted if the nephew could demonstrate that, on the proper construction of the contract, he and old Mr Beswick had no intention at the time of contracting that Mrs Beswick should have the right to enforce the provision. In our view, the nephew would not be able to satisfy that onus of proof so that Mrs Beswick would have the right of enforcement.

7.47   In *Junior Books Ltd v Veitchi & Co Ltd*,[33] it may be that Veitchi's sub-contractual obligations, including the obligation to use reasonable care in laying the floor, purported to benefit Junior Books, who were presumably expressly identified as beneficiaries. However, since Veitchi's sub-contract was part of a wider chain of contracts, under which Junior Books' rights for breach of Veitchi's obligations, were to lie against the head-contractor under the head-contract, we consider that the presumption of an enforceable right would be rebutted. Junior Books would therefore have no right to enforce Veitchi's obligations to the head-contractor.

7.48   We have already explained why, in *White v Jones*,[34] Mr Barratt's daughters could not use our reform to sue Mr Jones' and Messrs Philip Baker-King & Co for the breach of their contractual obligations to Mr Barratt to prepare his will with due care and attention. This is because the solicitors' implied promise did not purport to confer a benefit on the daughters. Rather it was Mr Barratt who was to confer the benefit on the daughters through his will.

7.49   In *Woodar Investment Development Ltd v Wimpey Construction UK Ltd*,[35] the contract between Wimpey Construction UK Ltd and Woodar Investment Development Ltd provided for payment of part of the purchase price of a plot of land to Transworld Trade Ltd. The purchasers sought to terminate, and the vendors sued for damages, including the sum due to Transworld. Although a majority of the House of Lords held that the purchasers were entitled to terminate, so that the vendors had no claim for breach of contract, they also indicated that the vendors could not have obtained substantial damages in respect of the purchasers' failure to pay Transworld. Under

---

[32]   [1968] AC 58. See para 2.47 above. See also para 7.28 (example 1) above.

[33]   [1983] 1 AC 520. See para 2.14 above. See also para 7.38 (example 11) above.

[34]   [1995] 2 AC 207. See paras 7.19-7.27 and para 7.36 (example 9) above.

[35]   [1980] 1 WLR 277. See para 7.29 (example 2) above.

our proposals, Transworld could have brought proceedings for the due sum directly. The contract purported to confer a benefit on Transworld, who was expressly identified and, in our view, the purchasers could not have rebutted the presumption that Transworld was intended to have the right to enforce the payment obligation.

7.50 In *Trident General Insurance Co Ltd v McNiece Bros Proprietary Ltd,*[36] Trident had taken out a liability insurance policy which, in its definition of "assured" purported to cover McNiece, a principal contractor. When one of its employees was injured, McNiece sought to rely on its rights under the policy. While there was no clear consensus as to the basis on which the claim was upheld, the High Court of Australia by a majority held that McNiece could enforce the contract. Under our proposals, McNiece would have a right to enforce the contract. The contract purported to confer a benefit on McNiece, who was identified in the contract by class ("all Contractors and Sub-Contractors") and there was nothing to rebut the presumption that it was intended that McNiece should have a right to enforce the contract.

7.51 In *Green v Russell,*[37] an employer took out a personal accident group insurance policy which named the employer as the "insured" and certain of his employees as the "insured persons". The recital to the policy stated that, "Whereas the insured is desirous of securing payment of benefits as hereinafter set forth to any insured person in the event of his sustaining accidental bodily injury..."; and one of the clauses in the policy stated that, "The company shall be entitled to treat the insured as the absolute owner of this policy and shall not be bound to recognise any equitable or other claim to or interest in the policy and the receipt of the insured or the insured's legal representative alone shall be an effectual discharge". One of the employees named in the policy died in a fire at the employer's premises. The question at issue was whether money paid, or about to be paid, by the insurers to the employee's mother should not be deducted from her claim under the Fatal Accidents Acts 1846-1908 on the basis that, under section 1 of the 1908 Act, it was "paid or payable on the death of the deceased under any contract of assurance or insurance". The Court of Appeal decided that the sum did fall within section 1 and should therefore not be deducted. But in doing so, it decided that the deceased had had no right, legal or equitable, to payment of the sum: there was no contractual claim because of the privity rule and there was no trust as it was not the employer's intention to constitute itself a trustee. On the face of it, this reasoning means that the employer has an absolute discretion whether to hand on to an employee the money paid by the insurance company on this sort of policy. One impact of our reforms is that such group personal accident policies could be reworded so as to give the third party employee the undoubted right to enforce the policy (without having to create an immediate trust of the promise). More difficult is the question whether a policy, such as that in the *Green* case, would give

---

[36] (1988) 165 CLR 107. See paras 2.67-2.69 and para 7.31 (example 4) above.

[37] [1959] 2 QB 226. See para 7.33 (example 6) above.

employees a right of enforceability under the second limb of our test. It is our view that, *once paid*, the sum is best regarded as being held on trust for the employee, or that the employer is otherwise accountable to the employee for the sum, so that the insurance contract does purport to confer a benefit on the employees (who, in the *Green* case were expressly identified by name). The fact that the money is first channelled through the employer, and that payment to the employer discharges the insurer, is a matter of administrative convenience and does not rebut the presumption that the third party is intended to have a right of enforceability (so that it can enforce the insurer's obligation to pay the employer).[38]

4. The Rejected Tests

7.52   It is worth clarifying that our recommended test of enforceability does not conform precisely to any of the six tests set out in the Consultation Paper,[39] albeit that it comes close to option (iii). We have rejected the other tests both because they did not command majority support among consultees and because each is flawed in some way. Option (i) is ambiguous and, on one interpretation, is too wide and, on another, too narrow.[40] Option (ii) contains no reference to the parties' intentions to confer a legal right on the third party. Option (iv) would potentially lead to too much uncertainty and, in some respects, may be too narrow.[41]

7.53   Our recommended test is furthest away from options (v) (reliance by third party) and (vi) (third party benefited). We think that it may be useful for us to clarify in a little more detail the clear differences between our approach and those two options. Those two options not only do not seek to effect the parties' intentions to confer legal rights on third parties, which we regard as crucial, but would also produce unacceptably wide liability. Option (v) on the face of it would mean, for example, that a person who buys a home on the faith of a new motorway being built would be able to sue the builder for loss caused (eg extra petrol costs) if the motorway is not completed on

---

[38] This reasoning derives some support from the judgment of Pearce LJ (the other substantial judgment being given by Romer LJ with whom Hodson LJ agreed). Pearce LJ said, at pp 246-247, "It is true that the company are entitled (as a matter of convenient machinery) to deal direct with the policy holder, and to treat him as if he alone were intended to get the benefits of all the insured persons. But the terms of the agreement as a whole make it clear that (whatever may be Green's legal or equitable rights against the policy holder) the £1,000 payable on Green's death is intended by the parties to be a benefit to Green's estate, and is not intended for the pocket of Russell. Moreover, I think that the terms of the agreement as a whole show that the parties envisage payment of the £1,000 direct to the policy holder and payment over by him to Green's estate. Thus the second payment, namely, by the defendant to the plaintiff, is a payment envisaged by the contract, and is clearly in my view a sum paid under a policy of assurance within the terms of the Fatal Accidents (Damages) Act, 1908". Indeed if the employer were simply able to keep the insurance payments for itself, it would seem that the insurance policy might be void under the Life Assurance Act 1774, section 3. See, generally, *Chitty on Contracts* (27th ed, 1994) paras 39-007-39-010.

[39] See para 7.1 above.

[40] See paras 4.6 and 7.11 above.

[41] See para 4.17 above.

time. Again if a boxer cancels a fight in breach of his contract with the promoter, application of this option would appear to mean that he could be sued by the television companies who had arranged to televise the fight and by all those who have bought tickets to watch the fight.[42] Option (vi) would produce an even wider, and even more unacceptable, liability than option (v). That is, it would be sufficient for a third party to show that it would have gained from due adherence to the contract and it would be irrelevant that the third party had not relied on the contract. It would mean, for example, that all those whose property would have been enhanced in value by the building of a new road or a new shopping centre would be able to sue if, in breach of contract, the road or shopping centre is not built on time (or at all).[43] The fact that they have not bought their properties on the faith of those developments (or have not otherwise relied on those developments) would not matter.

5. A Special Test of Enforceability for Consumers?

7.54   Some consultees argued that a test of enforceability based on effecting parties' intentions would not go far enough in protecting consumers. Rather they urged us to go beyond effecting the contracting parties' intentions and to *impose* a measure of consumer protection. In effect, their suggestion was that, where the third party is a consumer, reform should be based on options (v) and (vi). Clearly third party consumers stand to gain from our proposals. For example, under our proposals a manufacturer and retailer could expressly confer legal rights on the purchaser to enforce the contract as regards the quality of the goods purchased, thereby affording the purchaser a remedy if the retailer became insolvent.[44] Again a retailer and a purchaser could in their contract expressly confer a right of enforceability on a third party for whom the goods are being bought. Indeed where a contractual provision in the contract of sale purports to confer a benefit on a third party, who is expressly identified, the third party will have a right of enforceability subject to the retailer establishing that, on the proper construction of the contract, the retailer and purchaser did not intend to confer that right.[45] Similarly where a lead holiday-maker makes a

---

[42]   In Consultation Paper No 121, para 2.19, we gave the further example of a report prepared by a firm of auditors under a contract with a company and put into more or less general circulation. Such a report may foreseeably be relied on by third parties for any one of a variety of different purposes but we do not think that all those parties should have the right to sue in contract for their losses in the event of the report having been negligently prepared. *Cf Caparo Industries plc v Dickman* [1990] 2 AC 605 (no tortious duty of care owed by auditor to potential investor).

[43]   It is to be noted that the US Second Restatement draws a distinction between such incidental beneficiaries and intended beneficiaries, and that incidental beneficiaries are not permitted to enforce purported benefits under contracts: United States Restatement (2d) - Contracts, American Law Institute (1981) §§ 302 & 315. See paras 4.17-4.18 above.

[44]   Without such an express term, the purchaser would normally have no such right because even if expressly identified as a beneficiary of the manufacturer's contract with the retailer, the chain of contracts giving the purchaser a remedy against the retailer for the manufacturer's breach means that on a proper construction of the contract, construed in the light of the surrounding circumstances, the manufacturer and retailer do not intend to confer a legal right of enforceability on the third party.

[45]   See example 14 in para 7.41 above. Contrast example 15.

booking for a holiday for a number of persons on terms set out in a booking form, the other members of the party will be able to sue in the event of a breach of contract (subject to the proper construction of the contract being that the parties did not intend to confer that legal right).[46] Again in a construction contract between a head-contractor and the owner a subsequent owner or tenant who is expressly given legal rights to enforce the contract will be able to do so: as, subject to rebuttal, will the subsequent owner or tenant on whom the contract purports to confer a benefit and who has been expressly identified.[47]

7.55 However, while our proposals will therefore mean that consumer third parties will have rights that they do not at present have, our proposals do not automatically give consumers such rights. We consider that the automatic conferring of contractual rights on third parties who are consumers rests on policy considerations that need to be tackled in relation to specific areas. We do not think that they can properly be addressed through the kind of general reform with which we are here concerned. Indeed we think that it would be dangerous - in terms of producing a potential conflict of reform proposals - for us here to embark on specific measures of consumer protection when there are other reform initiatives under discussion in specific areas, based on protecting consumers. We have in mind particularly consumer guarantees[48] and the rights of subsequent purchasers or tenants to sue for defective construction work.[49] Rather our strategy is to reform the general law of contract, based on effecting contracting parties' intentions, which then leaves the way free for more radical consumer protection measures in future in specific areas.

7.56 We therefore recommend that:

(9)   **there should be no special test of enforceability for consumers in our proposed legislation.**

---

[46]   See example 13 in para 7.40 above.

[47]   See example 10 in para 7.37 above.

[48]   See European Commission, *Green Paper on Guarantees for Consumer Goods and After-Sales Services*, COM (93) 509 final, 1993. See also *Consumer Guarantees*, a Consultation Document issued by the Department of Trade and Industry, February 1992.

[49]   See, eg, *Latent Defects Liability and 'Build' Insurance*, a Consultation Paper issued by the Department of the Environment, April 1995, paras 33-39.

PART VIII
DESIGNATION, EXISTENCE AND ASCERTAINABILITY OF THIRD PARTY

1. Designation

8.1   It is inherent in the test of enforceability that we have recommended in Part VII above that the third party be expressly identified whether by name (for example, Joe Bloggs), class (for example, "stevedores", "subsequent owners", "subsequent tenants"), or description (for example, "person living at 36 Coronation Street" or "B's nominee"). So, in applying the first limb of our recommended test, one cannot expressly confer a right of enforcement on a third party other than by expressly identifying that third party by name, description or class. And the presumption in the second limb of our recommended test of enforceability is only triggered where there is express identification by name, description or class. It follows that, under our recommended reforms, third party rights cannot be conferred on someone who is *impliedly* in mind. We consider that the possibility of such an implication would give rise to unacceptable uncertainty.

8.2   At the other extreme, we are also of course rejecting a requirement that the third party be expressly identified by name. This was provisionally rejected in the Consultation Paper[1] and that rejection was supported by consultees. The objection to express designation by name is that it would prevent the conferral of a legally enforceable right upon a third party who was identified by class or description only (including those who do not exist at the time of contract). This would mean, for example, that it would be impossible for an employer and contractor to provide in a construction contract for the conferral of rights on future occupiers of the premises under construction.

8.3   We should clarify that, in our view, it is a sufficient identification by description (or class) if the third party is referred to in the contract as "B's nominee". In the New Zealand first instance decision of *Coldicutt v Webb & Keeys*[2] it was held that the nominee could sue because he had been designated by description and the only purpose of adding a reference to him was to give him the right to sue on the contract. The contract was one for the sale of land to "Webb or his nominee". Hillyer J said:-

> the requisite ingredients of that section [section 4 of the Contracts (Privity) Act 1982] are present. There is a promise in the agreement for sale and purchase by Mr Keeys to sell the land. The sale may be to a nominee. A benefit is thus conferred or purported to be conferred. The first plaintiff is not designated by name, however he is designated by description as a nominee and he is not a party to the deed or contract. Turning to the proviso to the section, there is nothing in the contract itself

---

[1]   Consultation Paper No 121, para 5.19.

[2]   Unreported, High Court, Whangerei, 17 May 1985, A50/84.

to indicate that it was not intended to create an obligation enforceable at the suit of the nominee.

8.4   While the approach in *Coldicutt* has been rejected by subsequent New Zealand cases,[3] we see no valid objection to it.[4] Indeed it is significant that the New Zealand Law Commission in its *Contracts Statutes Review*[5] preferred *Coldicutt* to the conflicting cases as being "supportable in principle and satisfactory in its result". The Commission concluded, however, that the interpretation of section 4 should be left to the courts to resolve and that the conflict in the cases did not merit an amendment of the Contracts (Privity) Act 1982.

2. Existence of Third Party

8.5   In the Consultation Paper,[6] the provisional view was expressed that it should be possible to create rights in a third party who was not in existence (or ascertained)[7] at the time that the contract was made, since otherwise a remedy would be denied to prospective beneficiaries such as an unborn child or a future spouse. However, whether a third party was ascertained at the time of the contract might be relevant in determining whether the contracting parties intended to confer on him a right to enforce the contract. This provisional view was overwhelmingly supported by consultees.

---

[3]   In *McElwee v Beer* (Unreported, High Court, Auckland, 19 February 1987, A 445/85, Wylie J) it was held that (i) assuming a nomination results in a benefit to the nominee, it is the nomination, not the contract (or the promise under the contract) that confers it; (ii) a nomination does not in itself confer a benefit for mere nomination leaves all the benefits with the original party to the contract; and (iii) a person designated by description connotes a person identifiable at the time of the contract, not someone who by capricious choice of the contracting party may subsequently be brought within the description. In *Field v Fitton* [1988] 1 NZLR 482, the New Zealand Court of Appeal supported (iii) above, observing that whether or not a nominee is sufficiently designated will depend on whether words of qualification are added to allow a bare nominee to be sufficiently identified. In *Karangahape Road International Village Ltd v Holloway* [1989] 1 NZLR 83, Chilwell J held that a benefit conferred on a nominee is not one conferred by the promise, but by the independent act of the contracting party, and that, in any event, section 4 could not apply because the nominee was not specified or particularised.

[4]   This is not to deny that, in the context of the particular contract, it may be that the nominee cannot otherwise satisfy the test of enforceability. This was the alternative ground of reasoning in *Field v Fitton* [1988] 1 NZLR 482. Bisson J said, at p 494, "The second difficulty is that the proviso to s 4 is fatal to the first respondents as there is on the proper construction of this contract no intention to create an obligation on the appellants enforceable at the suit of the first respondents alone. The mere addition of the words 'or nominee' without more, is not sufficient in this case... on the proper construction of the agreement to impute an intention to the parties to create, in respect of the benefit to a named purchaser an obligation on the part of the vendor enforceable at the suit of a bare nominee."

[5]   *Contract Statutes Review*, Report No 25 (1993) p 224.

[6]   Consultation Paper No 121, paras 5.20, 6.8.

[7]   A third party is 'ascertained' if he or she both exists and can be named.

8.6   We therefore recommend that:

    (10) there should be an "avoidance of doubt" provision to the effect that the third party need not be in existence at the time of the contract. (Draft Bill, clause 1(3))

8.7   The view was also expressed in the Consultation Paper[8] that it should not be necessary for the third party to be in existence (or ascertained) at the time of acceptance of the benefit by another third party, as appears to be required by section 55(6)(b) of the Queensland Property Law Act 1974.[9] It was felt that this would have adverse consequences for some members of a class of beneficiaries. For example, it would appear to mean that, where an employer has agreed with union representatives to review employees' salaries at regular intervals, and has also expressly provided that the agreement should be legally enforceable by the employees,[10] the benefit of this agreement would be enjoyed only by those members of the work-force who accepted it at its inception and not those who subsequently joined the company. Although the opinions of consultees were not specifically sought on this question, no consultee disagreed with our provisional view.

8.8   We therefore recommend that:

    (11) there should be no requirement that the third party be in existence at the time of acceptance by another third party.

3. Pre-Incorporation Contracts: A Special Case?

8.9   The common law rule is that a company which is not incorporated at the time that a contract is made on its behalf cannot enforce that contract, despite a purported later ratification of it.[11] Nor is the contract enforceable against the company. Section 36C of the Companies Act 1985[12] provides that the purported agent for the unincorporated company is liable on the contract. A pre-incorporation contract is therefore generally enforceable as between the signatory parties and remains valid as between them.

---

8   Consultation Paper No 121, para 5.21.

9   Section 55(6)(b) reads: "'beneficiary' means a person other than the promisor or promisee, and includes a person who, at the time of acceptance is identified and in existence, although that person may not have been identified or in existence at the time when the promise was given."

10   A collective agreement is not legally enforceable unless it is in writing and there is an express provision that it is legally enforceable: Trade Union and Labour Relations (Consolidation) Act 1992, s 179.

11   It is a contract made by an agent (the promoter) on behalf of a non-existent principal (the company) and leads to personal liability of the agent: *Kelner v Baxter* (1866) LR 2 CP 174.

12   As inserted by the Companies Act 1989, s 130.

8.10   It is clear that a reform which permits the conferral of rights on a third party not yet in existence may extend to a third party which is a company that has not yet been incorporated. Thus the interrelationship between our proposed reform and the rules governing liability on pre-incorporation contracts needs to be considered. Under our proposed reform, where a promoter/promisee contracts with a promisor to confer a benefit on a non-existent company, the company, once it comes into existence, could enforce the benefit if it could satisfy the test of enforceability. On the face of it, this would seem to derogate from the pre-incorporation contracts rule.

8.11   However, we agree with the New Zealand Law Commission[13] that a contract on behalf of a third party is not the same thing as a contract for the benefit of a third party. The former involves the third party becoming a party to the contract, and to all of its rights and obligations, after its incorporation. The latter is the situation that we are dealing with, where the third party is not, and will not become, a party to the contract, but will simply acquire a right to sue to enforce provisions of the contract. The third party company will not become subject to the obligations of the promoter under the contract, and so, for example, the obligation to pay for goods or services supplied to a company under a pre-incorporation contract would remain the promoter's. Thus, our proposed reform of the third party rule would not have the effect of rendering valid as against the third party company contracts that would otherwise be invalid.

8.12   We should also mention at this stage - although the point is discussed fully in Part X below[14] - that, while our reform does not enable obligations to be imposed on third parties, the third party's entitlement may be subject to conditions so that a failure to comply with the condition can give the promisor a defence or set-off. Our recognition that a company's right under a pre-incorporation contract may be conditional should not be misconstrued as permitting obligations under a pre-incorporation contract to be imposed on the company.[15]

8.13   Our general approach is supported by developments in New Zealand. The New Zealand Contracts (Privity) Act 1982 contained no specific provision to deal with pre-incorporation contracts. The law on pre-incorporation contracts in New Zealand was amended by the New Zealand Companies Amendment Act (No 2) 1983, introducing a new section 42A into the New Zealand Companies Act 1955, which permits the ratification of contracts made in the name of or on behalf of a non-existent company within a specified or reasonable time after the incorporation of the company. The

---

[13]   *Contract Statutes Review* (1993) para 5.18. It was stated that the special company law rules on pre-incorporation contracts and the provisions of the Contracts (Privity) Act 1982 could happily co-exist and that no amendments were warranted.

[14]   See paras 10.24-10.32 below.

[15]   It also follows from this that there is no question of our proposed legislation undermining s 36C of the Companies Act 1985 which was designed to implement Article 7 of the First Company Law Directive (Dir 68/151) which rests on the company not having assumed the obligations arising under the pre-incorporation contract.

Contracts (Privity) Act 1982 has been held since its enactment to apply to pre-incorporation contracts by the New Zealand courts,[16] a conclusion which has not been affected by the specific legislation dealing with the matter in company law. The New Zealand courts have maintained the distinction which we draw between a company becoming a full party to a contract made for it or on its behalf prior to its incorporation, and enforcing a contract as a third party whether made before its incorporation or not.

8.14 Consequently, we do not believe that we need to qualify recommendation 10 in order to preserve the rules governing pre-incorporation contracts.[17] We accept however that our proposals for reform may provide a route by which at least one of the effects of those rules may be avoided. Given that the rules governing pre-incorporation contracts have been described as "clearly unjust",[18] we believe that the accordance of a right of suit to the newly incorporated company in circumstances where this clearly matches the contracting parties' intentions goes some way towards doing greater justice to those involved than the present position.

8.15 In the Consultation Paper, we invited views on whether the issue of pre-incorporation contracts should be addressed in any reform of the third party rule, or whether it would be best left to specialist company legislation.[19] The preponderance of consultees' opinions was in favour of leaving general reform of pre-incorporation contract law to specialist legislation while accepting that there should be no restriction on a corporate third party's right to enforce an otherwise enforceable contract simply because it was entered into before the third party's incorporation.

---

[16] *Palmer v Bellaney* (1983) ANZ ConvR 467, holding that the Contracts (Privity) Act 1982, s 4, applied in the case of a contract made by X "as agent for a company to be formed" and that the company could accordingly enforce the contract. Although criticised (Farrar and Russell, *Company Law and Securities Regulation in New Zealand*), this interpretation was supported in *Speedy v Nylex New Zealand Ltd* (unreported, H Ct, Auckland, 3 February 1989, CL 29/87) by Wylie J. Cf *Cross v Aurora Group Ltd* (1989) 4 NZCLC 64,909 where a contract had been entered into on behalf of "Cross Property Management Ltd, a company currently being formed". In the event, Cross Property Management Ltd was not in the process of formation at the time of contract, but instead the promoter's solicitors had bought a shelf company and subsequently changed its name to Cross Property Management Ltd. It was held that section 4 could not apply to allow Cross to take the benefit of the contract, as there was no sufficient identification of the shelf company as being Cross for these purposes. Wylie J (at p 64,913) held that "Designation is a strong word, a positive word and means something more than a mere contemplation or possibility".

[17] It is perhaps noteworthy that reform of this doctrine has itself been advocated: in 1962 the Jenkins Committee recommended that companies should be given statutory power to adopt contracts made in their names or on their behalf before incorporation (Report of the Company Law Committee (Cmnd 1749), para 54(b)); and reform has been effected in New Zealand: Companies Amendment Act (No 2) 1983, s 15, introducing a new s 42A into the Companies Act 1955.

[18] *Pennington's Company Law* (7th ed, 1995) p 108.

[19] Consultation Paper No 121, paras 5.22-5.23, 6.9.

8.16   We therefore recommend that:

   **(12) the proposed legislation should contain no special provisions governing
           pre-incorporation contracts.**

4. Ascertainability of Third Party and Certainty

8.17   A few consultees pointed out that it must be possible to ascertain who is the third
        party at the time the right accrues. Thus, a third party who is to receive money or
        services under a contract would need to be capable of being ascertained with certainty
        at the time at which the promisor's duty to perform arose. Where the third party is to
        receive the benefit of an exclusion or limitation clause under the contract, the third
        party should be ascertainable with certainty by the date at which the liability falling
        within the exclusion or limitation clause was incurred. We agree, but it is hard to see
        that this represents anything more than the straightforward application of the normal
        principle that to be valid a contract, or contractual provision, must be sufficiently
        certain.

8.18   We therefore recommend that:

   **(13) although no legislative provision on this is necessary, a third party shall
           have no right to enforce a contract or contractual provision unless he or
           she is capable of being ascertained with certainty at the time when the
           promisor's duty to perform in the third party's favour arises, or when
           a liability against which the provision seeks to protect the third party is
           incurred.**

PART IX
VARIATION AND CANCELLATION

1. Provisional Proposals and Consultation

9.1 It was suggested in the Consultation Paper that a question central to reform of the third party rule was that of when the parties, after having agreed to confer a right on a third party, should be permitted to vary or cancel that right.[1] To allow the contracting parties an unlimited power to vary the contract would mean that the third party would not have a right that he could confidently rely on; on the other hand, to restrict the right to vary could be seen as an unacceptable fetter on the parties' freedom of contract. While most consultees favoured the ideas that (i) there should be some opportunity for the original parties to cancel or vary the contract but that (ii) there should be a cut-off point after which the contract could not be varied or cancelled without the consent of the third party, no clear view emerged from consultation as to what that cut-off point should be.

9.2 In the Consultation Paper, several tests for a cut-off point (or, as one might otherwise phrase it, the time of crystallisation of the third party's right) were outlined:[2]

   (i)   when the third party becomes aware of the contract;

   (ii)   when the third party adopts the contract either expressly or by conduct;[3]

   (iii) when the third party accepts or assents to the contract;[4]

   (iv)   when the third party materially alters his position in reliance on the contract;[5]

   (v)   when the third party either materially changes his position in justifiable reliance on the promise, or brings suit on it, or manifests assent to it at the request of the promisor or promisee.

9.3 We suggested that the central choice lay between (ii), (iii) and (iv). Consultees were divided between these. Options (ii) and (iii) were criticised on the grounds that the meaning of adoption or acceptance was unclear. Some consultees argued that the

---

[1]   Consultation Paper No 121, para 5.28. Variation or cancellation by the parties must be distinguished from a term (or statutory provision) which permits one of the parties unilaterally to alter the contracted-for work. A third party's rights are subject to such a term: see, eg, paras 9.37, note 30, and 10.31 below.

[2]   Consultation Paper No 121, para 5.27.

[3]   See section 11(3) of the Western Australia Property Law Act 1969.

[4]   Under section 55(6)(a) of the Queensland Property Law Act 1974, "'acceptance' means an assent by words or conduct communicated by or on behalf of the beneficiary to the promisor ...".

[5]   This is the primary test favoured in New Zealand: see Contracts (Privity) Act 1982, s 5(1).

concept of reliance in option (iv) was unclear, that its use could lead to artificial acts of reliance, that a choice had to be made between mere "reasonable" reliance and "detrimental" reliance, and that reliance could occur without the knowledge of either of the contracting parties.

9.4 We also asked "whether modification should be permitted where the contract allows it (either expressly or impliedly) regardless of adoption, acceptance or material reliance or at least where the third party knows (or should reasonably have been aware) that the contract permits modification even though he subsequently adopts, accepts or materially relies on the contract."[6] A large majority of consultees were in favour of permitting contractual provisions which preserve the right of the contracting parties to vary or cancel the contract to prevail over the crystallisation of a third party's rights.

2. The Two Extreme Positions

(1) Variation or Cancellation at Any Time

9.5 A number of consultees favoured allowing revocation at any time. Some others argued that revocation should be permitted at any time unless the third party had in some form provided payment for the benefit conferred upon it. These consultees were for the most part among those who were opposed to any reform of the doctrine of privity of contract, and therefore most likely saw this as a means of preserving the powers of the original contracting parties to the fullest extent possible. This option would preserve the ability of the contracting parties to agree between themselves to alter the contract at any time, in the same manner as if there were no third party rights involved.

9.6 Similarly some consultees saw the imposition of any limit on the power of the contracting parties to vary or cancel the contract as an attack on the doctrine of consideration. They argued that, if a third party's rights were allowed to crystallise so as to become irrevocable by the contracting parties, this would effectively mean enforcing gratuitous promises (or at best, promises supported only by reliance or detrimental reliance) made to the third party. This is a fundamental and important point. We have, however, dealt with it in Part VI above. We there explained that we saw no objection to accepting that, while formally, our proposed reform does not affect the requirement of consideration, at a deeper policy level, and within the area of third party rights, it may represent a relaxation of the importance attached to consideration.[7]

9.7 If the contracting parties were able to vary or cancel the contract at any time the impact of reforming the law, by giving a third party an entitlement to sue, would be marginal. As the New Zealand Contracts and Commercial Law Reform Committee pointed out, if reform of the third party rule is to have any substantial effect, there

---

[6] Consultation Paper No 121, para 5.31.

[7] See paras 6.13-6.17 above.

must be some limit on the parties' power to vary or cancel the third party beneficiary's rights without the third party's consent, even if it is only to prevent them doing so once judgment has been given in his or her favour.[8] If this were not the case, the reform would amount to little more than a procedural device to allow the third party to sue in his or her own name when for some reason the promisee was not prepared to act, and would not guarantee the third party any rights at all under the contract. The third party would be left in much the same position as at present.[9]

9.8 At the core of this issue is a conflict between preserving the freedom of the contracting parties to implement their intentions as they see fit at any particular time, and allowing the creation of effective third party rights so that a third party can arrange its affairs with some certainty.[10] We consider that the former policy is outweighed by the latter.

9.9 We therefore reject the view that the contracting parties should be permitted to vary or cancel at any time a contractual provision that is enforceable by a third party.

(2) No Variation or Cancellation

9.10 At the other extreme, a number of consultees favoured a rule which would not permit any variation or cancellation of a contractual provision enforceable by a third party.[11] But the majority agreed with our provisional view that to refuse to permit variation or cancellation at all would be too restrictive.[12] Where the third party is not even aware of the promise it is hard to see any conceivable injustice to the third party in allowing the contracting parties to vary or cancel the contract. We therefore reject this approach as creating too great a fetter on the ability of the contracting parties to change their original intentions.

---

[8] *Privity of Contract* (1981) para 8.3.1.

[9] That is, under the present law the third party will not get performance unless both parties decide that they want to honour the terms of the original contract, whereas a reform allowing variation or cancellation at any time would mean that the third party would not be able to secure performance where both parties agree to vary the terms of the original contract.

[10] See para 3.2 above.

[11] This was also the approach provisionally favoured by the Scottish Law Commission subject to there being a term in the contract providing for cancellation or variation: see Memorandum No 38 *Constitution and Proof of Voluntary Obligations: Stipulations in Favour of Third Parties* (1977) para 33.

[12] See Consultation Paper No 121 para 5.29. Indeed it was pointed out to us that the inability to vary or cancel benefits subsequently is one of the disadvantages of using a deed poll to overcome the doctrine of privity: see para 2.8, note 27, above.

3. Possible "Crystallisation" Tests

9.11   It is obvious from the above discussion that we consider that any reform will require some degree of constraint on the contracting parties' rights to vary the contract, but that this should not amount to a total bar on variation. In other words, along with the majority of consultees, we consider that there should be a 'crystallisation' test. We now move to consider what that test should be.

(1) Awareness

9.12   We reject at the outset a test which requires merely that the third party is aware of the terms of the contract, although it is the solution that was favoured by a few consultees. It is the crystallisation point that is most favourable to third parties and comes close to rejecting altogether a right to vary. However, we see variation or cancellation as causing no injustice to a third party who, while aware of the terms of the contract, has no wish to take advantage of them or who does not believe that the promise will be performed or that he or she has an entitlement to performance. Indeed he or she may even renounce the contract. Of course, it might be argued that such a third party is most unlikely to object to a variation or cancellation by the contracting parties so that no dispute would arise. But a dispute might arise where the third party changes its mind about wanting the promise performed after the contracting parties have varied or cancelled the contract. We therefore reject "awareness" as an appropriate crystallisation test.

9.13   In our view, this leaves reliance, detrimental reliance, acceptance or adoption as the major possible tests. In choosing between them, it is first necessary to clarify what each means.

(2) Reliance

9.14   Reliance on a promise, in our view, means "conduct induced by the belief (or expectation) that the promise will be performed or, at least, that one is legally entitled to performance of the promise." The reliance need not be detrimental: that is, the conduct need not make the plaintiff worse off than before the promise was made. To give two illustrations. Say A promises B to pay C £500. C then goes out and buys some shares, which he would not have risked buying but for A's promise of the £500. The shares have now tripled in value. Here C has relied on A's promise without being worse off than he was before the promise was made. Or say A promises B to pay C £500 and C, on hearing of this and because of it, immediately pays some outstanding bills. By so doing C has relied on the promise. But there is no necessity in showing reliance to go on to prove that, if A were to break the promise, C would be in a worse position than if the promise had never been made.

(3) Detrimental Reliance

9.15   Detrimental reliance means that the third party's conduct in reliance on the promise renders him or her worse off than he or she would have been if the promise had never been made. In the example of C buying shares in the previous paragraph, C would have detrimentally relied if the shares had fallen in value. Again a person detrimentally relies if he or she passes up profitable opportunities on the strength of the promise.

(4) Acceptance

9.16 Although a third party, unlike an offeree, is not normally being requested to respond, we consider that in defining what is meant by acceptance, some help can be derived from the well-known notion of "acceptance" of an offer in a standard bilateral contract. In that context, acceptance means communication of one's assent. This is supported by the legislation in Queensland which uses "acceptance" by the third party as the test for crystallisation of its rights, and defines "acceptance" as "an assent by words or conduct communicated by the beneficiary to the promisor...."[13] However, this definition leaves open whether "communication of one's assent" means that one's acceptance must be received by the promisor or whether it is sufficient that one communicates one's assent even though the promisor does not know of it (for example, by posting a letter). We return to that issue below.[14]

(5) Adoption Expressly or by Conduct

9.17 This was the crystallisation test favoured by the Law Revision Committee in 1937 and by the Western Australia Property Law Act 1969.[15] However, the phrase does not appear to have been defined in any case law and the difficulty is to know what it means. One possibility is that it means the same as "acceptance" (as defined above). Another is that it means either "acceptance" or "reliance". We consider that the ambiguity of the phrase means that it is best avoided.

4. Choice of Test

9.18 Having ruled out "adoption" as insufficiently clear in its meaning, we are left with three main possible crystallisation tests: reliance, detrimental reliance, and acceptance. After much deliberation, we have decided that the appropriate balance between avoiding injustice to a third party and allowing the contracting parties to change their minds is achieved by having a test whereby *reliance or acceptance* by the third party crystallises his or her rights.

9.19 In arriving at that test we have first had to make a choice between reliance and detrimental reliance. We have opted for the former. The essential injustice caused to a third party by the privity rule is that that party's reasonable expectations of the promised performance are disappointed. Reliance serves to indicate that expectations have been engendered in the third party. To require the reliance to be detrimental tends to shift the focus away from protecting the plaintiff's expectation interest to protecting the plaintiff's reliance interest. In other words, an insistence that reliance

---

[13] Section 55(6)(a) Queensland Property Law Act 1974.

[14] See para 9.20 below.

[15] See paras 4.2-4.7 above.

be detrimental makes it very difficult (albeit not impossible) to explain why the third party is entitled to performance of the promise, or its monetary substitute in the form of expectation damages, rather than damages for reliance loss (as, for example, for tortious misrepresentation).[16] A useful analogy is the doctrine of promissory estoppel, which, like our reform is concerned with the enforcement of certain promises by those who have not provided consideration. There the debate has raged for many years as to whether the promisee needs to have merely relied, or must have detrimentally relied, on the promise in order to fall within the doctrine. Although the matter cannot be regarded as entirely settled, there seems to be an emerging consensus to the effect that mere reliance is sufficient.[17]

9.20 But while we consider that reliance by the third party should be the primary test for the crystallisation of the third party's rights, we also think it necessary to have an alternative test of acceptance. This is primarily because, in our view, a third party who has (successfully) communicated its assent to the promisor ought to be secure in its entitlement without also having to show reliance on the promise. Furthermore, an acceptance enables the promisor to know exactly where it stands. In this respect, we think that the standard posting rule (that acceptance of an offer takes place when the letter is posted)[18] is here inappropriate. To apply the rule that a valid acceptance takes place on the posting of a letter (subject to exceptions) would mean that a third party could crystallise his rights not only without the promisor knowing anything about it but, more crucially, without the promisor even being able to foresee it (because, for example, the promisor did not know that the third party had come into existence). And in contrast to the reliance test (as discussed below)[19] it would seem impracticable and overelaborate to suggest that the posting rule should only apply where it was reasonably foreseeable that a postal acceptance would be made.

9.21 It has been suggested to us that an alternative test of acceptance is unnecessary because reliance encompasses acceptance (on the basis that reliance means "any conduct induced by the promise"). We do not agree. Acceptance by communicating one's assent is conduct designed to secure performance of the promise; it is not conduct induced by the belief that the promise will be performed or that one is legally

---

[16] See A Burrows, *Remedies for Torts and Breach of Contract* (2nd ed, 1994) pp 171-178.

[17] See, eg, Lord Denning in *Central London Property Trust Ltd v High Trees House Ltd* [1947] KB 130; *W J Alan & Co Ltd v El Nasr Export and Import Co* [1972] 2 QB 189; Treitel, *The Law of Contract* (9th ed, 1995) p 105; *Chitty on Contracts* (27th ed, 1994) paras 3-070-3-071; E McKendrick, *Contract Law* (2nd ed, 1994) p 93.

[18] See, eg, *Household Fire Insurance Co Ltd v Grant* (1879) 4 Ex D 216. The posting rule contrasts with the standard rule for instantaneous means of communication (eg telex and telephone) that the acceptance is valid only when received: see, eg, *Entores Ltd v Miles Far East Corp* [1955] 2 QB 327; *Brinkibon Ltd v Stahag Stahl and Stahlwarenhandels GmbH* [1983] 2 AC 34. The position in relation to fax and E-mail is, arguably, unclear: see Treitel, *The Law of Contract* (9th ed), pp 25-26.

[19] See paras 9.27-9.30 below.

entitled to performance of the promise. A third party who writes to the promisor saying "I do not want to take advantage of your promise" is not relying on the promise even though his conduct is induced by the promise. Similarly a third party who writes out of fear that the promise will otherwise be withdrawn saying "I want to take advantage of your promise" is accepting the promise but is not relying on it.

9.22 On the other hand we do not see the need for an additional alternative test of the third party "bringing suit on the promise". In our view, a third party who brings suit on the promise is relying on that promise in that it is embarking on conduct based on the belief that it is legally entitled to performance of the promise.

9.23 We are supported in our view that the best crystallisation test is reliance or acceptance by the fact that an approach of alternative tests was favoured by many consultees and that the precise approach of reliance or acceptance was particularly popular.

9.24 Some consultees preferred a single test of acceptance. A merit of this would be that the contracting parties would know where they stood before proceeding to vary or cancel the contract. However, we consider that any problems caused by the 'unilateral' nature of reliance are sufficiently catered for by modifying the reliance test so as to require that the promisor could reasonably have foreseen/anticipated that the third party would rely on the promise. This is discussed further below.[20] The obvious objection to a single acceptance test is that many third parties will rely (and even detrimentally rely) without having communicated their assent. As the contracting parties will not normally ask for communication of assent (although if they do, this will displace the reliance test as is explained below)[21] only those third parties who know the law can be expected to communicate assent. If acceptance alone were the test, one could even have a situation where the third party is present when the contract is made and is told of the beneficial promise, yet because he does not communicate his assent, the parties would be free to revoke despite reliance (including detrimental reliance) by the third party.

9.25 We should add the perhaps obvious point that where a contract contains more than one provision that is enforceable by a third party, only those provisions which the third party relies upon or accepts should become irrevocable (although, of course, the third party could rely on or accept all the provisions).

9.26 We therefore recommend that:

(14) **the contracting parties' right to vary or cancel the contract or, as the case may be, the contractual provision should be lost once the third party has relied on it or has accepted it ("acceptance" meaning "an**

---

[20] See paras 9.27-9.30 below.

[21] See paras 9.37-9.42 below.

assent by words or conduct communicated by the third party to the promisor"). The posting rule, applicable to the acceptance of offers sent by post (and possibly by some other means),[22] should not apply. (Draft Bill, clause 2(1) and (2))

5. The Reliance Test : Further Details

(1) Need the Promisor Be Aware Of, or Foresee, the Reliance?

9.27   A number of consultees considered that the third party's reliance should only crystallise its rights if the contracting parties, or one of them, was aware of the reliance. It was also suggested by one consultee that reliance should only count if it was reasonably to be anticipated. These suggestions stem from a fear about the consequences of the unilateral nature of reliance. The contracting parties may purport to vary or cancel a contract at a time when they do not know that the third party has relied; the promisor may then go on to perform in favour of someone else (that is, a fourth party). Although the promisor may have a claim in restitution against the party to whom performance was rendered, this will not always be so and the promisor will in any event normally have to bear the risk of the insolvency of that party.

9.28   In our view, the correct resolution of this difficulty rests on recognising that the promisor generally ought to check with the third party before revoking or cancelling the contract. In normal circumstances a promisor who has entered into a contract which, under our recommendations, is enforceable by a third party (because the parties have intended to confer legal rights on the third party) ought to realise that that third party is likely to rely on the contract and that he is not free to resile from the contract simply by obtaining the consent of the promisee. It follows from this that the unilateral nature of reliance only causes difficulty where the promisor could not reasonably be expected to check with the third party because the promisor did not realise that the third party knew of the contract. Indeed in the case of a third party who was not in existence at the time the contract was made, it may even be that the promisor did not realise that the third party had come into existence. To deal with this sort of problem we consider that the reliance test should be qualified so that reliance should only count where, unless the promisor is actually aware that the third party has relied, the promisor could reasonably have foreseen that the third party would rely on the promise.

9.29   It should be added that this qualification will create some incentive for a third party, who knows the law, to 'accept' the promise by communicating its assent. For if the third party goes ahead and relies without acceptance it runs some risk in certain circumstances of falling foul of the qualification.

---

[22]   See para 9.20, note 18, above.

9.30   We therefore recommend that:

   **(15) the reliance test should be qualified so that reliance should only count
           where (unless the promisor is aware that the third party has relied) the
           promisor could reasonably have foreseen that the third party would rely
           on the promise.** (Draft Bill, clause 2(1)(b) and 2(1)(c))

(2) Material Reliance

9.31   It was suggested to us that the third party's reliance should only count if it was
        material. And in New Zealand the Contracts (Privity) Act 1982, s 5(1)(a) requires
        that "the position of a beneficiary has been materially altered by the reliance of that
        beneficiary ... on the promise ...".[23] It is not entirely clear what the word 'material',
        in the phrase 'material reliance', refers to. In particular it is ambiguous as between the
        causal potency of the promise and the seriousness of the conduct induced by the
        promise. Even if one confines it to the latter, with the aim being to rule out trivial acts
        of reliance, we consider that it would be a recipe for litigation; for where is the line is
        to be drawn between trivial and non-trivial reliance? This is especially so given that
        we have clarified that the relevant test is reliance and not detrimental reliance. In our
        view, the importance of reliance is in indicating that expectations have been
        engendered in the third party, and the triviality of the reliance seems irrelevant to that.

(3) Protection of the Third Party's Reliance or Expectation Interest?

9.32   Some consultees doubted whether a third party should be entitled to expectation
        damages, where the promise for the third party has become irrevocable because of the
        third party's reliance and yet the parties have purported to vary or cancel the contract
        so that the promisor does not perform. They argued that, in this situation, the third
        party should be confined to recovering its reliance loss.

9.33   We have already touched on this question.[24] We believe that there is no good reason
        to restrict damages to the reliance measure. The reform that we are concerned to
        introduce allows third parties to 'enforce' contracts and we see no reason why the
        normal contractual measure of recovery (the expectation measure) should not apply.
        Again the analogy of promissory estoppel may be thought helpful; for that doctrine is
        not confined to protecting the plaintiff's reliance interest.[25]

---

[23]   There has been no judicial consideration of this provision: New Zealand Law Commission
       Contract Statutes Review (1993) para 5.30. The New Zealand Contracts and Commercial Law
       Reform Committee's Report, *Privity of Contract* (1981); para 8.3.5 uses both the terms
       "materially alter" and "injurious reliance" in a manner which suggests that the Committee did
       not regard the two as coterminous.

[24]   See para 9.19 above.

[25]   See A Burrows, 'Contract, Tort and Restitution - A Satisfactory Division or Not?' (1983) 99
       LQR 217, 239-244.

(4) Burden of Proof

9.34 As it can be difficult to prove reliance, it was suggested to us that the burden of proof would be very important and that the burden should lie on the contracting parties to show that the third party had not relied. Although we see the force in the argument, there are great difficulties in proving a negative and, in view of the fact that our proposals are concerned to confer rights upon a third party, we consider that the burden of proving the existence of those rights should be laid at the door of the third party. Again, this continues the analogy with promissory estoppel, as the party seeking the protection of the estoppel has the burden of proving reliance.[26]

(5) Reliance by Someone Other Than the Third Party

9.35 The New Zealand legislation prevents variation or cancellation of the third party's right once the third party's position has been materially altered by reliance on the promise by either the third party or by *any other person*.[27] In other words, the New Zealand provision extends to situations where someone other than the third party (ie one of the contracting parties or a fourth party) acts in reliance on the expected benefit to the third party, and the third party suffers detriment because of this reliance. An example of this may be where a parent or guardian of a child third party beneficiary has acted on the assumption that the child will be provided for by the benefit under the contract and has not therefore made any provisions for the child. The question was not raised in the Consultation Paper of whether acts of reliance should only count if undertaken by the third party, although we received one comment favouring the provisions of the New Zealand legislation on this issue.

9.36 We have decided not to follow the New Zealand approach on this question. First, we feel that that approach would make the reform unattractive to contracting parties, as we do not believe that contracting parties envisage themselves as effectively becoming insurers for any loss that the third party may suffer as a result of fourth party actions. Secondly, to allow the actions of fourth parties to constitute reliance would not sit well with the analogy we have been drawing with promissory estoppel. Thirdly, and perhaps most importantly, we have acknowledged that, while there are arguments for requiring the contracting parties to have knowledge of any reliance before their rights are fettered, it is not unreasonable to expect them to check whether the third party has actually relied. However, we think that it would be unreasonable to expect the contracting parties to check whether any other party has relied in such a way as to alter the third party's position, particularly as the third party may not know that its position has been so altered. To provide otherwise would be to place too heavy a burden on the contracting parties, and could result in the situation where the contracting parties have had their rights abrogated, yet neither they nor the third party know of this.

---

[26] Although Lord Denning's judgment in *Brikom Investments v Carr* [1979] QB 467 may be interpreted as reversing the burden of proving reliance.

[27] Contracts (Privity) Act 1982, s 5(1)(a).

6. Reservation of a Right to Vary or Cancel

9.37   It was provisionally recommended in the Consultation Paper that the parties should be able to reserve the right to vary or cancel the third party's right even after the latter had adopted, accepted or relied on that right.[28] There seemed to be broad agreement among consultees that the parties should have power to reserve to themselves or even to one of them[29] such a right to vary or cancel. This view was particularly prevalent among consultees involved in the construction industry, highlighting the fact that collateral warranties often provide for variation.[30]

9.38   It could be argued that any attempt to preserve the contracting parties' rights to vary negates the value of the third party's right: if the parties can vary the contract at any stage, even after reliance on it or acceptance of it by the third party, it would seem that the third party has few guaranteed rights. However, the third party's rights may be defined and limited by the terms of the contract,[31] and it would seem inconsistent to allow the contracting parties to make a contract that confers a benefit on a third party which is conditional upon an external factor, but not one which is conditional upon their own future intentions.

9.39   A number of consultees thought that the parties should only have such a right if the third party was aware, or perhaps should have been aware, of the reservation: otherwise, there might be a danger that the third party beneficiary could be misled. The New Zealand Contracts (Privity) Act 1982, section 6 provides that the parties may not operate such a clause unless the third party knew of it before it materially altered its position in reliance on the promise. This gives the third party the opportunity to consider the fact that it is not guaranteed the right of enforcement before it chooses to rely on the promise. This is part of a wider issue relating to the extent to which, in this legislation, one can fully deal with the possibility of the third party being misled as to its entitlement.[32]   In line with our basic commitment to respecting the intentions of the contracting parties, and not causing unnecessary uncertainty, we have concluded that this legislation should only go so far as to require that the reservation of a right to vary or cancel is expressly provided for.

---

[28]   Consultation Paper No 121, para 5.27.

[29]   Cf New Zealand Contracts (Privity) Act 1982, s 6(b).

[30]   Almost all construction contracts of any complexity contain a clause permitting the employer, or the architect or engineer on behalf of the employer, to order variations to the work. Though often called "variations", such changes are not variations to the contract but only to the work, since they are contemplated by the original contract. The third party's rights, since they are conferred by the contract, would clearly be subject to such variations.

[31]   See para 10.4 below.

[32]   See para 13.10 point (iv) below.

9.40   We therefore recommend that:

(16)   the contracting parties may expressly reserve the right to vary or cancel the third party's right irrespective of reliance or acceptance by the third party. (Draft Bill, clause 2(3)(a))

7.   Can the Relevant Crystallisation Test be Laid Down in the Contract?

9.41   We consider that, by an express term, the parties should be able to lay down in the contract a crystallisation test different from reliance or acceptance. That is, they should be able to reserve a right to vary or cancel the contract until, for example, the third party has accepted by writing (so that reliance would not count and nor would an oral acceptance).

9.42   We therefore recommend that:

(17)   the parties, by an express term, should be able to lay down a crystallisation test different from reliance or acceptance. (Draft Bill, clause 2(3)(b))

8.   Crystallisation Where There Is More Than One Third Party

9.43   Although this was not put out to consultation, it is perhaps worth clarifying that, in our view, where there is more than one third party, who can satisfy the test of enforceability, reliance on or acceptance of the contract (or satisfaction of whatever other crystallisation test is expressly laid down in the contract) by each third party should be needed to crystallise that third party's rights.[33] The practical effect of this will vary depending on whether the promise is intended to confer enforceable rights that are to be separately, or jointly, enjoyed with other third parties. For example, where A contracts with B to pay C £100 and D £150, it is clear that any crystallisation of C's rights or consent by C cannot affect D's rights and vice versa. On the other hand, a contract between A and B to benefit C and D jointly, where D has neither accepted nor relied (indeed D may not yet be alive) but C has accepted or relied, could not be varied to exclude D unless C consents: but it could be varied to exclude D if C does consent.[34]

---

[33]   The issue of releases where there is more than one third party is dealt with at para 11.9 below.

[34]   The main two alternative approaches to this question of jointly entitled third parties would, in our view, produce obviously unacceptable results. These two alternatives are: (i) requiring the consent to variation of each jointly entitled third party (including the consent of those who may not yet be alive) once the rights of one of them have crystallised; or (ii) allowing a variation or cancellation of the rights of all of them (despite the known refusal to consent of a third party whose rights have already crystallised) unless and until the rights of each of them have crystallised.

9.44   We therefore recommend that:

   (18) although no legislative provision on this is necessary,[35] where there is more than one third party who satisfies the test of enforceability, the relevant crystallisation test would need to be satisfied by each third party in order to crystallise that third party's rights.

9. Creating Irrevocable Rights

9.45   We did not put forward any provisional view as to whether effect should be given to a term in the contract (enforceable by the third party) that the contract is irrevocable and, while we drew attention to the position under US law,[36] we did not expressly seek consultees' views on this point.

9.46   We do not see the attraction, nor the justification, for holding the contracting parties to a contract which the third party has neither relied upon nor accepted. In our view this would be an unreasonable fetter on the contracting parties' freedom of contract which could not be justified by reference to any injustice to another party. In any event, this would cut across the standard contractual principle that the parties are free to vary any term of the contract, even a 'no-variation' term. We therefore consider that any provision of a contract for the benefit of a third party which purports to render that contract irrevocable should be as open to variation or discharge as any other contractual term. Similarly if the parties have expressly laid down a crystallisation test different from reliance or acceptance, they should be free to vary it prior to reliance or acceptance by the third party.

9.47   We therefore recommend that:

   (19) a contractual term to the effect that the contract is irrevocable should be as open to variation or cancellation by the contracting parties as any other term.

10. Judicial Discretion to Authorise Variation or Cancellation

9.48   The New Zealand Contracts (Privity) Act 1982, section 7, gives the court a discretion to authorise a variation or discharge of the contract if "it is just and practicable to do so", despite a material reliance which would otherwise have crystallised a third party's rights. The legislation further provides that the court which orders a variation or

---

[35] We have taken the view throughout this Report that legislative provisions dealing with where there is more than one third party with a right of enforceability are unnecessary and that the law to be applied follows directly, or by analogy, from the normal principles applicable to a plurality of creditors. See also paras 11.9-11.10 below. See generally Treitel, *The Law of Contract* (9th ed, 1995) pp 529-533. In leaving these matters to the courts to determine, we have also been influenced by the facts that (i) these matters were not put out to consultation; and (ii) these matters do not appear to have been dealt with in the legislation reforming privity in, eg, New Zealand, Western Australia or Queensland.

[36] Restatement (2d) Contracts, § 311(1) prevents discharge or modification by the contracting parties if a term of the promise creating the duty so provides. See Consultation Paper No 121, para 5.29.

discharge may also order that such sum as it considers just to compensate the third party who has relied on the promise be paid by the promisor. In the Consultation Paper we provisionally recommended that the courts should not have a residual discretion to authorise variation or discharge for reasons of justice.[37] Most consultees agreed on grounds of certainty. However, there was a minority view that a measure of judicial discretion to authorise variation or discharge was desirable. We have been persuaded that that is a preferable approach.

9.49 We particularly have in mind situations where the contracting parties wish to vary or cancel the contract but cannot reasonably ascertain whether the third party has relied on the contract so that his consent is required. This may be, for example, because the third party simply refuses to say whether it has relied or not or cannot reasonably be contacted to ascertain whether it has relied or not. It is of course possible to seek a declaration of rights under the contract without involving the court in authorising a variation or cancellation, but such a declaration would not aid the parties if they wished to vary and there was found to have been reliance. We also have in mind situations where, although consent is known to be required, the contracting parties are locked into the contract because the third party cannot reasonably be contacted in order for consent to be obtained or because the third party is mentally incapable of consenting to a variation.

9.50 Therefore we now consider that the courts should be given a limited discretion to authorise variation or cancellation and on such terms (including as to the payment of compensation to the third party) as seems appropriate. The discretion should extend to where the third party is mentally incapable of consenting, or cannot reasonably be contacted in order for consent to be obtained, or where the parties cannot reasonably ascertain whether the third party's consent is required. We would not expect such a limited discretion to create any significant degree of uncertainty.

9.51 We therefore recommend that:

(20) **there should be a judicial discretion to authorise a variation or cancellation (and on such terms, including as to the payment of compensation to the third party, as seems appropriate) in certain limited circumstances irrespective of reliance or acceptance by the third party. The discretion should extend to where the parties cannot reasonably ascertain whether the third party's consent is required for the cancellation or variation of the contract; or where the third party's consent cannot be obtained because his whereabouts cannot reasonably be discovered or because he is mentally incapable of giving his consent.** (Draft Bill, clauses 2(4) to 2(7))

---

[37] Consultation Paper No 121, paras 5.32-5.33, 6.13.

PART X
DEFENCES, SET-OFFS AND COUNTERCLAIMS

1. Introduction

10.1   In the Consultation Paper, we provisionally recommended that the rights of the third party against the promisor should be subject to the promisor's defences, set-offs and counterclaims which would have been available to the promisor in an action by the promisee.[1] But we invited views on the scope of the defences, set-offs and counterclaims that should be relevant and, in particular, on whether, in the case of a set-off or counterclaim, a promisor may only rely on matters arising from the contract in which the promise is contained or may also set up against the third party set-offs and counterclaims arising out of other relations between the promisor and the promisee.[2]

10.2   There are always problems in the law of obligations in defining what constitutes a defence. For these purposes, however, we use the term to refer essentially to matters which affect the existence, validity and enforceability of the whole contract or of the particular provision benefiting the third party. We therefore include as defences matters which render the contract void (for example, fundamental mistake) or voidable (for example, the promisee's misrepresentation, duress or undue influence) or that have led to the contract being discharged (for example, frustration or serious breach by the promisee). Similarly we treat as a defence the failure of a condition which was the basis for the promise to benefit the third party.[3] In contrast, we do not include as defences matters which bar a particular remedy such as that specific performance is not available of a contract for personal service. The normal rules relating to remedies are applicable to the third party's action in line with recommendation 2 above and we do not think that all restrictions on the promisee's remedies (for example, that the promisee is guilty of laches so as to rule out specific performance or that the promisee has failed in its duty to mitigate its loss) should carry across to bar or restrict automatically the third party's remedy. Nor do we regard as defences, procedural restrictions on the enforcement of the contract such as arbitration clauses (unless of the *Scott v Avery*[4] type) or jurisdiction clauses. We also exclude from the notion of defences variation or cancellation by the contracting parties: that

---

[1]   Consultation Paper No 121 paras 5.24 to 5.25, 6.10. We pointed out in para 5.24 that our provisional recommendation is analogous to the rule that the assignee of a chose in action takes the benefit of it "subject to equities". See *Chitty on Contracts* (27th ed, 1994) paras 19-039 to 19-040. We also provisionally recommended, at paras 5.16 and 6.5, that rights created against a contracting party should be governed by the contract and be valid only to the extent that it is valid, and may be conditional upon the other contracting party performing its obligations under it.

[2]   *Ibid.*

[3]   Alternatively one can say that the promised benefit is a conditional one, and where the condition is not fulfilled, the promise does not apply: see paras 10.24-10.32 below.

[4]   (1856) 5 HL Cas 811; 10 ER 1121. See para 14.17, note 23, below.

form of "defence" has been discussed in Part IX above and is subject to a separate regime which seeks to restrict the rights of the original contracting parties to change their minds once the third party has relied on or accepted the promise.

10.3   There is also some difficulty in certain contexts in distinguishing set-offs and counterclaims. Nowadays both constitute cross-claims for monetary remedies, whether the cross-claim is for a debt or liquidated damages or unliquidated damages. However, a set-off may be narrower in that it appears that sometimes the set-off must arise out of the same transaction as the plaintiff's claim, whereas the only limitation on pleading a counterclaim is that trial of both the claim and counterclaim will not "embarrass or delay the trial or [be] otherwise inconvenient."[5]   A set-off is also narrower in that it cannot exceed the amount of the plaintiff's claim and, in effect therefore, operates as a defence.

10.4   There can be little doubt that defences going to the existence, validity and enforceability of the whole contract, or of the particular contractual provision being enforced by the third party, should be of equal relevance whether the promisee or the third party is suing. If the promise was induced by the fraud or undue influence of the promisee, or has been discharged by reason of the promisee's repudiatory breach or by reason of the doctrine of frustration, or was given subject to a condition that has not been fulfilled, the third party should have no greater rights to enforce it than would the promisee. The third party would otherwise clearly be getting something that it was never truly intended to have. Not surprisingly, there was little dissent from this on consultation.[6]   However, the position in respect of set-offs and counterclaims is less straightforward.

2. Precedents for Reform
(1) Law Revision Committee/Western Australia/Queensland
10.5   The Law Revision Committee's Report accepted the proposition that the third party's right should be subject to all defences which would have been available against the promisee.[7] This consequently formed part of the amendments to the law effected in

---

[5]   RSC, O 15, r 5. See also 0 15, rr 2-5 and Commentary; O 18, r 17.

[6]   The contrary argument was put by some consultees who argued that the third party's right was a direct, not a derivative, one, so that only defences relevant to the third party's own conduct should be available to the promisor.

[7]   Law Revision Committee, Sixth Interim Report (1937) para 47: "...the promisor should be entitled to raise against the third party any defence, such as fraud or mistake, that would have been valid against the promisee".

Western Australia[8] and in Queensland.[9] It is noteworthy that neither the Law Revision Committee, nor the Western Australian nor Queensland draftsmen, specifically mentioned set-offs or counterclaims within their recommendations or provisions.[10] While it may be that the term "defences" was intended to include set-offs, it cannot be taken to include counterclaims.

(2) United States

10.6   The Second Restatement[11] provides that a contract which is voidable or unenforceable at the time of its formation can create no superior right in a third party, and that where a contract "ceases to be binding in whole or in part because of impracticability, public policy, non-occurrence of a condition, or present or prospective failure of performance, the right of any beneficiary is to that extent discharged or modified". Thus, the third party's claim is subject to such factors as lack of formation or of consideration, lack of capacity on the part of the contracting parties, fraud or mistake, as tending to vitiate the contract itself; and to any limitations or conditions imposed on the third party's right by the terms of the contract or by the general law.[12] However, it appears that matters arising from other transactions between the promisor and the promisee are not relevant to the third party's claim unless the contract says so.

(3) New Zealand

10.7   The New Zealand Contracts (Privity) Act 1982, section 9(2),[13] provides that,

> [T]he promisor shall have available to him, by way of defence, counterclaim, set-off, or otherwise, any matter which would have been available to him...(b) If (i) The beneficiary were the promisee; and (ii) The promise to which the

---

8   Western Australian Property Law Act 1969, s 11(2)(a): "...all defences that would have been available to the defendant in an action or proceeding in a court of competent jurisdiction to enforce the contract had the plaintiff in the action or proceeding been named as a party to the contract shall be so available".

9   Queensland Property Law Act 1974, s 55(4): "...any matter which would in proceedings not brought in reliance on this section render a promise void, voidable or unenforceable, whether wholly or in part, or which in proceedings (not brought in reliance on this section) to enforce a promissory duty arising from a promise is available by way of defence shall, in like manner and to the like extent, render void, voidable or unenforceable or be available by way of defence in proceedings for the enforcement of a duty to which this section gives effect".

10   See similarly, H McGregor, *Contract Code drawn up on behalf of the English Law Commission*, (1993) s 641, pp 286-7.

11   Restatement (2d) Contracts, § 309.

12   *Corbin on Contracts*, (1951 with supplements) vol 4 para 818. Vol 4 pp 266-273 instances lack of consideration, illegality, lack of capacity, fraud, mistake, lack of formality and non compliance with any requisite condition as "facts that affect the contract in its formation, operating to determine the primary legal relations of the parties". A third party's rights would be limited by such facts.

13   See New Zealand Contracts and Commercial Law Reform Committee, *Privity of Contract* (1981) para 8.2.6. and Appendix, p 75.

proceedings relate had been made for the benefit of the promisee; and (iii) The proceedings had been brought by the promisee.

The formulation is, however, limited by section 9(3) of the Act, which permits a set-off or counterclaim only where this "arises out of or in connection with[14] the deed or contract in which the promise is contained".

3. Options for Reform

10.8   Although we did not specifically address the matter in this way in the Consultation Paper, we now believe that it is helpful to recognise that there are three main possible options as to the scope of the relevant defences, set-offs or counterclaims. First, a third party's claim could be subject only to defences affecting the existence or validity of the contract or the particular contractual provision purporting to benefit the third party. Other defences, set-offs and counterclaims available against the promisee would not be available against the third party. Secondly, the third party's claim could be subject to defences, set-offs or counterclaims, which arise from or in connection with the contract and which would have been available in an action brought by the promisee. This is the option that was essentially favoured in New Zealand.[15] Thirdly, the third party's claim could be subject to all defences, set-offs or counterclaims which would have been available in an action brought by the promisee.

10.9   We believe that, of these, the first and third are respectively too narrow and too wide. The third is too wide given that the third party is not simply stepping into the shoes of the promisee. Moreover, it would be extremely difficult for the third party to discover the whole range of counterclaims that the promisor had against the promisee. The first seems too narrow given that the third party's right derives from the contract. It would prevent the promisor raising any set-off or analogous defence. If B sells goods to A and the contract price is to be paid to C, and B in breach of warranty delivers goods that are not of the standard contracted for, it would seem that, just as in an action for the price by B, so in an action by C, A should be entitled to set up the damages for breach of warranty in diminution or extinction of the price.[16] Again if B induces A to make the promise to benefit C by a fraudulent or negligent misrepresentation, and yet A cannot, or does not wish to, rescind the contract, it would seem that A ought to be able to set off damages for the misrepresentation against a claim by C. Admittedly, to ignore set-offs would still enable the promisor to bring a claim against the promisee. But bringing a claim may be less advantageous

---

[14]   We understand that the words "in connection with" were added in order to safeguard the promisor's remedies in respect of misrepresentation inducing the contract.

[15]   See also Manitoba Law Reform Commission, *Privity of Contract* (1993) pp 63-64 and 77. Having stated that "[t]hird party rights are essentially derivative and not independent and direct" the Commission recommended following the approach in the New Zealand Contracts (Privity) Act 1982 (but without the equivalent of s 9(4)(b): see para 10.10 note 17 below).

[16]   Strictly speaking, the right to set up damages in diminution or extinction of the price is not a set-off (see *Mondel v Steel* (1841) 8 M & W 858; 151 ER 1288) although it is a defence.

than being able to rely on a set-off; apart from the costs the promisor would be seriously prejudiced if the promisee became insolvent.

10.10   In substance, we therefore prefer the second of the three options (that is, the New Zealand approach), which was also the option favoured by the majority of consultees. However, we consider it misleading and unnecessarily complex to include a reference to counterclaims as well as to set-offs. In New Zealand, the inclusion of counterclaims was thought to necessitate section 9(4) of the New Zealand Contracts (Privity) Act 1982, which lays down that: "(a) The beneficiary shall not be liable on the counterclaim, unless the beneficiary elects, with full knowledge of the counterclaim, to proceed with his claim against the promisor; and (b) If the beneficiary so elects to proceed, his liability on the counterclaim shall not in any event exceed the value of the benefit conferred on him by the promise". While we would not have thought section 9(4)(a) to be necessary, a clause along the lines of section 9(4)(b) seems essential if counterclaims are included.[17] In other words, if one includes counterclaims, one needs a separate clause clarifying that there is no question of the third party being *liable* to the extent that the counterclaim exceeds the value of the benefit received by the third party under his claim. There would otherwise be an infringement of the principle that reform of the third party rule is intended to enable the enforcement of benefits by third parties, not to impose burdens. A reference to set-offs only would avoid the need for such an additional clause. Moreover, as one is concerned only with set-offs or counterclaims that arise out of or in connection with the contract, it is difficult to see that the wider scope of counterclaims as opposed to set-offs would be relevant. We are also concerned that the reference to counterclaims - even if of lower value than the third party's claim - implies that the third party can be sued by the promisor for breach of an obligation under the contract. In other words, it is not obvious to us that one can allow the promisor to raise counterclaims while at the same time denying that the promisor can raise the same issues in a separate action against the third party. While it has been suggested to us that to exclude counterclaims might encourage an argument (even though fallacious) by a third party that he or she is not caught by a cross-claim of the promisor's because the cross-claim is a counterclaim and not a set-off, we think that the risks of a misunderstanding of our proposed reform are far greater if one includes counterclaims than if one excludes them.

---

[17]   The draft Bill attached to the Report of the New Zealand Contracts and Commercial Law Reform Committee had no equivalent to s 9(4)(b). In a mirror image to our thinking, the Manitoban Law Reform Commission, Privity of Contract (1993) p 63 recommended the equivalent of s 9(4)(a) without s 9(4)(b).

10.11 We have further departed slightly from the New Zealand approach[18] to the extent that we think it casts the net too wide to include all defences and set-offs "arising out of or in connection with the contract". For where the third party is seeking to enforce a particular contractual provision, rather than the whole contract, it would seem that the defence or set-off should have to be relevant to the particular contractual provision. Otherwise a defence or set-off relating to an entirely separate clause, having no direct relevance to the particular contractual provision being enforced, could be used as a defence or set-off to the third party's claim. For example, if C seeks to enforce a payment obligation to him contained in, say, clause 20 of a construction contract between A and B, C's right should not be limited by a defence or set-off that A has against B in respect of, say, clause 5 which has nothing to do with clause 20.

10.12 We therefore recommend that:

(21) the third party's claim should be subject to all defences and set-offs that would have been available to the promisor in an action by the promisee and which arise out of or in connection with the contract or, insofar as a particular contractual provision is being enforced by the third party, which arise out of or in connection with the contract and are relevant to that contractual provision. (Draft Bill, clause 3(2) and 7(2)(b))

10.13 It was pointed out that allowing the promisor to raise defences (or set-offs or counterclaims) might have serious implications for the third party. For example, one of the advantages of reforming the third party rule is said to be to enable the original parties to a construction contract to grant subsequent owners or occupiers of the building contractual rights to repair of the premises, without the need for collateral warranties to be given to each owner or occupier. But the rights of, say, a subsequent owner, would be diminished if they could be met by a defence that the contractor had against the employer. The defence might be quite unknown to the subsequent owner.

10.14 A similar problem might arise in the context of insurance. A head-contractor might take out a policy to cover itself and all sub-contractors working on a project. If the insurance company could use a defence available against the head-contractor as a defence to an action brought by the sub-contractor, the sub-contractor's claim might be defeated on the ground of, for example, misrepresentation or non-disclosure by the contractor (perhaps even in relation to a quite different aspect of the contract). This would make the insurance cover conferred on the sub-contractor unreliable.

---

[18] Note also that s 9(3) of the Contracts (Privity) Act 1982 applies the restriction "arising out of or in connection with the contract" to set-offs and counterclaims but not to defences. While it would seem to be the case that a defence which could be raised by the promisor against the promisee must inevitably 'arise out of or in connection with the contract' we have decided that it is marginally preferable to apply that restriction to both defences and set-offs. In particular, we would not wish to leave any room for an argument that what one may loosely call a 'set-off' is, strictly speaking, a defence not a set-off and therefore falls outside the restriction. For a case in which technical distinctions between defences and set-offs were raised, see *Henriksens Rederi A/S v THZ Rolimpex, The Brede* [1974] QB 233.

10.15   We accept that the third party's rights may be limited in this way. At root this is the consequence of the third party's rights deriving from the contract between the promisor and the promisee; and, in our view, to require, for example, the promisor to notify the third party of defences and set-offs would place an unfair burden on the promisor.[19] Our preference for the second of the above options reduces the risk for the third party, as against the third option. Moreover, if the contracting parties so wish, they can reduce the potential uncertainty for the third party, by including an express term in the contract to the effect that the promisor may *not* raise any defence or set-off that would be available against the promisee.[20] Conversely, and following the same logic of affording primacy to the contracting parties' intentions, we would also accept that the parties should be able to limit the value of the benefit to the third party by agreeing expressly that the third party's benefit is to be subject to *all* defences and set-offs that the promisor would have had against the promisee (that is, not just those that arise out of or in connection with the contract or, where a particular contractual provision is being enforced, that are relevant to that contractual provision).[21] The third party can only be entitled to what the contracting parties have agreed it should be entitled to.

10.16   We therefore recommend that:

(22)   **the contracting parties may include an express provision to the effect that the promisor may *not* raise any defence or set-off that would have been available against the promisee; conversely, the parties may include an express provision to the effect that the third party's claim is subject to *all* defences and set-offs that the promisor would have had against the promisee.** (Draft Bill, clause 3(3))

[19]   This is supported by the fact that the third party, as a volunteer, cannot be a bona fide purchaser without notice.

[20]   A hypothetical illustration may here be useful. Say B agrees with A, who is an art dealer, to purchase a painting as a gift for C, his niece. A and B expressly confer a right of enforceability on C for non-delivery. B owes A considerable sums for other art works purchased. B wishes to ensure that the transaction in C's favour is not affected by this fact. A and B expressly agree that A may only raise against C defences and set-offs that would have been available independently against her. We also here have in mind where A excludes his liability to B but expressly indicates that the exclusion is not to apply to C. Clearly we do not want recommendation 21 to mean that A can ignore the express indication and raise the exclusion against C.

[21]   The following hypothetical illustration may be helpful. Say A and B agree that A will pay C if B transfers his car to A. B owes A substantial sums of money from the collapse of B's business. A's claims against B do not arise from or in connection with the contract for the transfer of the car. Nevertheless A procures B's agreement to an express clause which entitles A to raise against a claim by C any matter which would have given him a defence or set-off to a claim by B.

4. Defences, Set-Offs and Counterclaims Available Only Against the Third Party

10.17   In the above discussion, as in the Consultation Paper, it has been assumed that the question at issue is whether a defence, set-off or counterclaim, that was available to the promisor against the promisee, should also be made available in an action by the third party. However, a number of consultees pointed out that a question also arises as to whether the promisor can raise any defences, set-offs or counterclaims that are specific to the third party alone and would not have been available to the promisor in an action by the promisee. For example, a tenant who is entitled to the benefit of a promise by the contractor to repair the premises might already owe the same firm money for alterations previously carried out to the premises. Similarly the contract between the promisor and the promisee may have been induced by a misrepresentation to the promisor, or undue influence exerted against the promisor, by the third party of which the promisee had no notice.[22] Consultees suggested that the promisor should be entitled to rely on such defences, set-offs and counterclaims. We agree and, although we have had some doubts as to whether a specific legislative provision on this is necessary - or whether, on the contrary, the standard rules on defences, set-offs and counterclaims would inevitably be applied to the third party's action in any event - we have ultimately decided that a clarificatory provision would be preferable.[23]

10.18   We should also emphasise that there is no objection here to including counterclaims. To include counterclaims would not infringe the principle that contractual burdens should not be imposed on the third party because what one here has in mind are independent claims that the promisor would, in any event, have had against the third party (for example, tort damages for a fraudulent or negligent misstatement by the third party inducing the contract). However, to avoid any possibility of our reform leading to a contractual burden being imposed on the third party, one must confine the counterclaims to those that do not arise from the contract.

10.19   We therefore recommend that:

   (23)   it should be made clear that, in addition to the third party's claim being subject to defences and set-offs that the promisor would have had available in an action by the promisee, the third party's claim is also to be subject to the defences, counterclaims (not arising from the contract)

---

[22]   Cf *Barclays Bank plc v O'Brien* [1994] 1 AC 180 which establishes that a contracting party (A) will only be able to set aside a contract that he has been induced to enter into by the undue influence or misrepresentation of a third party (C) if the other contracting party (B) had actual or constructive notice of the undue influence or misrepresentation or if the third party was acting as agent for B.

[23]   Section 9(2)(a) of the New Zealand Contracts (Privity) Act 1982 is directed to this point.

and set-offs that would have been available to the promisor had the third party been a party to the contract.[24] (Draft Bill, clause 3(4))

10.20   Similarly to recommendation (22), we consider that recommendation (23) should be subject to an express provision in the contract by which the contracting parties lay down that the third party's claim shall not be subject to defences, counterclaims (not arising from the contract), and set-offs that would otherwise have been available against the third party.[25] But we would not wish to allow the contracting parties to widen the range of counterclaims available against the third party as this might lead to the imposition of burdens. And in this context there can be no question of the contracting parties *expanding* the range of defences or set-offs because the promisor is already entitled to all the defences or set-offs that would independently have been available against the third party.

10.21   We therefore recommend that:

> **(24) the contracting parties may include an express provision to the effect that the promisor may *not* raise any defence, set-off or counterclaim that would have been available to the promisor had the third party been a party to the contract.** (Draft Bill, clause 3(5))

5. Thirty Party Enforcing an Exclusion or Limitation Clause

10.22   An analogous approach to that put forward in recommendations 21 and 23 above should apply where the third party seeks to enforce an exclusion or limitation clause in a claim (for example, in tort) that is brought against him by the promisor. That is, the third party should not be able to rely on an exclusion or limitation clause if it was invalid as between the contracting parties (for example, because induced by the promisee's fraud, duress or undue influence or because it falls foul of the Unfair

---

[24]   We have had some concern as to whether this recommendation achieves our desired result of preventing the third party enforcing the contract in the situation where the contract between the promisor and the promisee has been induced by a misrepresentation to the promisor, or undue influence exerted against the promisor, by the third party, of which the promisee had no notice. Had the third party *been a party to the contract,* would the promisor have been able to *rescind* the contract so as to have had a defence *to his claim?* We have been unable to find any authority on the question whether in multi-party contracts, the misrepresentation or undue influence of any of the parties to the contract entitles the promisor to rescind the contract so as not to be bound to perform the promise: cf Treitel, *The Law of Contract* (9th ed, 1995) p 531. But we tend to think that, even if the whole contract cannot be rescinded, (and note that *TSB Bank plc v Camfield* [1995] 1 WLR 430 rules out rescission on terms) the promisor does have a defence to a claim brought by a misrepresentor or a person who has exerted undue influence: see Treitel, *The Law of Contract* (9th ed, 1995) pp 342, 344-345.

[25]   The following hypothetical illustration may be helpful. A agrees with B to pay £5000 to C if B will transfer a number of cases of vintage wine to A. C is a creditor of B's. C is also the local garage owner and B is aware that A and C have recently had a disagreement about the quality of repairs done to A's car by C. B is concerned that A may seek to withhold part of the benefit destined for C by raising a counterclaim against C for the damage to his car. Consequently A and B include an express provision that A may raise no defences, set-offs or counterclaims of any nature whatever against a claim by C to enforce A's contractual obligation to pay the £5000.

Contract Terms Act 1977); or where the third party's own conduct (for example, fraud by the third party not known about by the promisee) renders the clause unenforceable by the third party. Yet in respect of exclusion and limitation clauses (and conceivably analogous types of clause) it is inappropriate to talk of defences available to the promisor. It seems preferable, therefore, to have a separate provision to the effect that the third party can only rely on the exclusion or limitation clause to the extent that he could have done so had he been a party to the contract (where this phrase means to include matters that affect the validity of the exclusion clause as between the contracting parties as well as matters affecting validity or enforceability that relate only to the third party).[26]

10.23   We therefore recommend that:

(25) **where the third party seeks to rely on the test of enforceability to enforce an exclusion or limitation clause (or conceivably an analogous type of clause) he may do so only to the extent that he could have done so had he been a party to the contract (where the phrase 'had he been a party to the contract' means to refer to matters that affect the validity of the clause as between the contracting parties as well as matters affecting validity or enforceability that relate only to the third party).** (Draft Bill, clause 3(6))

6. The Line Between Benefits and Burdens

10.24   As was explained in paragraph 2.1 above, our recommended reforms, in line with the provisional view in the Consultation Paper,[27] do not seek to change the present rule, or the exceptions to it, whereby parties cannot impose an obligation upon a third party. However, we went on in the Consultation Paper to explain that it was also our provisional view - and there was no dissent from this by consultees - that the contracting parties may impose conditions upon the enjoyment of any benefit by the third party.[28] If the third party took a benefit that was qualified or conditional but could ignore the qualification or condition, it would be getting something it was never intended to have. Although we wish to confirm our provisional view, this issue of conditional benefits is not entirely straightforward.

10.25   There is a distinction between imposing a burden on the third party and conferring a conditional benefit upon him. The distinction is an easy one to draw where the condition does not require performance by the third party. For example, a benefit which is made conditional on the third party reaching a certain age clearly imposes no

---

[26]   One cannot simply use the formulation that 'the third party may rely on the clause only to the extent that the *promisee* could have done so' because, for example, this would render unenforceable by the third party an exclusion clause in A's contract with B which excludes C's (but not B's) liability in tort to A.

[27]   Consultation Paper No 121, paras 5.36 and 6.17.

[28]   *Ibid.*

burden on the third party. If the third party sued for breach of contract before reaching the specified age, its claim would fail on the basis that there had been no breach because the condition for the promisor's performance had not occurred. Alternatively, one can say that the promisor would have a defence in line with recommendations (21) or (23) above.

10.26 Drawing the distinction is, perhaps, more difficult where the condition requires performance by the third party.[29] Take, for example, a contract between A and B in which A agrees to grant a right of way over its land to C on condition that C keeps it in repair. If C satisfies the test of enforceability, to what extent, if at all, is C bound by the repairing obligation?[30]

10.27 Our view is that C is 'bound' by the condition (the repairing obligation) in the very limited sense that A can use that condition as the basis of a defence or set-off to a claim by C to enforce the contract. In contrast, C would not be bound by the condition (the repairing obligation) in the sense that C can be sued for breach of that repairing obligation: that is, A cannot bring a claim or counterclaim against C for breach of contract. So where C fails to keep the right of way in repair, A would be entitled to withdraw that right (for example, by blocking it off) and would have a defence to any action by C for withdrawal of the right of way. In contrast if A sued C for breach of the repairing obligation that claim would fail because a third party cannot have burdens imposed on it by a contract to which it is not a party.

10.28 We recognise that the approach we are here taking constitutes a narrow view of the extent to which a person who takes a benefit must also take the burden. But our narrow approach is based on avoiding the possibility of the third party being overall worse off (unless bound by, for example, a contract or trust) by being given the right to enforce, and enforcing, a contract to which he was not a party. If conditions attached to the benefit are to be independently enforceable against the third party,

---

[29] We are here assuming that there is no contract between the third party and the promisor. The courts may find that terms conferring a conditional benefit on a third party actually give rise to a collateral contract between the third party and the promisor. For this to be the case, the term conferring the benefit would have to be construed as an offer made by the promisor to the third party, and the third party would have to accept this. So, for example, if A promises B to loan C £1000 provided C repays £1000 to A after a year, we would regard C's right of enforceability as normally being subject to C undertaking to repay the £1000 to A: that is, there would normally need to be a contract between A and C before C has rights (and duties). But if there is no contract between A and C, A would, in any event, normally have a restitutionary claim against C to recover the money paid on the basis of failure of consideration: see P Birks, *An Introduction to the Law of Restitution* (revised ed, 1989) chapter 7, esp pp 222-226; A Burrows, *The Law of Restitution* (1993) chapter 9, esp pp 251-253, 320-321.

[30] Another useful example is where a warranty, given by a construction company to a subsequent owner of the building, is subject to conditions as to inspection and maintenance by the occupier or to the payment of an annual fee to the construction company. A further example is a bank's undertaking to pay under a letter of credit against presentation of shipping documents. The beneficiary owes no duty to the bank to present anything but unless he does so he will not get paid.

rather than merely providing a defence or set-off to an action by him, it would be necessary for the third party to have undertaken to abide by those conditions: that is, it would be necessary for the 'third party' to be in a contractual relationship with the promisor.[31]

10.29 A useful, if not exact, analogy can be drawn between our willingness to permit the conferral of conditional benefits but not the imposition of burdens, and the law of assignment. One contracting party may not assign the burden of a contract to a third party.[32] Where, however, rights are assigned, the extent of the rights assigned are defined by the contract. Thus an exemption clause which is construed as defining the limits of the assignor's rights will be binding on an assignee.[33] Similarly, the assignment of a conditional benefit may require satisfaction of the condition if the remainder of the right assigned is to be enjoyed: the restrictions or qualifications may be an integral part of the right which the assignee must take as it stands.[34] However, it should be noted that a difference between our reform and assignment is that the assignor would normally be liable for breach of the conditions attached to the benefit assigned. In contrast, where a conditional benefit is conferred on a third party it is unlikely that the promisee will have guaranteed or contracted to procure the third party's performance of the condition.

10.30 A very important example of a condition being attached to the benefit enforceable by the third party (C) is where in the contract between A and B benefiting C, there is a clause excluding or limiting A's liability to C. C's right to enforce A's promise under our proposed Act must be subject to the exclusion or limitation clause.

10.31 We also think it important to clarify that the relevant condition may be that the promisee does not choose to exercise a discretion given to him to divert the benefit from the third party. Say, for example, A contracts with B to deliver goods to C or as B shall direct.[35] Assuming that C can satisfy the test of enforceability, it is plain that C's right is conditional on B not choosing to divert the goods to someone else. If B directs A to deliver to D instead of to C, C cannot sue A for non-delivery: that is, A

---

[31] We are here assuming that none of the standard exceptions to the 'burden' aspect of privity is applicable: see para 2.1, note 5, above.

[32] *Tolhurst v Associated Portland Cement Manufacturers Ltd* [1902] 2 KB 660, 668; *Pan Ocean Shipping Co Ltd v Creditcorp Ltd* [1994] 1 WLR 161. See also *Chitty on Contracts* (27th ed 1994) paras 19-043ff.

[33] *Britain & Overseas Trading (Bristles) Ltd v Brooks Wharf & Bull Wharf Ltd* [1967] 2 Lloyd's Rep 51. See also *Chitty on Contracts* (27th ed 1994) para 19-044.

[34] *Tito v Waddell (No 2)* [1977] Ch 106, 290, 302 per Megarry VC. It should be noted that after *Rhone v Stephens* [1994] 2 AC 310, the types of conditions which will be enforced will be strictly limited to those which are "relevant to the exercise of the right" (per Lord Templeman at p 322).

[35] For this sort of contract see, eg, *Mitchell v Ede* (1840) 11 Ad & El 888; 113 ER 651.

can raise against C the defence that A would have had against an action by B for non-delivery to C.

10.32 Therefore we recommend that:

(26) **the present general rule whereby parties to a contract cannot impose burdens upon third parties should be retained, although they may impose conditions upon the enjoyment of any benefits by them. The distinction between imposing burdens and conditional benefits (and hence the line between what falls outside our reform and what falls within it) depends on whether the condition is the basis merely of a defence or set-off to the third party's claim or whether, on the contrary, the condition is the basis of a claim or counterclaim by the promisor against the third party. This recommendation therefore ties in with recommendations (21) and (23) above and no further legislative provision is required.**

PART XI
OVERLAPPING CLAIMS

1. More Than One Plaintiff: Claims by the Third Party and by the Promisee

(1) Promisee's Rights

11.1   If our principal proposed reform is accepted, so that where the test of enforceability is satisfied a third party will have the right to enforce the contract, the question arises as to the promisee's rights. Does the recognition of the third party's rights mean that the promisee has no right to sue on the contract?

11.2   In the Consultation Paper,[1] the provisional recommendation was made that the promisor's duty to perform should be owed both to the third party and to the promisee: that is, the third party's rights should be additional to, and not at the expense of, the promisee's rights. This was supported by the vast majority of consultees. It also appears to be the position in the other common law jurisdictions that have departed from the third party rule.[2]

11.3   We are convinced that permitting a double action is the correct approach. There is no reason to remove a contractual right from the promisee (for which, in a contract supported by consideration, he or she has bargained) merely because the contract gives rights of enforcement to a third party.

11.4   We therefore recommend that:

(27)   **the promisor's duty to perform should be owed to both the promisee and the third party and, consequently, unless otherwise agreed between the contracting parties, the promisee should retain the right to enforce a contract even if the contract is also enforceable at the suit of the third party.** (Draft Bill, clause 4)

(2) Promisee's Rights Where Performance by Promisor to Third Party

11.5   It was provisionally proposed in the Consultation Paper that a promisor who performs his obligation to the third party should be discharged from any further obligation to

---

[1]   Consultation Paper No 121, para 5.34.

[2]   See, eg, the New Zealand Contracts (Privity) Act 1982, s 14(1)(a); Queensland Property Law Act 1974 s 55(7) (although those provisions are probably primarily concerned with preserving the third party's existing rights). See also Manitoba Law Reform Commission, *Privity of Contract* (1993) pp 64-5. The United States Restatement (2d) Contracts § 305(1) allows the promisee to enforce the promise; it speaks of the promise creating duties to both promisee and third party. Corbin states, "...several actions on one promise are not necessarily regarded as unjust...[this] is witnessed by the law of joint and several contracts". *Corbin on Contracts* (1951 with supplements) vol 4 para 824 cites *Baurer v Devenis*, 121 A 566, 570 (1923) per Wheeler CJ: "Nor can the injustice of possibly permitting two actions against a promisor be allowed the consideration heretofore given it. It was optional with the promisor whether he should engage in this performance for the third party. Having voluntarily so agreed, it is no hardship to require him to fulfil his agreement".

the promisee.[3] This seems self-evident and there was no dissent from it on consultation. This is also in accordance with section 305(2) of the United States Second Restatement which lays down that, "Whole or partial satisfaction of the promisor's duty to the beneficiary satisfies to that extent the promisor's duty to the promisee."

11.6   We therefore recommend that:

(28)   although no legislative provision on this is necessary, a promisor who has fulfilled its duty to the third party, whether wholly or partly, should to that extent be discharged from its duty to the promisee.

(3) Promisee's Rights Where Release of/Settlement with Promisor by Third Party

11.7   It was provisionally proposed in the Consultation Paper that a promisor who has been released by the third party should be discharged from any further obligation to the promisee.[4] However, it was pointed out to us on consultation that the performance of a single promise might benefit both promisee and third party, rather than being for the exclusive benefit of the third party. In that situation, at the very least, the promisee should not be deprived of his right of action by the third party's release of the promisor from further obligations to him. Our initial reaction to this was to think in terms of a provision which drew a distinction between releases where the contract was for the exclusive benefit of the third party and releases where the contract was for the benefit of both promisee and third party: only the former type of release given by the third party would operate to release the promisor's obligation to the promisee. But such a provision would not only be very complex but would run the danger of creating litigation on the issue of whether the contract was for the exclusive benefit of the third party or not. We have therefore ultimately opted for the simpler clearer solution that a third party cannot release the promisor's obligation to the promisee (unless otherwise agreed in the original contract). This seems to us to accord with the fact that the promisee is, after all, the contracting party and we think it right that the promisor should seek a release from him as well as from the third party. Moreover this approach follows from a standard principle, relating to a release given by a 'several creditor', namely that a several creditor can only give an effective release of an obligation owed to himself and not to someone else.[5] Of course, it would be a very odd situation where a third party wishes to release the promisor and the promisee does not wish to do so and yet the promisee has nothing to gain from performance.

11.8   We therefore recommend that:

(29)   although no legislative provision on this is necessary, a release given to the promisor by the third party should not discharge the promisor's

---

[3]   Consultation Paper No 121, para 5.34.

[4]   Consultation Paper No 121, para 5.34.

[5]   See Treitel, *Law of Contract* (9th ed, 1995) p 532.

obligation to the promisee (unless otherwise agreed in the original contract).

(4) Releases Where More Than One Third Party

11.9 Although not relating to a promisee's rights or to overlapping claims, this seems the most convenient place to mention releases where there is more than one third party, who has the right to enforce the contract. What is the impact of a release by one third party on the promisor's obligation to the others?[6] In our view, (and unless otherwise agreed in the original contract) this turns on whether the promise is intended to confer enforceable rights that are to be separately, or jointly, enjoyed with other third parties. If the promised benefit is to be enjoyed separately or independently, the release by one third party should not discharge the promisor's obligation to the other third parties. Say, for example, A contracts with B to pay C £100 and D £150. A release by C should not operate to discharge A's liability to D.[7] The promises of payment are independent of each other. The same would apply if terms in a construction contract are to be for the benefit of each subsequent occupier of the building. In contrast, if A contractually promises B to pay £100 to C and D jointly or to transfer land into the joint ownership of C and D, the promise is for the benefit of C and D jointly. A release given by either C or D should normally release A's obligations to C and D.[8] All these consequences follow directly, or by analogy, from standard principles relating to releases where there is a plurality of creditors.[9]

11.10 We therefore recommend that:

(30) **although no legislative provision on this is necessary,[10] the effect of a release of the promisor by one third party on the promisor's obligations to another third party is dependent (unless otherwise agreed in the original contract) on whether the promise is for the benefit of the third parties independently of each other, or whether it is for the benefit of the third parties jointly. If the promised benefit is to be enjoyed independently, the release by one third party should not discharge the promisor's obligation to the other third parties. But if the promise is for the joint benefit of the third parties, the release by one third party**

---

[6] An analogous issue is whether a variation or cancellation made by the contracting parties with the consent of one party (whose rights have crystallised) is valid vis-a-vis another non-consenting third party (whose rights have crystallised). For the somewhat similar question as to when there is a crystallisation of a third party's rights, where there is more than one third party, see para 9.43 above.

[7] In support of this see, eg, *Wilson & Co Inc v Hartford Fire Insurance Co*, 254 SW 266 (1923).

[8] This is to apply the standard law on releases given by joint creditors: a well-recognised exception is that, if the release is given by one joint creditor in clear fraud of another, the latter can have it set aside. See, eg, *Jones v Herbert* (1817) 7 Taunt 421; 129 ER 168; *Innell v Newman* (1821) 4 B & Ald 419; 106 ER 990; *Barker v Richardson* (1827) 1 Y & J 362; 148 ER 710; *Wallace v Kelsall* (1840) 7 M & W 264; 151 ER 765; *Phillips v Clagett* (1843) 11 M & W 84; 152 ER 725.

[9] See Treitel, *The Law of Contract* (9th ed, 1995) p 532.

[10] See para 9.44, note 35, above.

should normally discharge the promisor's obligation to the other third parties.

(5) Third Party's Rights Where Performance by Promisor to Promisee (Rather than to Third Party), or Release of/Settlement with Promisor by Promisee

11.11 This issue is closely linked with that of variation or cancellation of the third party's right by the contracting parties. The vast majority of consultees accepted our suggestion that, "[s]o long as the contract can still be varied, performance in favour of the promisee should arguably discharge the promisor and the third party would have no rights. Once the contract cannot be varied, the promisor should arguably have to perform in favour of his creditor, ie the third party."[11] We therefore now adopt this approach and consider that it should be extended to where the promisee releases or settles with the promisor.

11.12 Hence we recommend that:

(31) performance by the promisor to the promisee (rather than to the third party) and accepted by the promisee, or the release of the promisor by the promisee, should be straightforwardly regarded as a variation or cancellation of the contract and should therefore be governed by the recommendations in Part IX above.

11.13 A number of respondents suggested that this solution might be unfair if the promisor was not aware that the contract could not be varied when he rendered performance to the promisee. We do not agree. First, the promisor should take steps to discover whether the contract can still be varied before performing in a way that does not conform to his original obligation. Secondly, it would presumably be possible in most cases[12] for the promisor to recover money paid or the value of services rendered to the promisee by mistake via an action in restitution. Of course, there is the danger that in the meantime the promisee will have become insolvent, but that is a risk the promisor must take if he chooses unilaterally to vary the contract.

(6) Priority of Action?

11.14 If the promisee is to have a right of action, it must be asked whether he or she should be able to exercise that right at any time. It could be argued that some order of priority of actions should be developed; for if both the promisee and the third party sue in separate actions, the promisor would be confronted with the costs and inconvenience of two actions for enforcement of the same duty. It might be argued, for example, that the third party should have the first option to sue, and that it should

---

[11] Consultation Paper No 121, para 5.34.

[12] Where the money was paid or the services rendered under a mistake of fact. The dividing line between mistakes of fact and of law is difficult to draw. We have recommended that the distinction should be abolished: Restitution: Mistakes of Law and Ultra Vires Public Authority Receipts and Payments (1994) Law Com No 227.

only be open to the promisee to sue if the third party does not take the opportunity to sue. However, we regard the promisee and the third party as having separate rights so that it would seem wrong in principle to bar the promisee's claim by such a rule of priority of action. Rather the appropriate procedural approach in many cases (although we do not think that this should be a requirement) is for the third party to be joined as a party where the promisee sues.[13]

11.15 We therefore recommend that:

(32) there should be no order of priority between promisee and third party.

(7) Avoidance of Double Liability

11.16 The above recommendations (especially recommendation 27) may be thought to raise the problem of double liability: that is, of the promisor being liable to pay substantial damages to both the promisee and the third party for essentially the same loss. This problem will not arise if the promisee is entitled merely to nominal damages or if he or she is granted specific performance of the promisor's obligation to benefit the third party. Nor will there be a problem if the third party first recovered damages because then the promisee would be left with no corresponding loss outstanding.

11.17 We also do not think that there is a risk of double liability where the promisee recovers the third party's loss under one of the exceptions to the standard rule that the promisee is entitled to damages for its own loss only. Our understanding of the relevant law is that, in that situation, the third party could not subsequently recover substantial damages from the promisor under our proposals. In *The Albazero*[14], in which the House of Lords drew together the exceptions where the promisee can recover the third party's loss (for example, a consignee suing a carrier for damage to the owners' goods; and a bailee suing a tortfeasor for damage to his bailor's goods), Lord Diplock appeared to regard the promisee as being accountable for the damages received, in an action for money had and received, to the third party.[15] The duty to account means that the third party has no loss to recover from the promisor. And although the question of there being a duty to account was not specifically addressed in *Linden Gardens Trust Ltd v Lenesta Sludge Disposals Ltd*[16] it is important to note that Lord Browne-Wilkinson said that, where the third party itself had a direct cause of action, the rationale for allowing the promisee to recover the third party's loss was

---

[13] We discuss in paras 14.1-14.5 below the rules as to joinder, in the context of whether the promisee should be joined in an action by the third party. Those rules are equally applicable in the context of whether the third party should be joined in an action by the promisee. Note also that under RSC, O 4, r 9 the court has the power to order consolidation of actions where "some common question of law or fact arises in both...of them, or...the rights to relief claimed therein are in respect of or arise out of the same transaction or series of transactions, or ... for some other reason it is desirable to make an order".

[14] [1977] AC 774.

[15] [1977] AC 774, 845-846. See also Treitel, *The Law of Contract* (9th ed, 1995) p 550.

[16] [1994] 1 AC 85. See above paras 2.39-2.46.

inapplicable.[17] If so, the promisee would be unable to recover damages for the third party's loss where our Act gives the third party a right of enforceability.

11.18   The position is more difficult where the promisee recovers substantial damages for its own loss in circumstances where that loss is assessed on the basis that the promisee will "cure" the breach and yet the promisee does not then do so.[18] Say, for example, B has contracted for A to build a wall on C's land and C has been expressly given the right of enforceability. On a failure by A to build the wall, B recovers substantial damages on the basis that it will now pay for another builder to construct the wall. If the wall is not then built and C subsequently sues A, it would appear that C too has a claim against A for substantial damages. Or, let us assume that the promisee has a pre-existing liability to pay the third party £1000 and hence renders it a term of its contract with the promisor, in return for services rendered by the promisee, that the promisor pays £1000 to the third party. If the promisor fails to pay £1000 and if the third party can satisfy the test of enforceability, it would appear that both the promisee (because he will now have to find another £1000 to pay the third party) and the third party (in a subsequent action where the promisee has not paid him) have a claim against the promisor for damages (or the award of the agreed sum) of £1000.[19]

11.19   One possible answer to the risk of double liability in this situation is that, where the third party sues, the promisor could require the promisee to account to the third party for the damages recovered. In *Corbin on Contracts* there is the following illuminating passage: "The possibility of injustice to the promisor in allowing double recovery in separate actions appears to be slight. It is true that the third party may get judgment for the full value of the promised performance; also, that the promisee may get judgment for an equally large amount, being the amount of the debt owed by him to the third party - a debt that would have been satisfied by the promised performance. In neither suit does the jury have to consider the possibility that the promisor may later be compelled to perform under another judgment. But if the promisor does so perform, he is not without remedy. *If he satisfies the judgment of the promisee he has an equitable right that the promisee shall use the proceeds, other than costs, in satisfaction of the judgment obtained by the third party.* If he satisfies the judgment of the third party, this would operate to satisfy pro tanto the debt of the promisee to the third party and should also be provable in a supplementary proceeding to reduce the judgment of the

---

[17]   [1994] 1 AC 85, 115. See para 2.40 above.

[18]   A possible analogous problem is where the promisee recovers substantial damages representing the cost of cure and then the third party sues for specific performance. However, it would seem that in that situation the flexibility of the principles governing specific performance would enable the courts straightforwardly to avoid the promisor's double liability (eg, by refusing specific performance on the ground that damages are adequate or, possibly, by making the order conditional on the promisor being repaid its damages by the promisee).

[19]   *Quaere* whether the appropriate remedy for the third party lies in an action for the agreed sum. Note that, as is discussed below, the third party also has a claim against the promisee on the pre-existing liability. See paras 11.23-11.27, below.

promisee against the promisor".[20] For the equitable right referred to, Corbin relies on the case of *Joseph W North & Son Inc v North*.[21] Here the plaintiff bought the defendant's business and agreed to fulfil all outstanding orders to existing customers. The plaintiff also agreed to indemnify the defendant against existing liabilities. The plaintiff committed a breach, and the defendant sued on the indemnity, obtaining judgment. This did not discharge the plaintiff's duty to the existing customers, but it was held that he had an equity to avoid double liability for the same harm, and that the amount of the judgment should be so applied as to prevent such double liability.[22] Some support for such a proposition in English law may be deduced from *Loosemore v Radford*,[23] which was cited in *Joseph W North & Son v North*. In that case, the plaintiff was surety for the defendant's liability to X. Fearful that the defendant would default and that he would be left with inadequate remedies against him, the plaintiff obtained from the defendant a separate covenant to pay him the amount of the principal debt. The plaintiff then sued on this and recovered judgment for the full amount. The defendant appealed, pointing out that the plaintiff had not been called upon to pay under the guarantee. Parke B said that the defendant might have an equity that any sums he might pay to the plaintiff should be applied in discharge of his debt to X, but since the action was one at law, the plaintiff was entitled to recover full damages under his separate covenant with the defendant. Although not precisely on the point, the case seems to suggest that equity would prevent a debtor from being forced to pay twice for what was in substance the same loss. Such a principle, applied by analogy to our third party beneficiary situation, would prevent double liability of the promisor to both the promisee and the third party.[24]

11.20   It must be recognised, however, that the basis of this equitable right, if it exists at all, is unclear. Although one may be tempted to think that the principle against unjust enrichment is involved, it is not easy to see on what conventional ground the promisee is thought to be *unjustly* enriched at the expense of the promisor (or the third party). In our view, therefore, it is preferable to ensure the protection of the promisor by a

[20]   (1951, with supplements) vol 4, para 824 (emphasis added). See also Restatement (2d) Contracts § 305.

[21]   110 A 581 (1920).

[22]   Backes VC of New Jersey said, at p 582, "[T]he proposition that the complainant ought not to be twice mulcted (sic) in damages for breaches of covenants involving the same subject matter and resulting in a single injury, and that equity will protect against such evil consequences, is sound in principle and supported by authority". However he refused to find a trust in the complainant's favour of sums paid over under the first judgment, and instead held that a bare equity of appropriation of the proceeds of judgment existed, to the extinguishment of the defendant's dual liability so far as they might be necessary for that purpose and no more.

[23]   (1842) 9 M & W 655; 152 ER 277.

[24]   It must be noted, however, that there are cases which, arguably, cast doubt on the suggestion made in *Loosemore v Radford*. See *Re Law Guarantee Trust & Accident Society Ltd* [1914] 2 Ch 617; *Carr v Roberts* (1833) 5 B & Ad 78; 110 ER 721; *Re Walker, Sheffield Banking Co v Clayton* [1892] 1 Ch 621. See also Philips & O'Donovan, *The Modern Contract of Guarantee* (2nd ed, 1992) p 479.

statutory provision designed to avoid double liability.[25] And if the legislation is to include a provision to deal with this situation (where the promisee has recovered damages for its own loss) it would be prudent, so as to avoid confusion, to incorporate the exceptional situations where the promisee has recovered the third party's loss (although, as we have explained above,[26] we believe that, in any event, there would be no realistic prospect of double liability in those situations).

11.21   We therefore recommend that:

(33)   **where the promisee has recovered substantial damages (or an agreed sum) representing the third party's loss or assessed on the basis that the promisee will "cure" the breach for the third party, the third party will not be entitled under our proposed Act to an award which duplicates that sum and thereby imposes double liability on the promisor.** (Draft Bill, clause 5)

11.22   We should add that our concern here is to protect the promisor against double liability. We consider that it is best left to the courts to determine precisely when the promisee may be under a duty to account to the third party for the sum that the promisee has recovered. In the event of the promisee's insolvency, it will also be necessary for the courts to determine whether the third party has a proprietary remedy (through a trust or lien) or a personal remedy against the promisee.[27]

2.   More Than One Defendant: Claims by the Third Party Against the Promisor, and Against the Promisee on a Pre-Existing Liability

11.23   A situation discussed in the consultation paper was that of where the contractual benefit to the third party comprises the performance by the promisor of a pre-existing liability that the promisee owed to the third party. We provisionally recommended that, "where the promisor's performance is designed to discharge an existing obligation of the promisee to the third party, the third party should be able to pursue claims against either the promisor or the promisee, and his acceptance of benefits under the contract should discharge his rights against the promisee only to the extent that such obligation is thereby fulfilled".[28] Through that provisional recommendation, we were concerned to clarify that the giving of rights to the third party against the promisor does not automatically lead to it losing its rights against the promisee. While we adhere to that position, we believe that the position is so plain that no legislative provision to that effect is required.

---

[25]   See, analogously, s 7 of the Torts (Interference with Goods) Act 1977. Cf *O'Sullivan v Williams* [1992] 3 All ER 385.

[26]   See para 11.17 above.

[27]   See, analogously, *Lord Napier and Ettrick v Hunter* [1993] AC 713; *Hunt v Severs* [1994] 2 AC 350.

[28]   Consultation Paper No 121, para 6.16. See also para 5.35.

11.24   Of course this does not mean that the third party can recover twice over. Performance by the promisor will operate to discharge the promisee's pre-existing liability to the third party. Similarly, if the third party chooses to pursue the promisee, performance by the promisee will operate to discharge the promisor's contractual liability to the third party. In the latter situation, the promisee will be able to obtain an indemnity or reimbursement from the promisor: even if that is not provided for in the contract between the promisor and the promisee, this would be imposed by the law of restitution on the basis that, under legal compulsion, the promisee has discharged the promisor's liability where, as between the promisor and the promisee (according to their contract), the promisor is the primary debtor.[29] In the Consultation Paper[30] we also briefly questioned whether the third party should be required to pursue the promisor first before pursuing the promisee. We now confirm that, as is the standard position where a person has several separate rights against the same person, we do not believe that there should be any order of priority for enforcement of the third party's right.

11.25   However, several consultees drew attention to the need to ensure that, where the third party had agreed that the promisor's promise to perform will constitute a settlement or discharge of the promisee's obligation to him, the third party would not be permitted to resile from this by suing the promisee on the pre-existing obligation. We agree that this should be the legal position but we do not think that any legislative provision is needed to ensure this; the application of standard contractual principles is sufficient.

11.26   Therefore we recommend that:
        (34) **while no legislative provision to this effect is required, where a third party has pre-existing legal rights against the promisee, he should not lose those rights because the promisor and promisee enter into a contract whereby the promisor agrees to discharge the promisee's liability to the third party, but should acquire an additional right against the promisor;**
        (35) **while it is unnecessary for there to be a legislative provision on this, no compromise or settlement of the promisee's liability to the third party by the conferral of enforceable contractual rights against the promisor should be disturbed.**

11.27   The operation of those two recommendations can be illustrated as follows. Say, B owes C a sum of money. If B contracts with A that A will pay the sum to C then, under our proposals, C will have a third party action against A, provided C can satisfy the test of enforceability. Alternatively, C could sue B (recommendation 34). However, if C agrees with B that B's liability should be discharged by B securing A's

---

[29] See Goff and Jones, *The Law of Restitution* (4th ed, 1993) chapter 14; A Burrows *The Law of Restitution* (1993), chapter 7.

[30] Consultation Paper No 121, para. 5.35.

promise to pay C, then B should be discharged and C's only right of action would lie against A (recommendation 35). It should be emphasised that, for recommendation 35 to operate, B and C must have contracted to discharge B's liability; B would still remain liable if, for example, the true construction of the agreement was that C agreed not to sue B unless A defaulted on the obligation and A then does default.

PART XII
EXISTING EXCEPTIONS

1. Preserving Existing Exceptions

12.1   In the Consultation Paper, it was provisionally recommended that existing statutory exceptions to the third party rule should be preserved.[1] We made no provisional recommendations in relation to existing common law exceptions.[2] Some consultees suggested that the existing exceptions to the privity rule could best be preserved by statutory listing. We remain of the opinion that current statutory exceptions should be preserved, but we have concluded that this can be achieved by a general provision (to the effect that our proposed Act is to be without prejudice to any right or remedy of a third party which exists apart from the Act) rather than a more elaborate statutory listing. We also see no merit in attempting to abolish the common law exceptions, some of which give third parties more secure rights than will be given by our proposed reform. Others have developed through somewhat artificial and forced use of existing concepts, and we would expect that such exceptions would wither away as a consequence of our reform, which will render such artificiality unnecessary. Nor do we think that the common law exceptions should be listed or codified. Many of the common law exceptions are vague and shifting[3] and to codify or even list them might deprive the judges of flexibility in the development of the law in future. We would therefore recommend a general provision (as above) preserving the third party's rights at common law.

12.2   We therefore recommend that:

(36)   **the statutory and common law exceptions to the third party rule should be preserved by a statutory provision to the effect that our reform of the third party rule is to be without prejudice to any right or remedy of a third party which exists apart from our proposed Act;** (Draft Bill, clause 6(1))

(37)   **there should be no statutory listing or codification of the existing statutory and common law exceptions.**

12.3   In so far as one has in mind claims in the tort of negligence for pure economic loss as exceptions to the third party rule,[4] this seems an appropriate point to mention concurrent liability. In the Consultation Paper, we provisionally recommended that implementing legislation should not deal with the question of concurrent actions in

---

[1]   Consultation Paper No 121, para 5.38.

[2]   See para 3.5 note 5 above.

[3]   For example, the scope of the tort of negligence for pure economic loss has 'ebbed and flowed' over the last twenty years. See paras 1.4, 2.14 and 3.14 above.

[4]   See para 2.14 above.

contract and tort.[5] Most consultees accepted this and, since the publication of the Consultation Paper, the House of Lords in *Henderson v Merrett Syndicates Ltd*[6] has authoritatively ruled on the question by laying down that there is no automatic objection to allowing concurrent liability between tort and contract. We envisage that, analogously to the two-party situation, a third party's right under our proposed Act will be concurrent with, and will not knock out, a third party's rights in tort; and, in the light of *Henderson v Merrett*, we certainly do not believe that there is anything to be gained by dealing with this question in our proposed legislation.

12.4　We therefore recommend that:

(38)　there should be no legislative provision in our proposed legislation dealing with the issue of concurrent liability in tort and contract.

2.　Should Existing Legislation Conferring Rights of Enforceability on Third Parties Preclude a Third Party Taking Rights under Our Proposed Legislation?

12.5　We have found very difficult the question of the interrelationship between our reform and the existing preserved statutory exceptions. At first blush, one might have thought that our proposed legislation and existing statutory exceptions could easily sit alongside each other. That is, one might have thought that, where the third party has a right of enforceability under another enactment and under our proposed Act, he could simply choose which statute to invoke;[7] and that where the third party does not have a right of enforceability under another Act, but would have under our proposals, our proposed Act should plainly apply. Moreover, we do not accept as a general proposition that, just because a statute has in the past conferred rights of enforceability on some third parties, that represents a deliberate legislative choice that in no circumstances shall other third parties have the right to enforce the type of contract in question. We would emphasise that the basic policy of our reform - that the intentions of the contracting parties to confer legal rights on third parties should be upheld - is a compelling one and should not lightly be displaced by arguments that this would clash with the policies underlying other statutes.

12.6　Nevertheless it has been persuasively suggested to us that in three areas to permit third parties to claim a right of enforceability under our proposed Act would both contradict

---

[5]　Consultation Paper No 121, paras 5.39 and 6.20.

[6]　[1995] 2 AC 145. See generally, A Burrows, "Solving the Problem of Concurrent Liability" (1995) 48(2) CLP 103.

[7]　However, the very existence of a right of enforceability under another statute may sometimes mean that, as regards the second limb of our proposed test of enforceability, the parties do not have an intention to confer rights on a third party other than under the other statute. One should also note that some restrictions on a third party's right (eg monetary or time limits) under another statute would also operate as restrictions under our Act by reason of our proposals on defences or remedies (see recommendation 2 in Part III above, and recommendations 21 and 23 in Part X above).

the policy underlying the relevant legislation and would cause unacceptable commercial uncertainty.[8] The three areas are first, contracts for the carriage of goods by sea; secondly, contracts for the international carriage of goods by road, rail or air; and thirdly, contracts contained in a bill of exchange, promissory note or other negotiable instrument.

(1) Contracts for the Carriage of Goods by Sea

12.7 The relevant statute in mind here is the Carriage of Goods by Sea Act 1992 and the problems drawn to our attention relate both to third parties who have rights of action under that Act (that is, who on the facts in question have the right to enforce the contract), and to those who do not (whom for convenience we label "new third parties").

12.8 Under the 1992 Act a third party (a consignee or sub-buyer) takes the rights and, where he exercises his rights, incurs the liabilities (of the original consignor) under the contract of carriage: that is, the Act permits the enforcement by subsequent holders of a bill of lading, or by persons entitled to delivery under ship's delivery orders or sea waybills, of the terms of the contract of carriage only on terms that such a person also becomes subject to the liabilities of the contract of carriage.[9] Thus, a holder of a bill of lading who seeks to take advantage of the terms of the contract of carriage in order to sue the carrier for short delivery, say, or for damage to the cargo while in transit, will also become liable to the carrier for claims for unpaid freight or for demurrage charges. Furthermore, the basic model for the 1992 Act is one of assignment so that the third party's rights are transferred from the promisee leaving the promisee with no rights of enforcement. In both these respects, the promisor is better off under the 1992 Act than it would be under our proposed Act; that is, under our scheme, a third party takes the benefits but not the burdens of a contract (except to the extent that the benefits are conditional); and the promisor is liable to the promisee as well as to the third party. It would be unacceptable if the provisions of the 1992 Act - specifically

---

[8] But the objection of creating uncertainty, if thought a problem, could be solved by confining the operation of our reform in respect of certain types of contract to the first limb of the test of enforceability.

[9] Carriage of Goods by Sea Act 1992, s 2(1), "... a person who becomes - (a) the lawful holder of a bill of lading; (b) the person who ... is the person to whom delivery of the goods to which a sea waybill relates is to be made by the carrier in accordance with that contract; or (c) the person to whom delivery of the goods to which a ship's delivery order relates is to be made in accordance with the undertaking contained in the order, shall (by virtue of becoming the holder of the bill or, as the case may be, the person to whom delivery is to be made) have transferred to and vested in him all rights of suit under the contract of carriage as if he had been a party to that contract"; s 3(1), "Where ... the person in whom rights are vested [by virtue of the foregoing] - (a) takes or demands delivery from the carrier of any of the goods to which the document relates; (b) makes a claim under the contract of carriage against the carrier in respect of any of those goods; or (c) is a person who, at a time before those rights were vested in him, took or demanded delivery from the carrier of any of those goods, that person shall (by virtue of taking or demanding delivery or making the claim or, in a case falling within paragraph (c) above, of having the rights vested in him) become subject to the same liabilities under that contract as if he had been a party to that contract".

tailored, as they are, to the demands of the shipping industry - could be undermined to the detriment of a promisor by a third party (who falls within the 1992 Act) choosing to sue under the provisions of our proposed reform rather than under the 1992 Act.[10]

12.9   Turning to "new third parties" it is clear that the policy of the Carriage of Goods by Sea Act 1992 was to confine the enforcement of contracts of carriage covered by the Act to certain third parties only (namely, subsequent holders of a bill of lading or persons entitled to delivery under a sea waybill or a ship's delivery order). Yet under our proposals other third parties could be given rights to enforce such a contract. That the Act was intended to exclude enforcement by other third parties clearly emerges from the following passage in the Law Commission's Report[11] which led to the Act:-

> Consultants suggested several different ways of extending the 1855 [Bills of Lading] Act beyond bills of lading. One suggestion was to adopt an agreed definition of the type of document to be covered in legislation, without naming any documents specifically. The holder of such a document would be able to assert rights of action against the carrier. By defining the class of document to which the Act applies, it would be easier to construe into the Act a wider range of documents including those currently in use and others as yet unthought of, thus ensuring that the Act would have a lengthy shelf-life. Another solution eschews any sort of documentary approach and instead would allow any third party to vindicate rights against a carrier who had become obliged to deliver goods to him. However, on balance, we recommend that legislation should enumerate a number of specified documents. We prefer the certainty of an approach which makes it clear which documents are covered by the Act and which are not. Since we have adopted an evolutionary approach to reform, we have built on the foundations of the 1855 Act, retaining those features of the Act which have worked well... Those shipowners, cargo interests and their legal advisers whom we have consulted want to know which documents are included in legislation and which are not. They do not want the certainty of the 1855 regime overthrown in favour of an untried technique which makes no mention of any sort of document with which they are familiar, but rather makes everything depend on the concept of legal obligation, which is seen as too imprecise and uncertain.

12.10   It is our view, therefore, that, at least as regards new third parties, it would indeed in general contradict the policy of the Carriage of Goods by Sea Act 1992 if a third party

---

[10]   We are not convinced, however, that such a third party could so outflank the 1992 Act by suing under our proposed Act. As regards the promisee's rights, the effect of the 1992 Act would surely be that under clause 4 of our draft Bill (implementing recommendation 27) the promisee would have no greater right to enforce the contract under our proposals than under the 1992 Act. And where another statute automatically attaches burdens to the third party's rights, nothing in our proposed Act removes those burdens.

[11]   Rights of Suit in Respect of Carriage of Goods By Sea (1991) Law Com No 196; Scot Law Com No 130, para 5.2.

-were able to rely on our proposed Act to enforce contracts covered by the 1992 Act; and we therefore consider that our proposed Act should not apply to contracts covered by the 1992 Act.[12] Having said that, we are most anxious to preserve the operation of our Act as regards exclusion and limitation clauses in such contracts.[13] Nothing in the 1992 Act was directly concerned with the problem of the enforceability of such clauses and there is therefore, in this respect, no clash of policy between our proposals and the 1992 Act.

12.11   We therefore recommend that:

     (39)   **a third party shall have no right of enforceability under our proposed Act in the case of a contract for the carriage of goods by sea governed by the Carriage of Goods by Sea Act 1992 except that a third party can enforce an exclusion or limitation of liability in such a contract if he satisfies the test of enforceability.** (Draft Bill, clause 6(2)(a) and 6(3)(a))

(2) Contracts for the International Carriage of Goods by Road, Rail or Air

12.12   Contracts for the international carriage of goods[14] by road or rail, or cargo by air, are governed by international conventions that are given force in England by various statutes.[15] One possible problem posed for our proposals by the conventions is that in some situations, where third parties are given rights to enforce international contracts of carriage, they also take some or all of the burdens under the contracts.[16] To allow

---

[12]   A "contract of carriage", for the purposes of the 1992 Act, is defined in s 5(1) of the Act.

[13]   See paras 2.19-2.35 above.

[14]   Although the international carriage of passengers and their baggage is also governed by international conventions, it will be rare for a third party who has been injured or whose baggage has been lost or damaged to assert rights under our proposed Act (rather than, eg, in tort) and, even if he or she does, we do not think that this would clash with the policy of the conventions. We therefore confine ourselves to considering the carriage of goods and cargo.

[15]   International carriage of goods by road is governed by the Geneva Convention on the Contract for the International Carriage of Goods by Road 1956 (CMR) given statutory force by the Carriage of Goods by Road Act 1965, as amended by the Carriage by Air and Road Act 1979. International carriage of goods by rail is governed by Appendix B (CIM) of the Berne Convention concerning International Carriage by Rail 1980 (COTIF) given statutory force by the International Transport Conventions Act 1983. International carriage of cargo by air is governed by the Warsaw Convention 1929, as amended by the Hague Protocol 1955, and by the Guadalajara Convention 1961 (dealing with the rights and liabilities of the "actual carrier") given statutory force by the Carriage by Air Act 1961 and by the Carriage by Air (Supplementary Provisions) Act 1962. Also relevant is Part B of Schedule 2 to the Carriage by Air (Application of Provisions) Order 1967, SI 1967 No 480 made under s 10 of the Carriage by Air Act 1961, which sets out (with amendments) the original Warsaw Convention and the Guadalajara Convention: by reason of article 5 of the 1967 Order those Conventions continue to apply in respect of international carriage that is not subject to the amended Warsaw Convention (presumably because the place of departure or destination of the carriage by air is within a State which ratified the Warsaw Convention in 1929 but did not ratify the Hague Protocol in 1955). The Montreal Protocol 1975, amending the Warsaw Convention, has been given statutory force by the Carriage of Goods by Air and Road Act 1979 but the relevant provisions of that Act are not yet in force.

[16]   See, eg, Article 14 of the Warsaw Convention 1929, as amended by The Hague Protocol 1955, given statutory force by the Carriage by Air Act 1961; Article 13(2) of the Geneva Convention on the Contract for the International Carriage of Goods by Road 1956 (CMR) given statutory

such third parties to have rights under our proposed Act might conflict with the conventions in that our proposals enable the creation of rights, which may be conditional, but do not enable burdens to be imposed on a third party.[17]

12.13   What about "new third parties"? It is arguable that the general philosophy of the air, road and rail conventions is to leave it to national law to determine precisely which third parties should have rights of enforceability, while subjecting all those who bring actions in respect of international conventions to particular restrictions and limitations.[18] Yet Article 54 of the COTIF (CIM) Convention on carriage of goods by rail appears to lay down definitively when consignors, consignees, and persons designated by consignees can bring actions against the railway arising from the contract of carriage; and if the consignor has rights of suit, the consignee does not, and vice versa.[19] If this is a correct interpretation of the Convention, our proposals could undermine it by allowing other third parties rights of action. It is also noteworthy that, whatever the policy of the Convention on carriage by road, section 14(2) of the Carriage by Road Act 1965 (giving the force of law in the United Kingdom to the CMR Convention) defines as "persons concerned" to whom the Convention applies: "(a) the sender, (b) the consignee, (c) any carrier who... is a party to the contract of carriage, (d) any person for whom such a carrier is responsible..., (e) any person to whom the rights and liabilities of any of the persons referred to in paragraphs (a) to (d) to this subsection have passed (whether by assignment or assignation of operation of law)." This would appear to rule out other third parties and, given that the Act is applicable to Scotland, it might be regarded as having deliberately ruled out claims by a third party under a *ius quaesitum tertio*.

12.14   For these reasons, we are satisfied that there is at least a danger that our proposed Act might be used to undermine the conventions (or implementing statutes) on the international carriage of goods. We therefore consider that our proposed Act should not apply to a contract for the international carriage of goods by road, rail or air to

---

force by the Carriage of Goods by Road Act 1965; Article 28(1) of Appendix B (CIM) the Berne Convention concerning International Carriage by Rail 1980 (COTIF) given statutory force by the International Transport Conventions Act 1983.

[17]   But as we point out in para 12.8, note 10, above where another statute automatically attaches burdens to the third party's rights, nothing in our proposed Act removes those burdens.

[18]   "[I]t is widely assumed that the CMR contains no general or definitive rule governing the identity of the person or persons entitled to sue the carrier". M Clarke, *International Carriage of Goods by Road: CMR* (2nd ed, 1991) p 178 and, generally, pp 178-198. This is also the position under the Warsaw Convention Art 24(1) if *Gatewhite v Iberia Airlines* [1990] 1 QB 326 is correct. The ambiguity is removed by Art 24 Montreal Protocol 1975, which will be given statutory force by the Carriage by Air and Road Act 1979 (relevant provisions not yet in force). See, generally, D Glass and C Cashmore, *Introduction to the Law of Carriage of Goods* (1989) para 3.32 (road), para 4.20 (rail), paras 6.33 and 6.36 (air); *Chitty on Contracts* (27th ed, 1994) para 34-052 (air), para 35-114 (rail), paras 35-150 to 35-151 (road).

[19]   Although less clear, see also Arts 12(4), 13 and 14 of the Warsaw Convention on carriage by air.

which the international conventions apply.[20] Again, however, we see no such danger in respect of a third party being given the right to rely on an exclusion or limitation clause in the carriage contract.[21]

12.15　We therefore recommend that:-

(40)　a third party shall have no right of enforceability under our proposed Act in the case of a contract for the international carriage of goods by road or rail, or cargo by air, governed by the relevant international conventions,[22] except that a third party can enforce an exclusion or limitation of liability in such a contract if he satisfies the test of enforceability.　(Draft Bill, clause 6(2)(b) and 6(3)(b))

(3) Contracts Contained in Bills of Exchange, Promissory Notes and Other Negotiable Instruments

12.16　As regards bills of exchange, promissory notes and (most) negotiable instruments,[23] the Bills of Exchange Act 1882 gives third party rights of enforceability only to those who are holders. Yet under our proposed Act it is conceivable that other third parties to a contract contained in a bill of exchange promissory note or other negotiable instrument would have rights to enforce that contract. We accept the force of the argument that it would both undermine the policy of the Act and cause unacceptable

[20]　Although there are some provisions dealing with carriage of goods by more than one mode of transport (see, eg, Art 2(1) of CMR and Art 31 of the Warsaw Convention) we are aware that there can be difficulties in deciding on the extent to which, if at all, the international conventions (and the Carriage of Goods by Sea Act 1992) apply to the "multimodal" carriage of goods. Insofar as none of the relevant international conventions applies to the contract of carriage in question, and nor does the Carriage of Goods by Sea Act 1992, we see no objection to a third party who can satisfy the test of enforceability being given rights under our proposed Act.

[21]　Although the road and rail conventions already appear to protect even independent contractors engaged by the carrier to perform the carriage : see Arts 3 and 28 of CMR ; Arts 50-51 of COTIF (CIM). For a useful discussion of Art 28 of CMR, see Hill and Messent, *CMR: Contracts for the International Carriage of Goods by Road* (1984) pp 149-152. In contrast, Art 25A of the Warsaw Convention (like the Hague-Visby Rules, see para 2.22, note 79, above) refers only to servants and agents. It should be emphasised that specific restrictions in the conventions on the rights of servants, agents or other third parties to rely on exclusions (in particular where the loss or damage has been caused by wilful misconduct) could not be outflanked by the third party relying on our Act because of recommendation 25 and draft bill clause 3(6).

[22]　The reference in clause 6(3)(b)(iii) of our draft Bill to "the Convention which has force of law in the United Kingdom by virtue of section 1 of the Carriage of Air Act 1961" is sufficiently wide to include - and we intend should be read as including - the carriage of cargo by air provisions of the Carriage by Air and Road Act 1979 as and when those provisions are brought into force. The 1979 Act is concerned to amend the Carriage by Air Act 1961 and to give force of law in the United Kingdom to the Montreal Protocol, amending the Warsaw Convention.

[23]　Those negotiable instruments falling outside the Bills of Exchange Act 1882 (eg, Eurodollar bonds, negotiable certificates of deposit, floating rate notes) are enforceable by third parties who are analogous to those with rights of enforceability under the Act. It would contradict commercial understanding and practice if our proposed Act were to treat differently negotiable instruments falling with the 1882 Act and those falling outside the 1882 Act. See R Goode, *Commercial Law* (2nd ed, 1995) pp 519-520, 627-631.

uncertainty[24] to open up the possibility of third parties who are not holders being able to sue on such contracts, and we therefore consider that our proposals should not apply to such contracts.

12.17   We therefore recommend that:-

(41)   **a third party shall have no right of enforceability under our proposed Act in respect of a contract contained in a bill of exchange, promissory note or other negotiable instrument.** (Draft Bill, clause 6(2)(c))

3. Should This Opportunity Be Taken to Reform the Third Parties (Rights Against Insurers) Act 1930 and the Married Women's Property Act 1882?

12.18   Two statutory exceptions to the third party rule are the Third Parties (Rights Against Insurers) Act 1930 ("the Third Parties Act") and the Married Women's Property Act 1882 ("the MWPA 1882"). In the Consultation Paper, views were specifically sought as to whether those two Acts should be reformed.[25]

(1) Third Parties (Rights Against Insurers) Act 1930

12.19   The operation of the Third Parties Act[26] has been the subject of criticism for some time and a number of consultees argued that it needed amendment. One problem, for example, is that third parties cannot prevent the insurer and insured compromising the insured's claim to the detriment of the third party's, even though both may be well aware of his claims. Similarly, since the rights which the Act confers on third parties are only those which the insured would have enjoyed, an obligation to "pay to be paid" will frustrate the right of the third party where the insured has become insolvent and therefore failed to pay. Again, a provision which renders the benefit under the insurance contract subject to a discretion on the part of the company to pay[27] may lead to the conclusion that since the insured had no "right" to an indemnity, the third party can have no such right transferred to it in the event of the assured's insolvency. The assured will have no right against the insurer until judgment is obtained by the third party.

---

[24]   Although the objection of uncertainty, if thought a problem, could be solved by confining the operation of our reform to the first limb of the test of enforceability: see para 12.6, note 8, above.

[25]   Consultation Paper No 121, para 5.38. See also paras 6.18-6.19.

[26]   See, eg, *Firma C-Trade SA v Newcastle Protection and Indemnity Association; Socony Mobil Oil Inc v West of England Shipowners Mutual Insurance Association (London) Ltd (The "Fanti" and The "Padre Island") (No 1)* [1991] 2 AC 1 (HL); *Post Office v Norwich Union Fire Insurance Society Ltd* [1967] 2 QB 363; *CVG Siderurgicia del Orinoco SA v London Steamship Owners' Mutual Insurance Association Ltd* [1979] 1 Lloyd's Rep 557; *Bradley v Eagle Star Insurance Co Ltd* [1989] AC 957; *Normid Housing Association Ltd v Ralphs and Mansell and Assicurazioni Generali* [1989] 1 Lloyd's Rep 265; *Nigel Upchurch Associates v Aldridge Estates Investments Co Ltd* [1993] 1 Lloyd's Rep 535; *Woolwich Building Society v Taylor, The Times,* 17 May 1994; *Cox v Bankside Members Agency Ltd* [1995] 2 Lloyd's Rep 437.

[27]   As is the case under the Rules of many shipowners' Protection & Indemnity Associations for certain types of benefits.

12.20 We consider that the issues involved in a reform of the 1930 Act are different than those involved in any general reform of the third party rule. They involve a balancing of rights between insurance companies, insolvent insureds and third party claimants which we cannot properly address in this project. Nevertheless, the response of consultees confirms that the operation of the Third Parties Act should be looked at in the near future. We have therefore pressed for a separate Law Commission project to be undertaken on the Third Parties Act and we are delighted that this project was approved (in June 1995) as an item on the Law Commission's Sixth Programme of Law Reform.[28]

12.21 We therefore recommend that:

(42) reform of the Third Parties (Rights Against Insurers) Act 1930 should not be covered in our general reform of the third party rule.

(2) Married Women's Property Act 1882

12.22 In the Consultation Paper,[29] views were invited on the proposal of the Law Revision Committee that section 11 of the MWPA 1882 should be extended to all life, endowment and education policies in which a particular beneficiary is named.[30] Section 11 of the 1882 Act presently provides that where a person takes out a policy of insurance on his or her own life expressed to be for the benefit of his or her spouse and/or children, a trust is created in favour of those purported beneficiaries. Consultees who addressed this issue were in favour of the proposed extension of the 1882 Act, and some suggested further extensions, such as enacting a provision similar to section 48 of the Australian Insurance Contracts Act 1984.

12.23 It is instructive to begin by considering the Australian provision. Section 48 permits a person who is not a party to a contract of insurance, but who is "specified or referred to in the contract... as a person to whom the insurance cover provided by the contract extends", to recover the amount of his or her loss from the insurer in accordance with the contract.[31] Thus, for example, the Australian legislation would permit the subsidiary of an assured company to bring a direct right of action against an insurer, where the policy was expressed to indemnify "the assured, all subsidiary, associated and related companies, all contractors, sub-contractors and suppliers" against a specified liability to another party, although the subsidiary company would not be in

---

[28] See Law Commission Sixth Programme of Law Reform (1995), Law Com No 234, Item 10.

[29] Consultation Paper No 121, para 6.19.

[30] Law Revision Committee, Sixth Interim Report, para 49. See para 4.3 above.

[31] Section 48 is set out in Appendix B below. Note that s 48 does not subsume the issue dealt with in England by the Third Parties (Rights Against Insurers) Act 1930. The Third Parties Act 1930 applies so as to permit a person who obtains a judgment or award against another person (who is insured against that claim but is insolvent) to enforce the judgment or award directly against the insurer. In contrast the Australian legislation would apply generally to permit a person *who is specified or referred* to in a contract of insurance as a potential beneficiary of that contract to bring a direct claim against the insurer.

privity of contract with the insurer.[32] Similarly, it would permit an employee who was specified as an insured under a corporate health insurance programme taken out by his or her employer to maintain a direct action against the insurance company.[33]

12.24   In respect of many insurance contracts, our reforms will have much the same effect as is achieved by the Australian Act. In particular, a liability insurance policy where an insurer is to indemnify specified third parties against legal liability will be enforceable under our reforms (whether under the first or second limb of the test of enforceability). Similarly most medical expenses insurance policies, taken out on behalf of employees, will be enforceable by employees under our reforms. The differences relate to the fact that the third party's right is more secure and automatic under the 1984 Act than under our reforms. In particular, our reforms leave open the possibility that even though a third party is expressed to be covered by the policy the contracting parties may intend that only the promisee and not that third party should have the right of enforcement. So, for example, some standard group personal accident insurance policies may fall outside our reform whereas they would fall within the 1984 Act. It would also appear that, once made, an insurance contract in Australia cannot be varied or cancelled by the original contracting parties: under our reforms variation or cancellation is possible before reliance or acceptance by the third party.

12.25   Accepting then, that the Insurance Contracts Act 1984, section 48, goes beyond our general reform, we face the question as to whether we should recommend an equivalent reform in this country. We have found this difficult. On the one hand, the Australian provision may be thought to reflect the expectations of assureds and third parties to whom the insurance is expressed to extend that such policies are enforceable by the third parties. It may also be argued that it reflects the standard good practice of insurers and assureds in ensuring that such third parties are paid. On the other hand, it is not obvious why the intentions of an assured and insurer to give the assured alone the right to enforce the policy should be overridden. It is also not obvious to us that the contracting parties should have no right to vary or cancel the contract prior to reliance or acceptance by the third party. Furthermore we are somewhat concerned that we did not put out to consultation the possibility of such a provision and we have therefore not had the benefit of a wide-range of views in relation to such a proposal. We note in this respect that the Australian legislation was introduced as a result of a specific review of the law governing insurance contracts by the Law Reform Commission of Australia.[34] One can add that there may be something to be gained by assessing the impact in practice of our general reform of privity before deciding

[32]   Cf *Trident General Insurance Co Ltd v McNiece Bros Pty Ltd* (1988) 165 CLR 107. See paras 2.67-2.69 above.

[33]   Cf *Green v Russell* [1959] 2 QB 226. See paras 3.25 and 7.51 above.

[34]   Australian Law Reform Commission, *Insurance Contracts*, Report No 20, 1982.

whether such an "industry-specific" reform is required. On balance, therefore, we have decided that it would be inappropriate in this project to recommend following Australia in affording automatic rights to third parties covered by insurance.

12.26   We also consider that it would not be sensible in this project to recommend the extension of the Married Women's Property Act 1882 in the manner proposed by the Law Revision Committee. In particular it is far from clear why a "trust" solution is more appropriate than one permitting variation or cancellation of the contract by the contracting parties prior to crystallisation of the third party's rights. It is also not clear what precisely the Law Revision Committee meant when using the term "endowment and education policies". Moreover, to extend the 1882 Act would, ideally, require more than its mere amendment and would instead require its repeal and replacement. This is because the Law Revision Committee's suggested amendment would take one outside the purpose of the Act which, in the long title, is specified as being "to consolidate and amend the Acts relating to the Property of Married Women". Again we consider that it would be preferable to wait to see how far our general reforms overcome perceived problems caused by the privity doctrine in relation to insurance contracts before giving non-parties to insurance contracts automatic rights of enforceability. And viewed against the wider Australian reform, we would be concerned that the Law Revision Committee's recommendations may be justifiably criticised as being an outdated and inadequate "half-way house".

12.27   We therefore recommend that:

(43)   **there should not be an extension of section 11 of the MWPA 1882 at this stage.**

PART XIII
CONSEQUENTIAL AMENDMENTS

1. Our General Approach

13.1   In this Part, we address the question of whether any of the many statutes passed on the basis of the third party rule (including statutory exceptions to it)[1] require amendment in the light of our reform.

13.2   It is important at the outset to clarify that we regard our proposed statute as carving out a general and wide-ranging exception to the third party rule, while leaving that rule intact for cases not covered by the statute.[2] Moreover, it is not intended that the statute should give the third party full "contractual rights" nor that the third party should simply be deemed to be a party to the contract. So, for example, if the third party were simply treated as having the same rights as a contracting party, the contracting parties could not vary or cancel the contract without the third party's consent, thus undermining our approach in Part IX. Nor would we wish to give the third party the right to terminate the contract (that is, to wipe away the contract for the future) for the promisor's substantial breach.[3]

13.3   It follows that, in our view, where statute has prescribed a particular regime to apply to "contracts", "deeds" and "agreements", and to "parties" to contracts, deeds and agreements on the understanding that only parties could enforce the rights and obligations created by those contracts, deeds and agreements, that understanding should continue to govern the interpretation of that particular statute, unless the contrary is specifically provided in the statute.

13.4   We therefore recommend that:

(44)   **our proposed statute should not be interpreted as giving the third party full "contractual rights" nor as deeming the third party to be a party to the contract. It follows that, although no general legislative provision on this seems necessary, "contracts", "parties" to contracts, and "contractual rights and obligations" should be construed as they would have been prior to the enactment of our proposed reform. However, to avoid contradiction, a legislative provision is required to make clear that the references to treating the third party as if a party to the contract for the purposes of recommendations (2), (23) and (25) above should not be**

---

[1]   Part XII (Existing Exceptions) did not consider "consequential amendments" to other statutes.

[2]   See para 5.16 above.

[3]   See para 3.33 above.

interpreted as treating the third party as if he were a party to the contract for the purposes of any other enactment.[4] (Draft Bill, clause 6(6))

13.5 The above recommendation clarifies that our proposed Act is not to undermine or, indeed, render uncertain the operation of other statutes affecting contracts. A much more difficult question is whether we ought, by consequential amendment, to extend a policy, that on the face of it has been worked out legislatively in respect of contracting parties only, to claims by third parties under our Act. Our general answer to that question is that it would be foolish to attempt such an exercise across the whole range of statutes. In effect it would require detailed consideration of every statute that has an impact on contracts,[5] and would involve proposing amendments on a statute by statute basis. To attempt this without specialist knowledge of each area and without the views of informed consultees would be a herculean task that would be likely to miss its mark. We should also emphasise that, given that statutes have been passed against the background of a large number of common law and statutory exceptions to the third party rule, we think it most unlikely that glaring policy problems will be left if we do not make consequential amendments reflecting our new statutory exception.

13.6 Having said that, we have considered in detail the interrelationship between our reform and a limited number of, what one may term, "core contract" statutes. These are statutes which are either central to one's thinking about contract or have been drawn to our attention as statutes which merit consideration in the light of our proposed reform. In addition to the main statutory exceptions to the third party rule[6] the enactments which we have looked at are as follows:- Gaming Acts 1845, 1892; Law Reform (Frustrated Contracts) Act 1943; Law Reform (Husband and Wife) Act 1964 (NI); Misrepresentation Act 1967; Defective Premises Act 1972; Supply of Goods (Implied Terms) Act 1973; Consumer Credit Act 1974; Unfair Contract Terms Act 1977; Civil Liability (Contribution) Act 1978; Arbitration Acts 1950, 1975 and 1979; Sale of Goods Act 1979; Limitation Act 1980; Supply of Goods and Services Act 1982: Building Act 1984; Companies Act 1985; Insolvency Act 1986;[7]

---

[4] An obvious example is section 3 of the Unfair Contract Terms Act 1977 which applies "as between contracting parties where one of them deals as a consumer or on the other's written standard terms of business".

[5] A LEXIS search of statutes performed by us using the search terms 'contract' or 'deed' or 'agreement' with 'party' or 'promisor/ee' or 'covenantor/ee' revealed over 800 entries.

[6] These are listed in paras 2.52-2.62 above.

[7] Although we have satisfied ourselves that any difficulties raised by the effect of our reform on the Insolvency Act 1986 are surmountable without amendment to the 1986 Act, we have had most concern about the impact of our proposals on company and individual voluntary arrangements (see ss 1-7 and 252-254 of the Insolvency Act 1986). We understand that the non-binding effect of voluntary arrangements on creditors who were not given notice of the voluntary arrangement meeting is considered to be a general defect in the insolvency legislation. As far as our Act is concerned, a particular difficulty concerns non-existent third parties (see para 8.6 above). While we consider that a non-existent third party who satisfies the test of enforceability would class as a 'creditor' under the 1986 Act, this will not be so where the third

Financial Services Act 1986; Minors' Contracts Act 1987; Consumer Protection Act 1987; Consumer Arbitration Agreements Act 1988; Contracts (Applicable Law) Act 1990; Civil Jurisdiction and Judgments Act 1982, 1991; Unfair Terms in Consumer Contracts Regulations 1994.

13.7   Our conclusion is that, even in relation to that limited range of enactments - and subject to two provisions on limitation periods and section 2(2) of the Unfair Contract Terms Act 1977 respectively - no consequential amendments are required. This is for one of two reasons; either the enactments are already sufficiently widely worded to apply to claims by third parties under our proposed statute and it is appropriate that they should so apply; or, if that is not so, amendment to render the enactments applicable to claims by third parties under our proposed statute is unjustified in terms of policy at least in this project. While we do not propose to set out the details of those two reasons in respect of each of the core contract statutes, we would like to set out our thinking on UCTA 1977 in some detail (because we have agonised most about it). We must also explain the amendment recommended to the Limitation Act 1980.

13.8   We therefore recommend that:

(45) subject to recommendations (46) and (47) below, no consequential amendment to other legislation is required by our proposals.

2. The Unfair Contract Terms Act 1977

13.9   We here set out why we believe that an extension of UCTA 1977 so as to restrict the ability of promisors to exclude liability to third parties should not be pursued in this project. The essential situation in mind is where there is an exclusion clause contained in the contract which, as a matter of construction, excludes or restricts the promisor's liability for breach of his obligations to the third party. Analogous to that is where the benefit to the third party is qualified by a condition. The third party may wish to argue that the exclusion or restriction (or condition) is unreasonable under section 3 of UCTA 1977. The difficulty for the third party is that, as it stands, section 3 of UCTA 1977 does not appear to apply to claims by third parties under our proposed Act. It can be argued that, as a matter of policy, UCTA ought to be extended to cover such a situation.   If this were not so, third parties would be left exposed to unreasonable exclusion clauses; third parties might be 'deceived' as to their entitlement; and one would be producing an 'uneven' law whereby, in an action by the promisee to enforce the promise for the third party, section 3 of UCTA 1977 would apply whereas, in our proposed direct action by the third party, UCTA 1977 would not apply.

party's right has been validly cancelled. It follows that, provided the debtor obtains the promisee's consent to cancel the third party's right, voluntary arrangements will not be hindered by our reform's recognition that rights of enforceability may be conferred on non-existent third parties. To avoid the need for the promisee's consent, it would appear that an amendment to the Insolvency Act 1986 would be needed to ensure that non-existent third parties who satisfy the test of enforceability do not class as creditors under the 1986 Act.

13.10   Despite the force of these arguments, we consider the following counter-arguments to be compelling:-

(i)   Our test of enforceability rests on effecting the intentions of the contracting parties to confer legal rights on the third party. To apply UCTA 1977 - much of which is concerned to protect consumers irrespective of the true construction of a contract - to claims by third parties would cut across that essential basis of our reform.

(ii)   Linked to (i) is the argument that the intentions of the contracting parties in respect of the legal entitlement of the third party have a more important active role under our reform than does the concept of 'intention to create legal relations' in determining whether the original contract is valid.[8] It follows that an exclusion of liability may merit greater respect as regards third party rights under our reform then it does in determining the legal entitlement of the contracting parties inter se.

(iii)   Our approach is not to give a third party exactly the same rights as if he had been a contracting party.[9] There is therefore no inconsistency in giving the promisee more secure rights than the third party.

(iv)   In applying the test of enforceability the common law rules as to the incorporation and construction of exclusion clauses[10] can go much of the way to stopping, for example, promisors relying on exclusion clauses hidden away in small print. And misrepresentation by the contracting parties to the third party as to the contents of the contract would potentially give the third party the right to recover its reliance loss for the tort of deceit or negligent misstatement.

(v)   While third parties will not be as well protected as they would be if we went ahead and amended UCTA 1977, they will of course have better rights under our proposals than they have under the present law.

(vi)   Under our proposals, UCTA 1977 will continue to operate to control exclusion clauses in respect of claims by the promisee to enforce the promise for the third party's benefit. So, for example, if the promisor has undertaken responsibility but has then limited it in the small print, UCTA 1977 s 3(2)(a) would apply: the promisor, when in breach of contract, would be limiting his liability by reference to the term in the small print. The limitation would only be valid if it were reasonable. If the problem was that the promisee was somehow misled into thinking that a third party would get enforceable rights when this was not what the contract provided, the promisee could

---

[8]   See para 7.7 above.

[9]   See para 13.2 above.

[10]   See Treitel, *The Law of Contract* (9th ed, 1995) pp 197-224. Bingham LJ's judgment in *Interfoto Ltd v Stiletto Ltd* [1989] QB 433 is particularly interesting in its references to a contractual principle of dealing in good faith.

rely on the present s 3(2)(b)(i): the promisor would be claiming to rely on the small print to 'render a contractual performance substantially different from that which was reasonably expected'.

(vii) If we were to recommend reform of UCTA 1977, some difficult questions of policy would be raised as to the precise extent and form of the amendments. In particular, we would have to decide whether reasonableness should be judged as between the promisor and the promisee or as between the promisor and the third party. And we would have to decide whether one can sensibly apply to third parties the notion of 'dealing as a consumer' in UCTA 1977. We might also be forced to deal, in respect of sections 6-7 of UCTA 1977, with tricky problems relating to the exclusion of implied terms in contracts for the sale of goods: for example, it is not absolutely clear that all contracts in which goods are bought for the benefit of third parties are classified as contracts of sale.[11] Without the benefit of consultees' views, we would prefer not to tamper with the definition of a contract of sale but this might be unavoidable if sections 6-7 were extended to cover claims by third parties under our proposed reform. Furthermore, it is possible that full protection of third parties against being 'misled' as to their entitlement would need to go much further than the control of exclusion or limitation clauses to include, for example, defences and variation or cancellation clauses that the third party did not know about. It would appear that such wide protection raises policy issues that go well beyond those underpinning UCTA 1977. We should emphasise, however, that we would not wish anything in our proposed legislation to be construed as hampering the protection of third parties by the judiciary through the application or extension of common law techniques.[12]

(viii) We believe that, as a matter of practical politics, one step should be taken at a time. To reform the privity doctrine to reflect the contracting parties' intentions is to take a relatively uncontroversial step. To combine that with an amendment which would in certain circumstances prevent promisors contracting out of conferring legal rights on third parties is much more controversial and might jeopardise the acceptance of our central reform.

(ix) Given that we are, in effect, departing from a long-established common law doctrine we think that there is much to be said for allowing a period of time for the effect of our reform to 'settle down' before pursuing consumer protection measures in relation to claims by third parties. Indeed it would be tantamount to 'shooting in the dark' to attempt such measures in advance of seeing what, if any, problems are thrown up in practice.

(x) Although we venture this argument with some diffidence, as the correct interpretation is far from clear, it *appears* that the Unfair Terms in Consumer

---

[11] See para 7.41, note 30, above.

[12] See para 1.10 above.

Contracts Regulations 1994, implementing EEC Council Directive 93/13, are inapplicable to conditions on, or exclusions of, a third party's rights.[13] If this is correct, the treatment of contracting parties and third parties in respect of "unfair terms" will be significantly different whatever one does about UCTA 1977.[14]

13.11 There are two final points to make in respect of the Unfair Contract Terms Act 1977. First, in the reverse situation, where the third party seeks to enforce an exclusion clause (A excluding C's liability to A in the tort of negligence) and it is the promisor who wishes to invoke UCTA 1977, there appears to be no difficulty. UCTA 1977 applies so as to render the clause void under section 2(1) (as regards negligently caused personal injury or death) or valid only in so far as reasonable as between the contracting parties under sections 2(2) and 11(1). No amendment to UCTA 1977 is required and, indeed, the situation is covered by recommendation 25 above.[15]

13.12 Secondly, we have been troubled by section 2(2) of UCTA 1977. Applying our policy that UCTA 1977 should not restrict a promisor excluding its liability to the third party, the promisor ought to be able to exclude its liability to the third party for the breach of a contractual duty of care. Yet, as it stands, section 2(2) (in contrast to, for example, section 3) would apply to a claim by a third party under our proposed Act for breach of a contractual duty of care. That is, the breach of the obligation to the third party would constitute the breach "of any obligation, arising from the express or implied terms of a contract, to take reasonable care or exercise reasonable skill in the performance of the contract".[16] We therefore consider that section 2(2) of UCTA 1977 should be amended so as to ensure that it does not apply in respect of a third party bringing an action under our proposed Act for the breach of a contractual duty of care. This amendment would not, of course, affect the operation of exclusion clauses in relation to claims by third parties in tort. Nor would it affect the operation of section 2(1) of UCTA 1977, which renders void the exclusion or limitation of negligently caused personal injury or death (assuming business liability). Admittedly, to leave section 2(1) unamended, and therefore applicable to claims by third parties under our proposed Act, may be regarded as a contradiction of our wish to effect the parties' intentions. But the exclusion or limitation of liability for negligently caused personal injury or death is an extreme case as is reflected by such a clause being

---

[13] See, for example, reg 5(1) "An unfair term in a contract concluded with a consumer by a seller or supplier shall not be binding on the consumer". See generally on the Unfair Terms in Consumer Contracts Regulations 1994, Treitel, *The Law of Contract* (9th ed, 1995) pp 245-259.

[14] Again, if this interpretation is correct, and given that in other EC countries third party rights to enforce contracts are well established, one can only assume that the Directive rests on a policy decision either that third parties do not merit the same protection as contracting parties or that, if they do, this should be a matter for the individual member states.

[15] See paras 10.22-10.23 above.

[16] Section 1(1)(a) UCTA 1977. In our view, this interpretation of s 1(1)(a) and s 2(2), as encompassing a claim by a third party under our proposed Act, is a valid one despite recommendation 44 (see para 13.4) above.

rendered automatically void. In our view, section 2(1) should apply to claims by third parties under our proposed Act for personal injury or death (albeit that such a claim will, presumably, be rare).

13.13   We therefore recommend that:

(46)   **section 2(2) of the Unfair Contract Terms Act 1977 shall not apply in respect of a claim by a third party under our proposed Act for the breach of a contractual duty of care.** (Draft Bill, clause 6(4))

3. Limitation Act 1980

13.14   In our view, the limitation period for actions brought by third parties to enforce a contract should be the same as the limitation period which would have applied if the third party had been a party to the contract. We therefore recommend an amendment to the Limitation Act 1980 making it clear that actions brought by third parties under our Act are to be treated as 'actions founded on simple contract' or as 'actions upon a specialty' for the purposes of the Limitation Act 1980.[17] We do not think that any other amendment of the 1980 Act is necessary (for example, sections 11 and 12 do not, in our view, require amendment).

13.15   We therefore recommend that:

(47)   **actions brought by third parties under our proposed Act are to be treated as "actions founded on simple contract" or as "actions upon a specialty" (depending on the nature of the contract) for the purposes of the Limitation Act 1980.** (Draft Bill, clause 6(5))

---

[17]   See sections 5 and 8 of the Limitation Act 1980.

PART XIV
MISCELLANEOUS ISSUES

1. Joinder of Promisee

14.1 In the Consultation Paper, we dealt with the issue of whether a third party, seeking to enforce a contract for his or her benefit, should be required to join the promisee as a party to that action.[1] This may be thought important given our recommendation that defences and set-offs that the promisor would have had in an action by the promisee should also be available in an action by the third party. There may also be questions as to whether the promisor and promisee have varied or cancelled the contract. Furthermore, in a situation where the promisee itself wishes to sue, joinder may be thought important as a means of saving the costs and inconvenience to the promisor of being exposed to two separate actions. Section 11(2)(b) of the Western Australia Property Law Act 1969 has a requirement that the promisee, as well as the promisor, be joined as a party to the litigation when a third party sues to enforce a contract made for his benefit. But such a requirement was rejected by the New Zealand Contracts and Commercial Law Reform Committee on the grounds that it could lead to unnecessary expense and possible problems as to service of the proceedings.[2]

14.2 A clear majority of consultees were against a requirement that the promisee be joined. They argued that it will often be unnecessary to join the promisee and to do so would then serve only to increase costs: and that it may be impracticable to join the promisee because of death, dissolution or absence abroad.

14.3 We agree and therefore recommend that:

(48) there should be no requirement that the promisee be joined as a party to the litigation when a third party sues to enforce a contract.

14.4 On the other hand, it was widely recognised by consultees that it will often be *desirable* for the promisee to be joined. We agree. The question at issue therefore is whether the existing Rules of the Supreme Court (and the equivalent County Court Rules) are adequate to enable or ensure the joinder of the promisee in circumstances where this is desirable. We believe that they are.[3] Under the present Rules of the Supreme Court:

---

[1] Consultation Paper No 121, para 5.26, 6.11. Note that it is a requirement for the enforcement of an equitable assignment that the assignor be joined in any action by the assignee against the debtor: see *Chitty on Contracts* (27th ed, 1994) paras 19-022-19-023.

[2] New Zealand Contracts and Commercial Law Reform Committee, *Privity of Contract* (1981) para 7.1.

[3] It should also be noted that we do not think that any amendment to the rules as to the award of costs are required as a result of our proposed reforms.

(i)   By Order 15, rule 4,[4] if both the third party and the promisee wish it, the promisee can be joined as of right.

(ii)   By Order 15, rule 6(2)(b),[5] the court (on its own motion or on application) can order the promisee to be joined as a plaintiff or as a defendant, albeit that no person can be added as a plaintiff without his consent.

(iii) By Order 16, rule 1,[6] the promisor can make the promisee a third party to the action.

14.5   We therefore recommend that:

(49) the existing Rules of Court are adequate to deal with joinder of the promisee in an action brought by a third party under our proposed reform.

2. Assignment of the Third Party's Right

14.6   Although we do not regard a third party under our proposed Act as having a "full" contractual right, his right under our proposals is clearly closely analogous to a contractual right and standard common law contractual principles should in general apply to it. We therefore see no good reason, and none was suggested to us, why the third party's right should not be assignable in the same way as a contracting party's rights under the contract.

---

[4] By O 15, r 4(1), "[T]wo or more persons may be joined together in one action as plaintiffs or as defendants with the leave of the Court or where - (a) if separate actions were brought by or against each of them, as the case may be, some common question of law or fact would arise in all the actions, and (b) all rights to relief claimed in the action (whether they are joint, several or alternative) are in respect of or arise out of the same transaction or series of transactions."

[5] By O 15, r 6(2), "[A]t any stage of the proceedings in any cause or matter the Court may on such terms as it thinks just and either of its own motion or on application -... (b) order any of the following persons to be added as a party, namely - (i) any person who ought to have been joined as a party or whose presence before the Court is necessary to ensure that all matters in dispute in the cause or matter may be effectually and completely determined and adjudicated upon, or (ii) any person between whom and any party to the cause or matter there may exist a question or issue arising out of or relating to or connected with any relief or remedy claimed in the cause or matter which in the opinion of the Court it would be just and convenient to determine as between him and that party as well as between the parties to the cause or matter."

[6] By O 16, r 1(1), "Where in any action a defendant who has given notice of intention to defend -... (c) requires that any question or issue relating to or connected with the original subject-matter of the action should be determined not only as between the plaintiff and the defendant but also as between either or both of them and a person not already a party to the action; then ... the defendant may issue a notice... containing a statement of the nature of the claim made against him and, as the case may be, either of the nature and grounds of the claim made by him or of the question or issue required to be determined."

14.7   We therefore recommend that:-

(50)   **although no legislative provision on this is necessary, a third party should be able to assign its rights under our proposed Act in an analogous way to that in which a contracting party can assign its rights.**

3. Contracts for the Sale of Land

14.8   One consultee raised a number of points regarding the impact of our proposals on contracts for the sale of land. Such a contract may be regarded as having a number of unusual features. For example, it is a specifically enforceable contract and transfers equitable title to the land. There is generally a period of time between the contract and the conveyance, by which latter method legal title passes. The contract usually provides for the payment of a deposit, which may nonetheless be repayable in certain instances where the contract is breached.[7] Since equitable title passes to the purchaser, the vendor becomes a trustee for the purchaser under the doctrine of conversion from the time of contract, with the vendor retaining certain rights over the land to protect his interest.[8] The most important of these is the unpaid vendor's lien.[9]

14.9   If B contracts with A to purchase land from A, conveyance to be made to C, and A defaults, who recovers the deposit paid by B? Is it B, or, assuming that C has a right to enforce the contract under our proposed reform, could it be C? In our view, the answer is clearly that B and not C is entitled to recover the deposit. It is trite law that an innocent party faced with a breach of a contract for the sale of land may recover his deposit, although a party in breach sometimes cannot.[10] In addition to the common law jurisdiction to permit recovery of deposits by a purchaser who is not in breach, section 49(2) of the Law of Property Act 1925[11] confers a wide discretion on the court to order "repayment" of any deposit even where it is the purchaser who is in breach of contract. The recovery of a deposit cannot be regarded as an "enforcement" of the contract so as to be one of the remedies available to a third party under our proposed

---

[7]   See *Cheshire and Burn's Modern Law of Real Property* (15th ed, 1994) pp 137-138; Law of Property Act 1925, s 49(2).

[8]   See *Cheshire and Burn's Modern Law of Real Property* (15th ed, 1994) pp 124-127. It has been said that "although the vendor because of his duties to the purchaser is called a trustee, it is wrong to argue that because he is so called he has all the duties of or holds the land on a trust which has all the incidents associated with the relationship of a trustee and his cestui que trust": *Berkley v Poulett* [1977] 1 EGLR 86, 93, *per* Stamp LJ. See also Gray, *Elements of Land Law* (2nd ed, 1993), pp 268-270.

[9]   See para 14.10 below.

[10]   This will depend on whether the sum paid is regarded by the courts as a genuine deposit or a part payment, in which latter case it is always recoverable provided that there has been a sufficient failure of consideration.

[11]   See *Universal Corporation v Five Ways Properties Ltd* [1979] 1 All ER 552; *Dimsdale Developments (South East) Ltd v De Haan* (1983) 47 P & CR 1.

reform.[12] The recovery of a deposit is a restitutionary remedy,[13] and is concerned to prevent the unjust enrichment of A at the expense of B (the payer).

14.10 We believe that the doctrine of conversion will operate to make A, as vendor, a trustee for C to whom the conveyance should be made.[14] The unpaid vendor's lien presents a different type of problem. If A contracts with B to purchase B's property, the purchase price to be paid partly to B and partly to C, does the lien benefit B as to the entire purchase price, or B as to his portion and C as to his, or B alone as to his portion? The answer to this appears to turn on whether one regards the security constituted by the unpaid vendor's equitable lien[15] as being designed to ensure that the purchaser performs its contract or rather as being designed to ensure restitution for the vendor.[16] If the former, B and C should each be entitled to an equitable lien for their respective portions of the purchase price. If the latter, B would be entitled to an equitable lien for the whole price (as representing the value of the land conveyed). Although this must be a matter for the courts to resolve, we would tentatively suggest that, in most circumstances, the former solution would be the most appropriate.

14.11 Finally, we were asked whether a third party with a right to enforce a contract for the sale of land would be a "purchaser" so as to fall within section 47 of the Law of Property Act 1925. If this were to be the case, the third party could insist on payment over to him by the vendor of the proceeds of any insurance maintained on property destroyed between contract and conveyance. We do not regard it as likely that, in a contract between A and B for the sale of land with conveyance to C, C would fall within the definition of "purchaser" in section 205(1)(xxi) of the Law of Property Act 1925, since he will not provide value, and does not actively take steps to acquire the property, being a mere passive recipient of a benefit.[17] Although this might seem to lead to inconvenient results, section 47 is rarely used in practice, and purchasers of

---

[12] See para 3.33 point (ii) above.

[13] See Goff & Jones, *The Law of Restitution* (4th ed, 1993) p 428ff.

[14] Using the maxim "Equity looks on as done that which ought to be done" (ie conveyance to C).

[15] The unpaid vendor's legal lien will be ignored for our purposes: it depends on possession and thus could not benefit a third party to whom payment of part of the purchase price was to be made.

[16] In a standard two-party contract, one need not choose between these two aims. See generally S Worthington, "Equitable Liens in Commercial Transactions" [1994] CLJ 263. Where title to land is unregistered, an unpaid vendor's lien is registrable as a Class C (iii) land charge under the Land Charges Act 1972. Where title is registered, the lien should be protected by lodging a caution or registering a notice, unless the vendor remains in actual occupation. In such circumstances, the lien can be protected under Land Registration Act 1925, s 70(1)(g) as an overriding interest: *Nationwide Anglia Building Society v Ahmed and Balakrishnan* (1995) 70 P & CR 381.

[17] Section 205(1)(xxi) defines "purchaser" as "a purchaser in good faith" for valuable consideration and includes a lessee, mortgagee or other person who for valuable consideration acquires an interest in property.

property generally maintain their own insurance. We would expect third parties with rights to enforce contracts for the sale of land to do the same.

4. Choice of Law

14.12   Our proposed statute, as part of English law, will not apply if the contract or (insofar as different choice of law rules can be applied to particular provisions of a contract)[18] the contractual provision alleged to be enforceable by the third party is governed by a foreign law. Whether a foreign law governs the contract (or contractual provision) is a matter for standard choice of law rules applicable to contract (including the Rome Convention on the Law Applicable to Contractual Obligations, given force in the United Kingdom by the Contracts (Applicable Law) Act 1990).[19] Where the third party is sued in tort but seeks to rely on our proposed Act to enforce an exclusion clause in a contract to which he is not a party, the standard choice of law rules may require that the exclusion clause is valid according to not only the choice of law rule for contract but also the choice of law rules for tort.[20]

14.13   We therefore recommend that:

(51)   **although no legislative provision on this is necessary, the standard choice of law rules applicable to contract (or, where the third party seeks to rely on an exclusion clause, the standard choice of law rules applicable to an exclusion clause operating as a defence to an action in tort) should determine whether our proposed Act applies in respect of facts involving a foreign element.**

5. Arbitration Agreements and Jurisdiction Agreements

14.14   Many contracts in common use in commerce and industry contain provisions obliging the reference of disputes to arbitration: or there may be a separate agreement to arbitrate. As was pointed out by various consultees, the Consultation Paper did not specifically consider the implications for arbitration of a reform of the third party rule. We seek to rectify that omission now. We have found this one of the most difficult issues that we have faced in this project.

14.15   Ultimately our recommendation is that arbitration agreements and jurisdiction agreements should fall outside our proposed reforms because such agreements cannot operate satisfactorily unless any entitlement of the third party to enforce the arbitration agreement carries with it a duty on the third party to submit to arbitration (or to comply with the jurisdiction agreement). Yet our reform is concerned only with the conferring of rights and benefits on third parties and not with the imposition of duties

---

[18]   See Dicey & Morris, *The Conflict of Laws* (12th ed, 1993) pp 1205-1208.

[19]   *Ibid*, ch 32.

[20]   *Ibid*, pp 1429-1430. Choice of law in tort is now largely governed by the Private International Law (Miscellaneous Provisions) Act 1995, Part III.

and burdens. In our view, a third party should in general[21] only be bound by an arbitration or jurisdiction agreement if it has agreed to be so bound in which case it becomes a true contracting party to the agreement and is no longer a third party to it.[22]

14.16　We were for a long time attracted by the idea that an arbitration agreement (or, analogously, a jurisdiction agreement) could operate as a procedural benefit to the third party and could also constitute a procedural condition on the third party's right to enforce the substantive promise. That is, if the third party wished to enforce its substantive right, it would be bound by the procedural condition to proceed via arbitration. So if A contracted with B to pay C £1000 for work done by B and there was an arbitration agreement referring to arbitration disputes relating to C's right to the £1000 our idea was that: (i) the arbitration agreement would be enforceable by C so that C could compel A and/or B to arbitrate as regards C's right to the £1000 notwithstanding that they did not wish to do so; and (ii) the arbitration agreement qualified C's right to the £1000, so that A and/or B would be entitled to a stay of litigation if C brought an action in the courts to enforce the promise of £1000.

14.17　We are now persuaded, however, that this approach is unacceptable for several reasons:

(i)　Our approach to conditional or qualified benefits rests on the condition or qualification operating as a defence that could be raised against the third party under recommendation 21 or 23. Yet it is clear law that an arbitration agreement (or a jurisdiction agreement) cannot be regarded as a defence to an action (unless an arbitration clause is of the *Scott v Avery*[23] type).[24] Rather

---

[21]　Ie subject to the possible application of the normal exceptions to the rule that a person who is not a party to the contract is not bound by it: see para 2.1 note 5 above. For example, a bailor may be bound by an arbitration or jurisdiction agreement in a contract of sub-bailment to which it is not a party.

[22]　For a possible analogy see the example of A contracting with B to loan £1000 to C to be repaid by C after a year, mentioned in para 10.26, note 29, above. In the event that the third party does bind itself to arbitrate by becoming a contracting party, procedural difficulties may arise involving, for example, the appointment of arbitrators. These difficulties would have to be solved by the application of the standard principles applying to multiparty arbitration agreements.

[23]　(1865) 5 HL Cas 811; 10 ER 1121. Although our recommendation is that arbitration agreements shall not confer a right of enforceability on a third party, we see no difficulty in allowing a *Scott v Avery* clause to operate as a defence under recommendation 21 above. Although C could not force A to arbitrate, if A refused to do so, A could no longer rely on the *Scott v Avery* defence. See Mustill and Boyd, *Commercial Arbitration* (2nd ed, 1989) p 164: "The second situation where a *Scott v Avery* clause is not available as a defence exists where the conduct of the defendant disentitles him from relying on it. [For example,] where the defendant has ... deprived the claimant of a proper opportunity to fulfil the condition precedent". See, eg, *Toronto Railway Co v National British and Irish Millers Insurance Co Ltd* (1914) 20 Com Cas 1: at p 23 Scrutton J said, "Conditions precedent may be waived by a course of conduct inconsistent with their continued validity...."

[24]　See Mustill and Boyd, *Commercial Arbitration* (2nd ed, 1989), ch 13.

the agreement is simply enforceable by and against the parties to it through a stay of litigation.

(ii) The qualification of the benefit approach cannot work where the third party is being sued in, for example, tort because there is then no substantive benefit to the third party that can be qualified. Say, for example, the third party is being sued by A in tort and there is an arbitration agreement between A and B that refers to arbitration all disputes arising out of the performance of the contract, including tort claims against B's sub-contractor (C). C can in no sense here be 'bound' to arbitrate. Yet it would plainly be unsatisfactory for C to be able to take the benefit of the arbitration clause without being so bound: C would otherwise be entitled to a stay of litigation of the tort action against him, while not being bound to arbitrate, hence leaving A without a forum for enforcing its tort claim against C. Even if one confined the operation of our proposed Act to arbitration (or jurisdiction) clauses relating to disputes as to the third party's right to enforcement under our Act - which in itself would constitute an unprincipled restriction - the same problem would apply if the third party were being sued in tort but was seeking to enforce an exclusion clause in the contract between A and B; that is, a conditional benefit approach cannot work where the enforceable benefit under our proposed Act is negative rather than positive.

(iii) It would seem that the qualification of the right approach could only, in any event, operate where the third party seeks to enforce the substantive promise. Yet A may wish to seek a declaration of its rights (for example, as to A's obligations to C) or may seek rescission of the contract on the basis of the promisee's fraud, even though C is not yet seeking to enforce the substantive promise. If the third party were not bound by the arbitrator's award, the declaration or rescission would be of little value to A. Yet it is hard to see how the qualification of the right approach can bind C to such an award of an arbitrator.

(iv) If the third party were entitled to, or bound to, arbitrate there would be difficulty in some situations in choosing the arbitrator. For example, what would be the position if the arbitrator is left to be agreed by the contracting parties or, as commonly happens, each party is to appoint an arbitrator and the two arbitrators are to choose an umpire? It is not at all clear that that sort of approach would be appropriate where a third party is involved in the arbitration.

14.18 We have therefore reluctantly come to the view that arbitration and jurisdiction clauses must be seen as both conferring rights and imposing duties and do not lend themselves to a splitting of the benefit and the burden.[25] Following on from that, one radical approach would be to bind the third party to those agreements in respect of a dispute affecting the third party's rights as if he were a party to them. While we have considered this possibility at length, we have ultimately rejected it essentially because it would contradict a central philosophy of our reform in that we are concerned only with the conferring of rights, and not the imposition of duties on third parties.[26] Our preferred approach therefore is that arbitration agreements and jurisdiction agreements should fall outside our reform and can neither be enforced by, nor are enforceable against, a third party.[27]

14.19 We therefore recommend that:

(52) **a third party shall have no rights of enforceability under our proposed reform in respect of an arbitration agreement or a jurisdiction agreement.** (Draft Bill, clause 6(2)(d) and (e))

6. Commencement of the Legislation

14.20 We do not intend that our reform should affect contracts entered into prior to the enactment of legislation based on our proposals. We further believe that any legislation should not commence its application until a reasonable time has been given for the professions and the public to become familiar with it and to redraft standard form contracts should they consider this to be desirable. We believe six months to be an appropriate time period.

14.21 We therefore recommend that:

(53) **the proposed legislation should not affect contracts entered into prior to its commencement date, which should be six months after receiving the Royal Assent.** (Draft Bill, clause 9(2))

---

[25] This derives support from the Privy Council's reasoning in *The Mahkutai* [1996] 3 WLR 1. Lord Goff said, at p13, that an exclusive jurisdiction clause "can be distinguished from terms such as exceptions and limitations in that it does not benefit only one party, but embodies a mutual agreement under which both parties agree with each other as to the relevant jurisdiction for the resolution of disputes. It is therefore a clause which creates mutual rights and obligations".

[26] If the third party were bound to arbitrate, without having agreed to do so, there is also some risk of there being a contravention of Article 6(1) of the European Convention on Human Rights, unless the arbitrator was "independent" as well as "impartial". And what is not clear, and raises concerns as regards English arbitrations, is whether an arbitrator, who is a member of the chambers to which one of the party's barristers belongs, would be regarded as 'independent'.

[27] We understand that the approach that we here recommend is supported by French law. In France, arbitration clauses are generally void, unless they are included in contracts made between certain commercial parties: see Code Civil, art 2061; *Code Commercial*, art 631. Subject to this, as against a third party beneficiary of a *stipulation pour autrui*, (see Consultation Paper No 121, Appendix, p 158), we understand that an arbitration clause is *res inter alios acta*, and the third party can neither be bound by it, nor take the benefit of it. However the third party beneficiary can independently bind himself by the arbitration clause, whether expressly or impliedly, and if he does so, is bound by it: *Code Civil*, art 1134.

SECTION D
SUMMARY

PART XV
SUMMARY OF RECOMMENDATIONS

We recommend that:-

Arguments for Reform

(1)   **The rule of English law whereby a third party to a contract may not enforce it should be reformed so as to enable contracting parties to confer a right to enforce the contract on a third party.** (Paragraph 3.29)

(2)   **A right to enforce the contract means (1) a right to all remedies given by the courts for breach of contract (and with the standard rules applicable to those remedies applying by analogy) that would have been available to the third party had he been a party to the contract, including damages, awards of an agreed sum, specific performance and injunctions; and (2) a right to take advantage of a promised exclusion or restriction of the promisor's rights as if the third party were a party to the contract.** (Paragraph 3.32 and draft Bill, clause 1(4) and 1(5))

The Form of the Legislation

(3)   **The third party rule should be reformed by means of a detailed legislative scheme.** (Paragraph 5.9)

(4)   **The legislation should not be construed as preventing judicial development of third party rights.** (Paragraph 5.11 and draft Bill, clause 6(1))

(5)   **The remedies available to the promisee in a contract enforceable by a third party should be left to the common law.** (Paragraph 5.17 and draft Bill, clause 4)

The Third Party Rule and Consideration

(6)   **The legislation should ensure that the rule that consideration must move from the promisee is reformed to the extent necessary to avoid nullifying our proposed reform of the doctrine of privity.** (Paragraph 6.8)

(7)   **Without prejudice to his rights and remedies at common law, a joint promisee who has not provided consideration should not be regarded**

164

as a third party for the purposes of our reform. (Paragraph 6.12 and draft Bill, clause 8)

The Test of Enforceability

(8)   **The test of enforceability should be as follows:**

(a) a third party shall have the right to enforce a contractual provision where that right is given to him - and he may be identified by name, class or description - by an express term of the contract (the "first limb");

(b) a third party shall also have the right to enforce a contractual provision where that provision purports to confer a benefit on the third party, who is expressly identified as a beneficiary of that provision, by name, class or description (the "second limb"); but there shall be no right of enforceability under the second limb where on the proper construction of the contract it appears that the contracting parties did not intend the third party to have that right (the "proviso"). (Paragraph 7.6 and draft Bill, clause 1(1) and 1(3) (the first and second limbs), clause 1(2) (the proviso) and clause 7(1) and 7(2)(a))

(9)   **There should be no special test of enforceability for consumers in our proposed legislation.** (Paragraph 7.56)

Designation, Existence and Ascertainability of the Third Party

(10)   **There should be an "avoidance of doubt" provision to the effect that the third party need not be in existence at the time of the contract.** (Paragraph 8.6 and draft Bill, clause 1(3))

(11)   **There should be no requirement that the third party be in existence at the time of acceptance by another third party.** (Paragraph 8.8)

(12)   **The proposed legislation should contain no special provisions governing pre-incorporation contracts.** (Paragraph 8.16)

(13)   **Although no legislative provision on this is necessary, a third party shall have no right to enforce a contract or contractual provision unless he or she is capable of being ascertained with certainty at the time when the promisor's duty to perform in the third party's favour arises, or when a liability against which the provision seeks to protect the third party is incurred.** (Paragraph 8.18)

Variation and Cancellation

(14)   **The contracting parties' right to vary or cancel the contract or, as the case may be, the contractual provision should be lost once the third**

party has relied on it or has accepted it ("acceptance" meaning "an assent by words or conduct communicated by the third party to the promisor"). The posting rule, applicable to the acceptance of offers sent by post (and possibly by some other means), should not apply. (Paragraph 9.26 and draft Bill, clause 2(1) and (2))

(15)   The reliance test should be qualified so that reliance should only count where (unless the promisor is aware that the third party has relied) the promisor could reasonably have foreseen that the third party would rely on the promise. (Paragraph 9.30 and draft Bill, clause 2(1)(b) and 2(1)(c))

(16)   The contracting parties may expressly reserve the right to vary or cancel the third party's right irrespective of reliance or acceptance by the third party. (Paragraph 9.40 and draft Bill, clause 2(3)(a))

(17)   The parties, by an express term, should be able to lay down a crystallisation test different from reliance or acceptance. (Paragraph 9.42 and draft Bill, clause 2(3)(b))

(18)   Although no legislative provision on this is necessary, where there is more than one third party who satisfies the test of enforceability, the relevant crystallisation test would need to be satisfied by each third party in order to crystallise that third party's rights. (Paragraph 9.44)

(19)   A contractual term to the effect that the contract is irrevocable should be as open to variation or cancellation by the contracting parties as any other term. (Paragraph 9.47)

(20)   There should be a judicial discretion to authorise a variation or cancellation (and on such terms, including as to the payment of compensation to the third party, as seems appropriate) in certain limited circumstances irrespective of reliance or acceptance by the third party. The discretion should extend to where the parties cannot reasonably ascertain whether the third party's consent is required for the cancellation or variation of the contract; or where the third party's consent cannot be obtained because his whereabouts cannot reasonably be discovered or because he is mentally incapable of giving his consent. (Paragraph 9.51 and draft Bill, clauses 2(4) to 2(7))

Defences, Set-Offs and Counterclaims

(21)   The third party's claim should be subject to all defences and set-offs that would have been available to the promisor in an action by the promisee and which arise out of or in connection with the contract or,

166

insofar as a particular contractual provision is being enforced by the third party, which arise out of or in connection with the contract and are relevant to that contractual provision. (Paragraph 10.12, draft Bill, clause 3(2) and 7(2)(b))

(22) The contracting parties may include an express provision to the effect that the promisor may *not* raise any defence or set-off that would have been available against the promisee; conversely, the parties may include an express provision to the effect that the third party's claim is subject to *all* defences and set-offs that the promisor would have had against the promisee. (Paragraph 10.16 and draft Bill, clause 3(3))

(23) It should be made clear that, in addition to the third party's claim being subject to defences and set-offs that the promisor would have had available in an action by the promisee, the third party's claim is also to be subject to the defences, counterclaims (not arising from the contract) and set-offs that would have been available to the promisor had the third party been a party to the contract. (Paragraph 10.19 and draft Bill, clause 3(4))

(24) The contracting parties may include an express provision to the effect that the promisor may *not* raise any defence, set-off or counterclaim that would have been available to the promisor had the third party been a party to the contract. (Paragraph 10.21, draft Bill clause 3(5))

(25) Where the third party seeks to rely on the test of enforceability to enforce an exclusion or limitation clause (or conceivably an analogous type of clause) he may do so only to the extent that he could have done so had he been a party to the contract (where the phrase 'had he been a party to the contract' means to refer to matters that affect the validity of the clause as between the contracting parties as well as matters affecting validity or enforceability that relate only to the third party). (Paragraph 10.23, draft Bill clause 3(6))

(26) The present general rule whereby parties to a contract cannot impose burdens upon third parties should be retained, although they may impose conditions upon the enjoyment of any benefits by them. The distinction between imposing burdens and conditional benefits (and hence the line between what falls outside our reform and what falls within it) depends on whether the condition is the basis merely of a defence or set-off to the third party's claim or whether, on the contrary, the condition is the basis of a claim or counterclaim by the promisor against the third party. This recommendation therefore ties

in with recommendations (21) and (23) above and no further legislative provision is required. (Paragraph 10.32)

Overlapping Claims

(27)   The promisor's duty to perform should be owed to both the promisee and the third party and, consequently, unless otherwise agreed between the contracting parties, the promisee should retain the right to enforce a contract even if the contract is also enforceable at the suit of the third party. (Paragraph 11.4 and draft Bill, clause 4)

(28)   Although no legislative provision on this is necessary, a promisor who has fulfilled its duty to the third party, whether wholly or partly, should to that extent be discharged from its duty to the promisee. (Paragraph 11.6)

(29)   Although no legislative provision on this is necessary, a release given to the promisor by the third party should not discharge the promisor's obligation to the promisee (unless otherwise agreed in the original contract). (Paragraph 11.8)

(30)   Although no legislative provision on this is necessary, the effect of a release of the promisor by one third party on the promisor's obligations to another third party is dependent (unless otherwise agreed in the original contract) on whether the promise is for the benefit of the third parties independently of each other, or whether it is for the benefit of the third parties jointly. If the promised benefit is to be enjoyed independently, the release by one third party should not discharge the promisor's obligation to the other third parties. But if the promise is for the joint benefit of the third parties, the release by one third party should normally discharge the promisor's obligation to the other third parties. (Paragraph 11.10)

(31)   Performance by the promisor to the promisee (rather than to the third party) and accepted by the promisee, or the release of the promisor by the promisee, should be straightforwardly regarded as a variation or cancellation of the contract and should therefore be governed by the recommendations in Part IX. (Paragraph 11.12)

(32)   There should be no order of priority between promisee and third party. (Paragraph 11.15)

(33)   Where the promisee has recovered substantial damages (or an agreed sum) representing the third party's loss or assessed on the basis that the promisee will "cure" the breach for the third party, the third

party will not be entitled under our proposed Act to an award which duplicates that sum and thereby imposes double liability on the promisor. (Paragraph 11.21 and draft Bill, clause 5)

(34) While no legislative provision to this effect is required, where a third party has pre-existing legal rights against the promisee, he should not lose those rights because the promisor and promisee enter into a contract whereby the promisor agrees to discharge the promisee's liability to the third party, but should acquire an additional right against the promisor. (Paragraph 11.26)

(35) While it is unnecessary for there to be a legislative provision on this, no compromise or settlement of the promisee's liability to the third party by the conferral of enforceable contractual rights against the promisor should be disturbed. (Paragraph 11.26)

Existing Exceptions

(36) The statutory and common law exceptions to the third party rule should be preserved by a statutory provision to the effect that our reform of the third party rule is to be without prejudice to any right or remedy of a third party which exists apart from our proposed Act. (Paragraph 12.2 and draft Bill, clause 6(1))

(37) There should be no statutory listing or codification of the existing statutory and common law exceptions. (Paragraph 12.2)

(38) There should be no legislative provision in our proposed legislation dealing with the issue of concurrent liability in tort and contract. (Paragraph 12.4)

(39) A third party shall have no right of enforceability under our proposed Act in the case of a contract for the carriage of goods by sea governed by the Carriage of Goods by Sea Act 1992 except that a third party can enforce an exclusion or limitation of liability in such a contract if he satisfies the test of enforceability. (Paragraph 12.11 and draft Bill, clause 6(2)(a) and 6(3)(a))

(40) A third party shall have no right of enforceability under our proposed Act in the case of a contract for the international carriage of goods by road or rail, or cargo by air, governed by the relevant international conventions, except that a third party can enforce an exclusion or limitation of liability in such a contract if he satisfies the test of enforceability. (Paragraph 12.15 and draft Bill, clause 6(2)(b) and 6(3)(b))

(41)   A third party shall have no right of enforceability under our proposed Act in respect of a contract contained in a bill of exchange, promissory note or other negotiable instrument. (Paragraph 12.17 and draft Bill, clause 6(2)(c))

(42)   Reform of the Third Parties (Rights Against Insurers) Act 1930 should not be covered in our general reform of the third party rule. (Paragraph 12.21)

(43)   There should not be an extension of section 11 of the Married Womens' Property Act 1882 at this stage. (Paragraph 12.27)

Consequential Amendments

(44)   Our proposed reform should not be interpreted as giving the third party full "contractual rights" nor as deeming the third party to be a party to the contract. It follows that, although no general legislative provision on this seems necessary, "contracts", "parties" to contracts, and "contractual rights and obligations" should be construed as they would have been prior to the enactment of our proposed reform. However, to avoid contradiction, a legislative provision is required to make clear that the references to treating the third party as if a party to the contract for the purposes of recommendations (2), (23) and (25) above should not be interpreted as treating the third party as if he were a party to the contract for the purposes of any other enactment. (Paragraph 13.4 and draft Bill, clause 6(6))

(45)   Subject to recommendations (46) and (47), no consequential amendment to other legislation is required by our proposals. (Paragraph 13.8)

(46)   Section 2(2) of the Unfair Contract Terms Act 1977 shall not apply in respect of a claim by a third party under our proposed Act for the breach of a contractual duty of care. (Paragraph 13.13 and draft Bill, clause 6(4))

(47)   Actions brought by third parties under our proposed Act are to be treated as "actions founded on simple contract" or as "actions upon a specialty" (depending on the nature of the contract) for the purposes of the Limitation Act 1980. (Paragraph 13.15 and draft Bill, clause 6(5))

Miscellaneous Issues

(48)   **There should be no requirement that the promisee be joined as a party to the litigation when a third party sues to enforce a contract.** (Paragraph 14.3)

(49)   **The existing Rules of Court are adequate to deal with joinder of the promisee in an action brought by a third party under our proposed reform.** (Paragraph 14.5)

(50)   **Although no legislative provision on this is necessary, a third party should be able to assign its rights under our proposed Act in an analogous way to that in which a contracting party can assign its rights.** (Paragraph 14.7)

(51)   **Although no legislative provision on this is necessary, the standard choice of law rules applicable to contract (or, where the third party seeks to rely on an exclusion clause, the standard choice of law rules applicable to an exclusion clause operating as a defence to an action in tort) should determine whether our proposed Act applies in respect of facts involving a foreign element.** (Paragraph 14.13)

(52)   **A third party shall have no rights of enforceability under our proposed reform in respect of an arbitration agreement or a jurisdiction agreement.** (Paragraph 14.19 and draft Bill, clause 6(2)(d) and (e))

(53)   **The proposed legislation should not affect contracts entered into prior to its commencement date, which should be six months after receiving the Royal Assent.** (Paragraph 14.21 and draft Bill, clause 9(2))

(Signed)   MARY ARDEN, *Chairman*

ANDREW BURROWS

DIANA FABER

CHARLES HARPUM

STEPHEN SILBER

MICHAEL SAYERS, *Secretary*

19 June 1996

APPENDIX A

Draft
Contracts (Rights of Third Parties) Bill

ARRANGEMENT OF CLAUSES

A

B I L L

INTITULED

An Act to make provision for the enforcement of a contract in certain circumstances by a person who is not a party to the contract; and for connected purposes.

A.D. 1996.

BE IT ENACTED by the Queen's most Excellent Majesty, by and with the advice and consent of the Lords Spiritual and Temporal, and Commons, in this present Parliament assembled, and by the authority of the same, as follows:—

5   **1.**—(1) Subject to the provisions of this Act, a person who is not a party to a contract (in this Act referred to as a third party) may in his own right enforce the contract if—

> (a) the contract contains an express term to that effect; or

> (b) subject to subsection (2) below, the contract purports to confer a
10   benefit on the third party.

(2) Subsection (1)(b) above does not apply if on a proper construction of the contract it appears that the parties did not intend the contract to be enforceable by the third party.

(3) The third party must be expressly identified in the contract by name, as a
15 member of a class or as answering a particular description but need not be in existence when the contract is entered into.

(4) For the purpose of exercising the rights conferred on him by this section there shall be available to the third party all such remedies as would have been available to him in an action for breach of the contract if he had
20 been a party to it, and the rules relating to damages, injunctions, specific performance and other relief shall apply accordingly.

(5) Where the contract excludes or limits the third party's liability in relation to any matter references in this Act to his enforcing it shall be construed as references to his availing himself of the exclusion or limitation.

25   (6) In this Act "the promisor" means the party to the contract against whom it is enforceable by the third party by virtue of this section and "the promisee" means the party to the contract by whom it is enforceable against the promisor.

Right of third party to enforce contract.

EXPLANATORY NOTES

Clause 1

Clause 1(1) sets out a two-limbed test for the circumstances in which a person who is not a party to a contract ("a third party") may enforce the contract (or any provision of it - see clause 7). The first limb is where the contract itself expressly so provides (clause 1(1)(a)). The second limb is where the contract purports to confer a benefit on the third party (clause 1(1)(b)) unless it appears on a true construction of the contract that the contracting parties did not intend him to have the right to enforce it (clause 1(2)). In addition, under either limb of the test of enforceability, clause 1(3) requires that the third party be expressly identified in the contract by name, class or description.

Clause 1(3) also lays down that the third party need not be in existence when the contract is made. This allows contracting parties to confer enforceable rights on, for example, an unborn child or a future spouse or a company that has not yet been incorporated.

Clause 1(4) provides that the courts may award all the remedies available to a plaintiff in an action for breach of contract to a third party seeking to enforce his rights under clause 1(1). The normal rules applicable to those remedies (for example, the rules on remoteness of damage, the duty to mitigate one's loss, or that laches bars specific performance) apply by analogy to the third party's action.

Clause 1(5) makes it clear that the Bill is to apply so as to entitle a third party to take advantage of an exclusion or limitation clause, as well as to enforce "positive" rights.

Variation and
cancellation of
contract.

2.—(1) Subject to the provisions of this section, where a contract is enforceable by a third party by virtue of section 1 above the parties to the contract may not without his consent vary or cancel the contract if—

(a) the third party has communicated his assent to the contract to the promisor;   5

(b) the promisor is aware that the third party has relied on the contract; or

(c) the promisor can reasonably be expected to have foreseen that the third party would rely on the contract and the third party has in fact relied on it.

(2) The assent referred to in subsection (1)(a) above—   10

(a) may be by words or conduct; and

(b) if sent to the promisor by post or other means, shall not be regarded as communicated to the promisor until received by him.

(3) A contract which is enforceable by a third party by virtue of section 1 above may expressly provide—   15

(a) that it shall be capable of cancellation or variation without the consent of the third party; or

(b) that his consent is to be required in circumstances specified in the contract instead of those specified in subsection (1) above.

(4) Where by virtue of the foregoing provisions of this section the consent 20 of a third party is required for the cancellation or variation of a contract the court may, on the application of the parties to the contract, dispense with that consent if satisfied—

(a) that the third party's consent cannot be obtained because his whereabouts cannot reasonably be ascertained; or   25

(b) that he is mentally incapable of giving his consent.

(5) The court may, on the application of the parties to a contract, dispense with any consent to a variation or cancellation of the contract that may be required by virtue of subsection (1)(c) above if satisfied that it cannot reasonably be ascertained whether or not the third party has in fact relied on 30 the contract.

(6) Where the court dispenses with a third party's consent it may impose such conditions as it thinks fit, including a condition requiring the payment of compensation to the third party.

(7) The jurisdiction conferred by subsections (4) to (6) above shall be 35 exercisable both by the High Court and a county court.

Defences etc.
available to
promisor.

3.—(1) Subsections (2) to (5) below apply where in reliance on section 1 above proceedings for the enforcement of a contract are brought by a third party.

(2) The promisor shall have available to him by way of defence or set-off 40 any matter that—

(a) arises from or in connection with the contract; and

(b) would have been available to him by way of defence or set-off in proceedings for the enforcement of the contract if those proceedings had been brought by the promisee.   45

EXPLANATORY NOTES

Clause 2

Clause 2 deals with the extent to which, once a third party has a right of enforceability in accordance with clause 1, the contracting parties can vary or cancel the contract without the third party's consent.

The contracting parties may not so vary or cancel the contract after the third party has communicated his assent to the contract to the promisor (that is, after the third party has accepted) (clause 2(1)(a)); or after the third party has relied on the contract, where the promisor is aware of that reliance (clause 2(1)(b)) or could reasonably be expected to have foreseen it (clause 2(1)(c)).

Clause 2(2) provides that the assent may be by words or conduct and that the "posting rule" - applicable to the acceptance of offers by post and possibly by some other means - does not apply (so that, for example, a letter of acceptance must be received by the promisor to be valid).

However, under clause 2(3), the above rules will be displaced by an express term of the contract providing that the contract can be cancelled or varied without the third party's consent or that the third party's consent is to be required in specified circumstances different to those specified in clause 2(1).

Clauses 2(4) to 2(5) give the court a power to dispense with the third party's consent (which is, or may be, required by virtue of clause 2(1)) where the third party's consent cannot be obtained because his whereabouts are unknown or he is mentally incapable of giving his consent (clause 2(4)) or where it cannot be ascertained whether the third party has in fact relied on the contract (clause 2(5)). The court may impose conditions on any such dispensation including that the third party is paid compensation (clause 2(6)).

Clause 3

Clauses 3(1) to (5) deal with the defences, set-offs and counterclaims available to the promisor in an action by the third party to enforce the contract.

Clause 3(2) makes available to the promisor any defence or set-off which arises from or in connection with the contract (or is relevant to the particular contractual provision being enforced by the third party - see clause 7(2)(b)) and which would have been available if the action had been brought by the promisee. So, for example, a void, discharged or unenforceable contract is no more enforceable by the third party than by the promisee.

(3) Subsection (2) above is subject to any express term of the contract as to the matters that are not to be available to the promisor by way of defence or set-off, and is without prejudice to any express term of the contract which makes available to the promisor by way of defence or set-off any other
5   matter which would have been so available in proceedings for the enforcement of the contract had they been brought by the promisee.

(4) The promisor shall also have available to him—

   (a) by way of defence or set-off any matter, and

   (b) by way of counterclaim any matter not arising from the contract,

10   that would have been available to him by way of defence or set-off or, as the case may be, by way of counterclaim against the third party if the third party had been a party to the contract.

(5) Subsection (4) above is subject to any express term of the contract as to the matters that are not to be available to the promisor by way of defence,
15   set-off or counterclaim.

(6) Where in any proceedings brought against him a third party seeks in reliance on section 1 above to enforce a contract (including, in particular, a contract purporting to exclude or limit any liability of his), he may not do so to the extent that he could not have done so (whether by reason of any
20   particular circumstances relating to him or otherwise) if he had been a party to the contract.

4. Section 1 above is without prejudice to any right of the promisee to enforce the contract.

Enforcement of contract by promisee.

5. Where by virtue of section 1 above a contract is enforceable by a third
25   party, and the promisee has recovered from the promisor a sum in respect of—

Protection of promisor from double liability.

   (a) the third party's loss in respect of the contract, or

   (b) the expense to the promisee of making good to the third party the default of the promisor,

30   then, in any proceedings brought by virtue of that section by the third party, the court shall reduce any award to the third party to such extent as it thinks appropriate to take account of the sum recovered by the promisee.

6.—(1) Section 1 above is without prejudice to any right or remedy of a third party which exists or is available apart from this Act.

Supplementary provisions relating to third party.

35   (2) Section 1 above confers no rights on a third party in the case of—

   (a) a contract for the carriage of goods by sea, except that a third party may by virtue of that section avail himself of an exclusion or limitation of liability in such a contract;

   (b) a contract for the carriage of goods by rail or road, or for the carriage of
40   cargo by air, which is subject to the rules of the appropriate international transport convention, except that a third party may by virtue of that section avail himself of an exclusion or limitation of liability in such a contract;

EXPLANATORY NOTES

Clause 3(4) makes it clear that the promisor also has available any defence or set-off, and any counterclaim not arising from the contract, which is specific to the third party (for example, a set-off arising from a linked contract between the promisor and the third party or a defence or counterclaim arising from the fact that, perhaps unknown to the promisee, the third party induced the promisor to enter into the contract by fraud).

Clauses 3(2) and (4) are subject to any express term of the contract which narrows or widens the defences or set-offs available under clause 3(2) (clause 3(3)) or narrows the defences, set-offs or counterclaims available under clause 3(4) (clause 3(5)).

Where a third party seeks to avail himself of an exclusion or limitation clause (or conceivably an analogous clause) in relation to proceedings brought against him, clause 3(6) seeks to ensure that an analogous approach to that set out in clauses 3(1) to 3(5) will be applied. This separate provision is needed because it is inappropriate in this context to talk of defences available to the promisor.

Clause 4

This preserves (and allows for the judicial development of) the promisee's right to enforce the contract. It clarifies that the third party's right is additional to, and not at the expense of, the promisee's right.

Clause 5

Where the promisee has recovered substantial damages (or an agreed sum) representing the third party's loss or assessed on the basis that the promisee will "cure" the breach for the third party, this clause ensures that the court can avoid an award to the third party which duplicates that sum and thereby imposes double liability on the promisor.

Clause 6

Clause 6(1) preserves the statutory and common law exceptions to the "third party rule" and allows for the judicial development of a third party's rights.

Clause 6(2) excludes from the Bill certain types of contracts. The types of contract covered by clauses 6(2)(a) and (b)—and see the definitional clause 6(3)—and (c) have been excluded primarily on the basis that to permit third parties a right of enforceability under this Bill would contradict the policy underlying legislation that already confers a right of enforceability on (some) third parties in respect of such contracts. However, a third party can avail himself of an exclusion or limitation clause under a contract otherwise excluded by clauses 6(2)(a) or (b).

(c) a contract contained in a bill of exchange, promissory note or other negotiable instrument;

(d) an agreement to submit to arbitration present or future disputes; or

(e) an agreement as to the court, or courts, which are to have jurisdiction to settle present or future disputes or are not to have such jurisdiction.   5

(3) For the purposes of subsection (2) above—

(a) "contract for the carriage of goods by sea" means a contract of carriage—

1992 c. 50.

(i) which is contained in or evidenced by a bill of lading or sea waybill to which the Carriage of Goods by Sea Act 1992 10 applies; or

(ii) under, or for the purposes of, which there is given an undertaking which is contained in a ship's delivery order to which that Act applies;

(b) "the appropriate international transport convention"—   15

1983 c. 14.

(i) in relation to a contract for the carriage of goods by rail, means the Convention which has force of law in the United Kingdom by virtue of section 1 of the International Transport Conventions Act 1983;

1965 c. 37.

(ii) in relation to a contract for the carriage of goods by road, 20 means the Convention which has force of law in the United Kingdom by virtue of section 1 of the Carriage of Goods by Road Act 1965; and

1961 c. 27.

1962 c. 43.

S.I. 1967/480.

(iii) in relation to a contract for the carriage of cargo by air, means the Convention which has force of law in the United 25 Kingdom by virtue of section 1 of the Carriage by Air Act 1961 or the Convention which has such force by virtue of section 1 of the Carriage by Air (Supplementary Provisions) Act 1962 (or either of the amended Conventions set out in Part B of Schedule 2 to the Carriage by Air Acts (Application of Provisions) Order 30 1967).

1977 c. 50.

(4) Section 2(2) of the Unfair Contract Terms Act 1977 (restriction on exclusion etc. of liability for negligence) shall not apply where the negligence consists of the breach of an obligation arising from the terms of a contract and the person seeking to enforce them is a third party acting by 35 virtue of section 1 above.

1980 c. 58.

(5) In sections 5 and 8 of the Limitation Act 1980 the references to an action founded on a simple contract and an action upon a specialty shall respectively include references to an action brought by virtue of section 1 above relating to a simple contract and an action brought by virtue of that 40 section relating to a specialty.

(6) A third party shall not by virtue of section 1(4) or 3(4) or (6) above be treated, for the purposes of any other Act (or any instrument made under any Act), as a party to the contract.

Enforcement limited to particular provisions of contract.

7.—(1) Section 1 above applies also where—   45

(a) the express term referred to in paragraph (a) of subsection (1) applies only to a particular provision of the contract; or

(b) it is only a particular provision of the contract that purports to confer a benefit as mentioned in paragraph (b) of that subsection.

EXPLANATORY NOTES

Clause 6(2)(d) and (e) - arbitration and jurisdiction agreements - have been excluded primarily because of the difficulties created by giving a third party a right to enforce such an agreement without being bound by it.

Clause 6(4) ensures that a third party cannot invoke section 2(2) of the Unfair Contract Terms Act 1977 to contest the validity of a clause excluding or limiting the promisor's liability under this Bill to the third party for negligently caused loss or damage (other than personal injury or death).

Clause 6(5) ensures that the standard limitation periods for actions for breach of contract under the Limitation Act 1980 apply to actions brought by third parties under this Bill.

Clause 6(6) ensures that those references in the Bill to the position "if the third party had been a party to the contract" are not to be interpreted as meaning that the third party should be treated as a party to the contract for the purposes of any other enactment (for example, section 3 of the Unfair Contract Terms Act 1977).

Clause 7

This is designed to ensure that the test of enforceability in clause 1 (and the rest of the Bill correspondingly) applies where the express term conferring the right of enforceability applies only to a particular provision of the contract, rather than the whole contract, or where it is only a particular provision, rather than the whole contract, which purports to confer a benefit. As regards clause 7(2)(b), see the explanatory note to clause 3(2) above.

(2) In any such case—

  (a) references in this Act to the enforcement of the contract, or to a contract being enforceable, by a third party shall be construed as references to the enforcement of the particular provision in question, or to its being enforceable, by a third party; and

  (b) the reference in section 3(2)(a) above to the contract shall be construed as a reference to the contract so far as relevant to that particular provision.

8.—(1) Where the persons to whom a contractual promise is made include a person who does not provide consideration for the promise, that person shall not be treated as a third party for the purposes of this Act.

(2) Subsection (1) above is without prejudice to any right or remedy of such a person in relation to the contract which exists or is available apart from this Act.

Joint promisee not providing consideration.

9.—(1) This Act may be cited as the Contracts (Rights of Third Parties) Act 1996.

(2) This Act comes into force at the end of the period of six months beginning with the day on which it is passed and does not apply in relation to contracts entered into before the end of that period.

(3) This Act extends to England and Wales only.

Short title, commencement and extent.

EXPLANATORY NOTES

Clause 8

For the reasons set out in paragraphs 6.9-6.12 of the Report, this clause is intended to leave it to the courts to decide on the precise rights of a joint promisee who has not provided consideration.

Clause 9

The Bill once passed is to come into effect on the expiry of a six month period. It does not apply to any contracts entered into prior to the end of that period.

APPENDIX B
Legislation From Some Other Jurisdictions[1]

1.   Western Australia

Property Law Act 1969, section 11:

"(2) Except in the case of a conveyance or other instrument to which subsection (1) of this section applies, where a contract expressly in its terms purports to confer a benefit directly on a person who is not named as a party to the contract, the contract is, subject to subsection (3) of this section, enforceable by that person in his own name but -

(a) all defences that would have been available to the defendant in an action or proceeding in a court of competent jurisdiction to enforce the contract had the plaintiff in the action or proceeding been named as a party to the contract, shall be so available;

(b) each person named as a party to the contract shall be joined as a party to the action or proceeding; and

(c) such defendant in the action or proceeding shall be entitled to enforce as against such plaintiff, all the obligations that in the terms of the contract are imposed on the plaintiff for the benefit of the defendant.

(3) Unless the contract referred to in subsection (2) of this section otherwise provides, the contract may be cancelled or modified by the mutual consent of the persons named as parties thereto at any time before the person referred to in that subsection has adopted it either expressly or by conduct."

2.   Queensland

Property Law Act 1974, section 55:

"(1) A promisor who, for a valuable consideration moving from the promisee, promises to do or refrain from doing an act or acts for the benefit of a beneficiary shall, upon acceptance by the beneficiary, be subject to a duty enforceable by the beneficiary to perform that promise.

(2) Prior to acceptance the promisor and promisee may without the consent of the beneficiary vary or discharge the terms of the promise and any duty arising therefrom.

(3) Upon acceptance -
    (a) the beneficiary shall be entitled in his own name to such remedies and relief as may be just and convenient for the enforcement of the duty of the

---

[1] The legislation produced in this publication is reproduced by permission but does not purport to be the official authorised version. We have been requested to advise readers that the authorised version of the Queensland legislation is available from GOPRINT Publications Division, PO Box 364, Woolloongabba Qld 4102, Australia. Telephone (07) 3246 3399.

promisor; and relief by way of specific performance, injunction or otherwise shall not be refused solely on the ground that, as against the promisor, the beneficiary may be a volunteer;

(b) the beneficiary shall be bound by the promise and subject to a duty enforceable against him in his own name to do or refrain from doing such act or acts (if any) as may by the terms of the promise be required of him;

(c) the promisor shall be entitled to such remedies and relief as may be just and convenient for the enforcement of the duty of the beneficiary;

(d) the terms of the promise and the duty of the promisor or the beneficiary may be varied or discharged with the consent of the promisor, the promisee and the beneficiary.

(4) Subject to subsection (1), any matter which would in proceedings not brought in reliance on this section render a promise void, voidable or unenforceable, whether wholly or in part, or which in proceedings (not brought in reliance on this section) to enforce a promissory duty arising from a promise is available by way of defence shall, in like manner and to the like extent, render void, voidable or unenforceable or be available by way of defence in proceedings for the enforcement of a duty to which this section gives effect.

(5) In so far as a duty to which this section gives effect may be capable of creating and creates an interest in land, such interest shall, subject to section 12, be capable of being created and of subsisting in land under the provisions of any Act but subject to the provisions of that Act.

(6) In this section-

(a) "acceptance" means an assent by words or conduct communicated by or on behalf of the beneficiary to the promisor, or to some person authorised on his behalf, in the manner (if any), and within the time, specified in the promise or, if no time is specified, within a reasonable time of the promise coming to the notice of the beneficiary.

(b) " beneficiary" means a person other than the promisor or promisee, and includes a person who, at the time of acceptance is identified and in existence, although that person may not have been identified or in existence at the time when the promise was given;

(c) " promise" means a promise-

(i) which is or appears to be intended to be legally binding; and

(ii) which creates or appears to be intended to create a duty enforceable by a beneficiary,

and includes a promise whether made by deed, or in writing, or, subject to this Act, orally, or partly in writing and partly orally;

(d) " promisee" means a person to whom a promise is made or given;

(e) " promisor" means a person by whom a promise is made or given.

(7) Nothing in this section affects any right or remedy which exists or is available apart from this section.

(8) This section applies only to promises made after the commencement of this Act."

3. The Commonwealth of Australia

Insurance Contracts Act 1984, section 48 :

"(1) Where a person who is not a party to a contract of general insurance is specified or referred to in the contract, whether by name or otherwise, as a person to whom the insurance cover provided by the contract extends, that person has a right to recover the amount of his loss from the insurer in accordance with the contract notwithstanding that he is not a party to the contract.

(2) Subject to the contract, a person who has such a right:

(a) has, in relation to his claim, the same obligations to the insurer as he would have if he were the insured; and

(b) may discharge the insured's obligation in relation to the loss.

(3) The insurer has the same defences to an action under this section as he would have in an action by the insured.

(4) Where a contract of life insurance effected by a person upon his own life is expressed to be for the benefit of a person specified or referred to in the contract, whether by name or otherwise, that second-mentioned person has a right to recover the moneys payable under the contract from the insurer in accordance with the contract notwithstanding that the second-mentioned person is not a party to the contract, and the moneys payable under the contract do not form part of the estate of the person whose life is insured and are not subject to his debts.

(5) Section 94 of the *Life Insurance Act 1945* does not apply in relation to a policy within the meaning of that Act that is entered into after the commencement of this Act."

4. New Zealand

Contracts (Privity) Act 1982:

" **1. Short Title and commencement-** (1) This Act may be cited as the Contracts (Privity) Act 1982.
(2) This Act shall come into force on the first day of April 1983.

2. Interpretation- In this Act, unless the context otherwise requires,-

" Benefit" includes-
(a) any advantage; and
(b) any immunity; and
(c) any limitation or other qualification of-
(i) An obligation to which a person (other than a party to the deed or contract) is or may be subject; or
(ii) A right to which a person (other than a party to the deed or contract) is or may be entitled; and
(d) Any extension or other improvement of a right or rights to which a person (other than a party to the deed or contract) is or may be entitled:

"Beneficiary", in relation to a promise to which section 4 of this Act apples, means a person (other than the promisor or promisee) on whom the promise confers, or purports to confer, a benefit:

"Contract" includes a contract made by deed or in writing, or orally, or partly in writing and partly orally or implied by law:

"Court" means-
(a) The High Court; or
(b) A District Court that has jurisdiction under section 10 of this Act; or
(c) A Small Claims Tribunal that has jurisdiction under section 11 of this Act:

"Promisee", in relation to a promise to which section 4 of this Act applies, means a person who is both-
(a) A party to the deed or contract; and
(b) A person to whom the promise is made or given:

"Promisor", in relation to a promise to which section 4 of this Act applies, means a person who is both-
(a) A party to the deed or contract; and
(b) A person by whom the promise is made or given.

3. Act to bind the Crown- This Act shall bind the Crown.

4. Deeds or contracts for the benefit of third parties- Where a promise contained in a deed or contract confers, or purports to confer, a benefit on a person, designated by name, description, or reference to a class, who is not a party to the deed or contract (whether or not the person is in existence at the time when the deed or contract is made), the promisor shall be under an obligation, enforceable at the suit of that person, to perform that promise: Provided that this section shall not apply to a promise which, on the proper construction of the deed or contract, is not intended to create, in respect of the benefit, an obligation enforceable at the suit of that person.

5. Limitation on variation or discharge of promise- (1) Subject to sections 6 and 7 of this Act, where, in respect of a promise to which section 4 of this Act applies,-
(a) The position of a beneficiary has been materially altered by the reliance of that beneficiary or any other person on the promise (whether or not that beneficiary or that other person has knowledge of the precise terms of the promise); or
(b) A beneficiary has obtained against the promisor judgment upon the promise; or
(c) A beneficiary has obtained against the promisor the award of an arbitrator upon a submission relating to the promise,-

the promise and the obligation imposed by that section may not be varied or discharged without the consent of that beneficiary.

(2) For the purposes of paragraph (b) or paragraph (c) of subsection (1) of this section,-

(a) An award of an arbitrator or a judgment shall be deemed to be obtained when it is pronounced notwithstanding that some act, matter, or thing needs to be done to record or perfect it or that, on application to a court or on appeal, it is varied:

(b) An award of an arbitrator or a judgment set aside on application to a Court or on appeal shall be deemed never to have been obtained.

6. Variation or discharge of promise by agreement or in accordance with express provision for variation or discharge- Nothing in this Act prevents a promise to which section 4 of this Act applies or any obligation imposed by that section from being varied or discharged at any time -

(a) By agreement between the parties to the deed or contract and the beneficiary; or

(b) By any party or parties to the deed or contract if -

(i) The deed or contract contained, when the promise was made, an express provision to that effect; and

(ii) The provision is known to the beneficiary (whether or not the beneficiary has knowledge of the precise terms of the provision); and

(iii) The beneficiary had not materially altered his position in reliance on the promise before the provision became known to him; and

(iv) The variation or discharge is in accordance with the provision.

7. Power of Court to authorise variation or discharge-(1) Where, in the case of a promise to which section 4 of this Act applies or of an obligation imposed by that section,-

(a) The variation or discharge of that promise or obligation is precluded by section 5(1)(a) of this Act; or

(b) It is uncertain whether the variation or discharge of that promise is so precluded,-

a Court, on application by the promisor or promisee, may, if it is just and practicable to do so, make an order authorising the variation or discharge of the promise or obligation or both on such terms and conditions as the Court thinks fit.

(2) If a Court-

(a) Makes an order under subsection (1) of this section; and

(b) Is satisfied that the beneficiary has been injuriously affected by the reliance of the beneficiary or any other person on the promise or obligation,-

the Court shall make it a condition of the variation or discharge that the promisor pay to the beneficiary, by way of compensation, such sum as the Court thinks just.

8. Enforcement by beneficiary-The obligation imposed on a promisor by section 4 of this Act may be enforced at the suit of the beneficiary as if he were a party to the deed or contract, and relief in respect of the promise, including relief by way of damages, specific performance, or injunction, shall not be refused on the ground that the beneficiary is not a party to the deed or contract in which the promise is contained or that, as against the promisor, the beneficiary is a volunteer.

9. Availability of defences-(1) This section applies only where, in proceedings brought in a Court or an arbitration, a claim is made in reliance on this Act by a beneficiary against a promisor.

(2) Subject to subsections (3) and (4) of this section, the promisor shall have available to

him, by way of defence, counterclaim, set-off or otherwise, any matter which would have been available to him-

(a) If the beneficiary had been a party to the deed or contract in which the promise is contained; or

(b) If -

(i) The beneficiary were the promisee; and

(ii) The promise to which the proceedings relate had been made for the benefit of the promisee; and

(iii) The proceedings had been brought by the promisee.

(3) The promisor may, in the case of a set-off or counterclaim arising by virtue of subsection (2) of this section against the promisee, avail himself of that set-off or counterclaim against the beneficiary only if the subject-matter of that set-off or counterclaim arises out of or in connection with the deed or contract in which the promise is contained.

(4) Notwithstanding subsections (2) and (3) of this section, in the case of a counterclaim brought under either of those subsections against a beneficiary,-

(a) The beneficiary shall not be liable on the counterclaim, unless the beneficiary elects, with full knowledge of the counterclaim, to proceed with his claim against the promisor; and

(b) If the beneficiary so elects to proceed, his liability on the counterclaim shall not in any event exceed the value of the benefit conferred on him by the promise.

10. Jurisdiction of District Courts- (1) A District Court shall have jurisdiction to exercise any power conferred by section 7 of this Act in any case where-

(a) The occasion for the exercise of the power arises in the course of civil proceedings properly before the court; or

(b) The value of the consideration for the promise of the promisor is not more than $12,000; or

(c) The parties agree, in accordance with section 37 of the District Courts Act 1947, that a District Court shall have jurisdiction to determine the application.

(2) For the purposes of section 43 of the District Courts Act 1947, an application made to a District Court under section 7 of this Act shall be deemed to be an action.

11. Jurisdiction of Small Claims Tribunal- (1) A Small Claims Tribunal established under the Small Claims Tribunals Act 1976 shall have jurisdiction to exercise any power conferred by section 7 of this Act in any case where-

(a) The occasion for the exercise of the power arises in the course of proceedings properly before that Tribunal; and

(b) The value of the consideration for the promise of the promisor is not more than $500.

(2) A condition imposed by the Small Claims Tribunal under section 7(2) of this Act shall not require the promisor to pay a sum exceeding $500 and an order of a Tribunal that exceeds any such restriction shall be entirely of no effect.

12. Amendments of Arbitration Act 1908- The Second Schedule to the Arbitration Act 1908 is hereby amended by inserting, after clause 10B (as inserted by section 14(2) of the Contractual Remedies Act 1979), the following clause:

"10C. The arbitrators or umpire shall have the same power as the Court to exercise any of the powers conferred by section 7 of the Contracts (Privity) Act 1982."

13. Repeal-Section 7 of the Property Law Act 1952 is hereby repealed.

14. Savings-(1) Subject to section 13 of this Act, nothing in this Act limits or affects-

    (a) Any right or remedy which exists or is available apart from this Act; or

    (b) The Contracts Enforcement Act 1956 or any other enactment that requires any contract to be in writing or to be evidenced by writing; or

    (c) Section 49A of the Property Law Act 1952; or

    (d) The law of agency; or

    (e) The law of trusts.

(2) Notwithstanding the repeal effected by section 13 of this Act, section 7 of the Property Law Act 1952 shall continue to apply in respect of any deed made before the commencement of this Act.

15. Application of Act-Except as provided in section 14(2) of this Act, this Act does not apply to any promise, contract, or deed made before the commencement of this Act."

APPENDIX C
List of Persons and Organisations who Commented on Consultation Paper No 121

Consultation took place in 1991 and closed on 30 June 1992. The descriptions of consultees may have altered since then.

GOVERNMENT BODIES
Local Authorities Associations
Lord Chancellor's Department

JUDICIARY AND PRACTITIONERS

(i)   Judiciary
His Honour Judge Bowsher QC
Council of H M Circuit Judges
The Hon Mr Justice May
The Hon Mr Justice Millett
The Rt Hon The Lord Mustill
His Honour Judge John Newey QC
Rt Hon Lord Justice Parker
The Hon Mr Justice Phillips
The Rt Hon Lord Jauncey of Tullichettle

(ii)   Barristers
Walter Aylen QC
Sir Wilfred Bourne KCB QC
R O Havery
G F Hawker
Chambers of Donald Keating QC
John Lindsay QC
Andrew Longmore QC
Robert Nelson QC
Christopher Thomas QC

(iii)   Solicitors
Allen & Overy
A G J Berg
Clifford Chance
Cyril Sweett & Partners
D M E Evans
Freshfields
J H L Leckie
G L Leigh
Lovell White Durrant
Masons
McKenna & Co
Norton Rose
R A Shadbolt
Simmons & Simmons
W H Thomas

LEGAL ORGANISATIONS
Family Law Bar Association
General Council of the Bar
Holborn Law Society
Institute of Legal Executives
The Law Society
Society of Public Teachers of Law

ACADEMIC LAWYERS
Professor John Adams, University of Kent
Professor Dr Christian V Bar, Universität Osnabrück
Professor Hugh Beale, University of Warwick
Andrew Bell, Manchester University
Professor Joost Blom, University of British Columbia
Professor Roger Brownsword, Sheffield University
Andrew Burrows, Lady Margaret Hall
Professor Hugh Collins, London School of Economics
Professor Brian Coote, University of Auckland
R O'Dair, University College London
Professor Aubrey Diamond, Notre Dame University
Professor Brice Dickson, University of Ulster
Professor M A Eisenberg, University of California
J D Feltham, Magdalen College Oxford
Professor Robert Flannigan, University of British Columbia
John G Fleming, University of California
Simon Gardner, Lincoln College Oxford
Roger Halson, University College London
Charles Harpum, Downing College Cambridge
Professor D J Hayton, King's College London
Peter Kincaid, MacQuarrie University
Professor Dr Werner Lorenz, Universität München
Professor Robert Merkin, Exeter University
Professor J R Midgley, Rhodes University
Professor Anthony Ogus, Manchester University
Dr F M B Reynolds, Worcester College Oxford
Colin Scott, London School of Economics
W J Swadling, Queen Mary and Westfield College London
Andrew Tettenborn, Pembroke College Cambridge
Professor G H Treitel, All Souls College Oxford
Professor A J Waters, University of Maryland
Dr Simon Whittaker, St John's College Oxford

OTHER ORGANISATIONS
Architects & Surveyors Institute
Association of British Insurers
British Bankers' Association
Building Employers Confederation
Chartered Institute of Arbitrators
Confederation of British Industry
Confederation of Construction Specialists
Construction Industry Council
Consumers' Association
Country Landowners Association
Federation of Civil Engineering Contractors
Finance and Leasing Association
Institute of Actuaries

Institute of Chartered Accountants
Institute of Civil Engineers
London Maritime Arbitrators Association
Motor Insurers' Bureau
National Federation of Consumer Groups
National Association of Estate Agents
National Consumer Council
Royal Institute of British Architects
Royal Institution of Chartered Surveyors
Securities and Futures Authority
Society of Construction Arbitrators
Wren Insurance Association Limited

OTHERS
John Barber
G M Beresford Hartwell
J M Kilby
Ove Arup Partnership

APPENDIX D

Participants at the Conference on Reform of the Law of Privity of Contract, held at the Institute of Advanced Legal Studies, Russell Square on 2-3 April 1992, which examined the Law Commission's Consultation Paper No 121

The descriptions of consultees may have altered since the date of the conference.

Jack Beatson, Law Commissioner
Andrew Bell, Manchester University
Andrew Burrows, Lady Margaret Hall
Professor Roger Brownsword, Sheffield University
Professor Hugh Collins, London School of Economics
R O'Dair, University College London
Professor Aubrey Diamond, Notre Dame University
Professor R Goode, St John's College Oxford
Roger Halson, University College London
Charles Harpum, Downing College Cambridge
Professor Robert Merkin, Exeter University
H McLean, Trinity College Cambridge
Professor Anthony Ogus, Manchester University
F Rose, St John's College Cambridge
Dr F M B Reynolds, Worcester College Oxford
Colin Scott, London School of Economics
W J Swadling, Queen Mary and Westfield College London
Andrew Tettenborn, Pembroke College Cambridge
Dr Simon Whittaker, St John's College Oxford

Printed in the UK for The Stationery Office Limited on behalf of the
Controller of Her Majesty's Stationery Office
Dd 5065578, 12/96, 22-0000, 39462, Ord 364304